Legitimacy and the Military

The Yugoslav Crisis

JAMES GOW

Pinter Publishers
London

© James Gow, 1992

First published in Great Britain in 1992 by
Pinter Publishers Limited
25 Floral Street, London WC2E 9DS

British Library Cataloguing in Publication Data

A CIP catalogue record for this book is available from the British Library
ISBN 1–85567–031–3

Typeset by Mayhew Typesetting, Rhayader, Powys
Printed and bound by Biddles Ltd, Guildford and King's Lynn

Legitimacy and the Military

Contents

Preface

The first two paragraphs and the last sentence of this book were written at the beginning of July 1991, just after fighting had broken out in Slovenia; the remainder, with the exception of one set of figures, was completed in January. At that stage a ninety-day moratorium had been declared on the Slovenian and Croatian declarations of independence to permit negotiations. In the meantime, as Slovenia secured the withdrawal of the Yugoslav People's Army from that republic (seemingly a precursor to acceptance of independence), the conflict shifted to Croatia and became much more violent than anything which had occured in Slovenia.

These events ensured the end of the Yugoslav state. They also, it seems to me, confirmed the book's conclusions. Legitimacy in Yugoslavia had passed from the Federation to the Republics; the army finally destroyed the remnants of federal legitimacy by acting against the republics and by aligning themselves with the Serbian Republican leadership and giving assistance to the Serbian 'Chetniks' (armed insurgents) operating in Croatia. Whereas non-intervention, restructuring and depoliticization might have formed the basis for relegitimation of both the army and the regime it served, instead the army intervened in the way most certain to guarantee the end of the Yugoslav state its leaders wished to preserve. Whatever would emerge from the ruins in the years to come, it could not be a return to the old Yugoslav state.

If there are any flaws in the book, then 'it's a fair cop' as they say. However, while I take responsibility for any errors, I would like to thank the people who have helped me. My apologies to those I may have forgotten; among those I remember are George Schopflin, John Allcock, Mike Clarke, Lawrie Freedman, Martin Edmonds, Mark Wheeler, Bisi Alaba, Janez Damjan and Joan Walker. I also wish to pay tribute to the late Duska Primozic, Milena and the Michalskis, and my parents – all of whom suffered along the way.

1 Introduction

At the end of June 1991, armed conflict erupted in Slovenia. On 25 June both Slovenia and Croatia declared themselves independent of the Socialist Federative Republic of Yugoslavia. Unlike Croatia, Slovenia immediately took control of frontier posts and erected some new ones. On 26 June, the Yugoslav People's Army (YPA) began to challenge Slovene control of the border posts. A day later, Slovenia was engulfed by violence as the YPA attempted to seize border posts and proceeded to bomb airports in Slovenia. As the federal Prime Minister confirmed after peace was restored, the army had been acting without political authority and out of control. Battle flared for about two weeks, before intervention by European Community (EC) peace brokers obtained a cease-fire, along with a ninety-day freeze on the implementation of independence. Those ninety days were available to conduct the real negotiations on how to end the existing Yugoslav state and rearrange relations between its six constituent republics; these talks had been stalled within Yugoslavia for over a year, but were necessary to provide a formal framework for Yugoslavia's *de facto* evolution into several state-like entities.[1]

The attack on Slovenia was the final blow for the post-war Yugoslav state. Ironically, it was dealt by an army acting outside political control and against its own interests. In its desire to preserve itself and the Yugoslav state, the YPA consistently acted in a way that pushed achievement of those aims further away. It also took on an increasingly Serbian character.[2] Had the army been able to change its perspective and institute radical and rapid restructuring, more of the Yugoslav state it sought to preserve would have been saved. As it was, as central political authority dwindled in the Yugoslav federation, the army became an increasingly prominent feature of the Yugoslav crisis. During the first six months of 1991, it deployed extensively throughout parts of Croatia and Bosnia and Hercegovina. Yet, in effect, those deployments protected Serb insurgents from the Croatian authorities. This kind of intervention only served to spur the Croatians and Slovenes (and, to a lesser extent, the Macedonians) in their moves to end the federation. Although a low profile and withdrawal from politics would have been of greater benefit to Yugoslavia, the army pursued an opposite course – partly out of fear for its own position, partly in the belief that it had a constitutional role to perform.

The YPA traditionally played a considerable role in domestic politics. In the 1970s, the military was judged by one analyst to play a more integral part in political affairs in Yugoslavia than in any other European communist state (only the advent of the martial regime in

Poland tempered this assessment).[3] Others noted the increasing prominence of YPA generals in the political arena since Tito's death.[4] It was not the growing physical presence of YPA officers that was significant, but the nature of what they said. In the 1970s, YPA members had clearly become numerically important in domestic politics, but 'the actual exercise of its political influence, or the ambitions of individual military figures'[5] were less clear. It could not have been interpreted as 'challenging' the party; instead it seemed a 'generally conservative',[6] not very critical supporter of the leadership. Indeed, within the party-army organization, military interest seemed to be confined to defence requirements and there existed 'a preoccupation with military-technical tasks'.[7]

In the early 1980s there was a marked change. The management of the economy, social order and the political system increasingly became topics for the YPA generals' critical attention.[8] The YPA, at least to outside observers, seemed increasingly to be at the heart of Yugoslav politics. How can we explain this apparently qualitative change in the generals' role? Will they extend their political role and institute military government? What is the effect of economic, social and political matters on military capability? How far can changes in military organization be related to extra-military factors? Such questions are embraced by just one: how can we understand civil-military relations in Yugoslavia?

Yugoslavia

If Poland is 'not so much a country as a state of mind',[9] Yugoslavia is a case of multiple schizophrenia. It is a tapestry of paradoxes: little, if anything is straightforward. The 'horrible truth' about Yugoslavia is its complexity; 'it cannot be simplified . . . without being distorted out of all recognition'.[10] The country is a mix of contrasting geographies, histories, cultures, religions, languages and economies, the sum of which cannot be comprehended without understanding of the various components. Moreover, it encompasses the political problems of centralism and federalism; of a 'totalitarian', 'Leninist' party in a plural, self-managing, multi-ethnic society; of authoritarianism and liberalism; of moulding theory into practice (and vice versa); of modernization and underdevelopment – the global North-South division is to some extent focused here; but more than this, of course, for forty years it has been where East meets West. Because of this, it is perhaps understandable that writing on Yugoslavia, particularly in newspapers, frequently contains errors and simplistic interpretations.[11] Although complexity makes it difficult to get a 'quick fix' on the country, it also makes Yugoslavia a fascinating, fruitful area to study. This has been so for students from many fields, but in particular it has been 'an almost ideal laboratory for political sociologists'.[12]

Political, sociological, cultural, religious and economic differences within Yugoslav frontiers surely owe something to the country's geography. There is a remarkable diversity of terrain for a small- to medium-sized country; several physiographic regions converge on Yugoslav territory. Distinct natural regions include the North–Eastern plains – on which half the inhabitants of Yugoslavia are to be found – the Pannonian lowlands of Serbia, the Vojvodina's version of the steppelands of the Ukraine and the *pusztas* of Hungary. In addition, most of the country is covered by mountains – albeit ones of enormous variation in size and type – and along the coast there is a small coastal strip trimmed with thousands of Adriatic islands. Between these regions, several intermediate zones are to be found. Concomitant with geophysical diversity is climactic variation: Titograd, for example, has an average monthly temperature 6°C greater than Cetinje only twenty-five miles to the East; annual rainfall in the former is half that in the latter.[13]

Differences in climate and relief partly reflect Yugoslavia's variation in other regards – for instance, the distribution of economic resources. It may also have played a part in the political and cultural division between East and West which predates the arrival of the South Slavs ('Yugoslav' means 'South Slav') by three or four centuries. The East-West divide between contemporary Yugoslavs reflects the way their ancestors fitted into a paradigm established in 285 AD by Diocletian and made permanent after another century by Theodosius; the modern line between the Latin alphabet and the Roman church in the West, and, in the East, the Cyrillic script and the Orthodox church corresponds to the old line separating the Roman from the Byzantine Empire.

The tensions that beset Yugoslavia in the late twentieth century may be traced in the early history of Slav settlement. The schism runs through contemporary Bosnia where Roman Catholic, Orthodox and Muslim populations coexist; to the North and West are the Catholics of Croatia-Slavonia, Dalmatia and Slovenia; to the South and East are Serbia, Kosovo, Montenegro and Macedonia. The South Slavs originated from the area around Kiev in the Ukraine. The exodus that began at the end of the fifth century saw the ancestors of the Slovenes settle in the sixth century and the Serbs and Croats between the seventh and tenth centuries. The lands upon which they settled formed part of either the Roman or Byzantine empires. Although both Croats and Serbs had independent medieval kingdoms and despite Slovene and Macedonian experiences in Slavonic empires, the early Roman or Byzantine religious and cultural imperial imprints remained.[14]

Muslims constitute the third major religious grouping in Yugoslavia. All are descended from ancestors who converted from Roman Catholicism. The Muslims live in two main areas. Those in the South, in Kosovo and around its borders, are ethnic Albanians who were islamicized by the Turks during the early stages of the Ottoman empire. The Albanians are the only national group in Yugoslavia to be able to claim a link with the pre-Roman inhabitants of the Balkans; Albanian is the only extant language to contain ancient Illyrian vocabulary.[15]

The other Muslim population is found in Bosnia. As indicated, the cut-off between Catholicism and Orthodoxy ran through Bosnia. As if this was not the cause of enough difficulties, the Bosnians decided to complicate matters by developing their own heretical church, the Bogomils ('the beloved of God') during the eleventh century. The Bogomils were persecuted by their fellow Christians so much that they happily and quickly embraced Islam when invading Turks over-ran them in 1463. The legacy of this rapid, voluntaristic conversion was the creation of an anomaly within the Turkish Empire: whereas Turks were brought into other parts of the empire to rule subject peoples (such as Serbian Slavs), a Slav-speaking, Allah-worshipping aristocracy flourished in Bosnia. The existence of this Slav-tongued aristocracy was Bosnia's distinguishing mark through four hundred years of Ottoman rule. Only in Montenegro, which remained an independent kingdom, albeit a very small one because it was inaccessibly mountainous, did another Slav-speaking clan system exist.

For a period of four to six hundred years, the bulk of Yugoslavs lived under imperial rule. Those formerly under Rome were under Austria–Hungary; on the other side of the divide was the Ottoman Empire. During the nineteenth century, the idea of a state in which all the Yugoslavs would live together was projected in both empires. However, the conceptions of unification were radically different.

The Croats and Slovenes living in the Habsburg Empire were strongly affected by the French revolution – which some of them experienced briefly thanks to Napoleon's troops. Twenty years after Napoleon's defeat, a Croat philologist, Ljudevit Gaj, founded the 'Illyrian Movement' which envisaged the eventual union of the Habsburg Slavs with the Serbs in an 'Illyrian' state. In the shorter term, they sought a politically autonomous Slav region within the Austro–Hungarian Empire – not a separate state.

Whereas the Croats sought national fulfilment through negotiation and constitutional measures, the Serbs turned to armed rebellion. In 1804, a revolt began against Turkish rule. Led by Djordje Petrovic (begetter of the Karadjordjevic dynasty), it was defeated by the Turks in 1813. After a period of Ottoman legal suzerainty, Serbia became a quasi-independent kingdom under Milan Obrenovic (in reality the realm was dependent on Austria for its independence from the Turks). The Obrenovic dynasty was troubled and was ultimately ousted in 1903, whereupon the Karadjordjevic heir, Peter, whose family had constantly disputed Obrenovic rule, became king. In the eleven years before the outbreak of the First World War, Serbia was the light for disaffected Slavs elsewhere, particularly after the Balkan Wars of 1912–13. In those wars, the Sandzak, Macedonia and Kosovo were annexed.

Serbian efforts had been directed towards national affirmation, For them, the idea of Yugoslavia was not a prime objective; it came some time after the assertion of national identity. The main concern of suzerain and independent Serbia outside its own borders was for ethnic Serbs living under foreign rule. The Yugoslav idea was weaker than in the Habsburg lands and was understood in terms of a 'Greater Serbia'.

The different aspects of the Yugoslav idea were evident from the beginning. As Banac has pointed out, linguistic policies were the key to national ideologies.[16] Gaj envisaged all the South Slavs giving up something to achieve a single literary language and cultural identity: Illyrian.[17] Croat political positions were based on the idea of concession. Illyrianism proved unattractive to other Yugoslavs.

To Serbs, Illyrianism seemed to be 'fundamentally calculated to stop the expansion of Serb national consciousness to its rightful limits'.[18] 'It is truly remarkable,' exclaimed one prominent anti-Illyrianist, 'that our Serb brethren of Roman dispensation . . . do not wish to call themselves Serbs, though they speak the Serbian language.'[19] This linguistic Serbianism derived from the work of Vuk Stefanovic Karadzic.

After the Turkish defeat of Karadjordjevic, Vuk had become an exile in Austria. Under the influence there of a Slovene, Jernej Kopitar, imperial censor for Slavonic languages, he worked on the standardization of the Serbian language; his phonetic Cyrillic alphabet was Gaj's model for a Croat version using Latin script. However, Vuk, reflecting the view of the philological establishment, saw most South Slavs as Serbs because both Serbs and a majority of Croats spoke the *stokavian* dialect; other Croats spoke the *cakavian* and the *kajkavian* dialects. (The nomenclature of South Slav dialects is derived from the use of *sto*, *ca*, or *kaj* to say 'what'.) Vuk and his supporters regarded all stokavian speakers as one nation, irrespective of political, cultural or religious features: that is, as Serbs.[20] For Serbs like Vuk the problem was to make Croats 'acknowledge that they are Serbs'. Moreover, they rejected the Illyrian idea completely, believing it would be 'crazy to abandon our famous name and to adopt another one which is dead and today has no meaning for itself'.[21] The different conceptions of a South Slav state were carried into the twentieth century. Serbia was a focus for Habsburg Slav aspirations; however, they could not see clearly how its interests might be at variance with their own.

The divergent strands of 'Yugoslavism' began to be brought together during and after the First World War. The first Yugoslav state was a child of the First World War settlement. The opposing conceptions of a Yugoslav state were represented by the Serbian government and the Yugoslav Committee which was composed of South Slav emigres from the Habsburg Empire.[22] The eventual arrangement was more suitable to the Serbs who, as a sovereign government, were generally in the stronger position. However, had the two groups not been drawn together, in spite of their differences, a Yugoslav state would have been as unlikely as it had been before 1914. Their mutual weaknesses meant that they had to use each other; for a Yugoslav state to appear, they had to work together. Using the Serbs gave the former Habsburg protagonists of Yugoslavia a Yugoslav state. But that state was one in which they would not be content.

The new country was formed as a constitutional monarchy; it had liberal–democratic forms and a king from the Serbian Karadjordjevic dynasty. (The country's name was 'The Kingdom of Serbs, Croats and Slovenes', but, following Banac,[23] for convenience it will only be referred to as 'Royal' or 'the first' Yugoslavia.) Democracy worked imperfectly and the South Slavs lived together uneasily for the first decade in the new country's history. In the late 1920s, there was a succession of constitutional, financial and agricultural crises. In 1929, Serbian domination of the defective democracy was succeeded by Serbian King Alexander's declaration of a dictatorship. Between then and the Second World War royal government became increasingly unpopular – in 1934, Alexander was assassinated on a visit to Marseilles. Large numbers of peasants could not be employed in a basically agrarian society; the country's socioeconomic structure decayed.[24]

On the eve of the Second World War, Royal Yugoslavia had run out of social, economic and political capital. Faced with the prospect of being crushed by Hitler's army unless Yugoslavia acceded to the Axis, the Regent, Prince Paul, signed. A group of predominantly Serb officers, outraged that their country should be so humiliated (and ignorant of the lack of alternatives open to Paul), promptly performed a military *coup*. This was the signal for Hitler's army to invade and overrun the Yugoslav army inside a week.[25]

Between 1941 and 1945, there followed a bloody war of liberation combined with a multi-sided civil war. Victory belonged to communist-organized forces, led by Tito. From 1943 onwards, they established a system of government on liberated territory; after the war, they took power throughout the country. The new country was given a federal constitution modelled on that of the USSR. This meant an apparent solution to the Belgrade-based centralism of interwar Yugoslavia as six sovereign republics of different national bases voluntarily joined the new state. However, like its model, it was federal in form, but highly centralistic in practice.

Newly born communist Yugoslavia turned to the Soviet Union for more than a constitutional draft. Its political ties were very close and help was sought to rebuild the economy. In the initial years of the post-war world, Yugoslavia was the Soviet Union's most faithful and admiring supporter within the Cominform, the Moscow-based association through which communist parties everywhere could be Soviet controlled. Various problems resulted in Stalin's expelling Yugoslavia from the Cominform in 1948. From 1949 onwards, Tito's regime looked to the West for assistance, but it always retained a position outside either the Western or the Eastern camps – fostering the Non-aligned Movement which held its first meeting in Belgrade in 1961. Yugoslavia's efforts to be neither Western nor Eastern in its external policies were matched by the development of internal ones which were neither Stalinist nor capitalist. The system of socialist self-management retained socially protective measures while introducing market forms. Concomitant with this was limited political liberalization. Political and economic liberalization increased incrementally; the changes were codified in fresh constitutions, the last of which came into force in 1974.

The 1974 Constitution remained in force in the 1980s. It confirmed the devolution of power to the republics – which meant that they had in reality what the 1946 Constitution had promised in principle. In addition, this constitution gave substantial, but less than complete, power to two provinces within Serbia. Yugoslavia had become a country of six republics – Serbia, Croatia, Slovenia, Bosnia and Hercegovina, Macedonia, Montenegro – and two autonomous provinces – Vojvodina and Kosovo. The devolution of power to eight constituent parts of the federation necessarily reduced central authority. The constitution was framed so as to limit the influence of Belgrade as the capital of both Yugoslavia and Serbia.

New political structures complemented the constitution. At the federal level, the 'head of state' became a collegiate presidency composed of a representative from each of the eight federal entities, an *ex officio* general and President for Life, Tito – who was 'President of the Presidency', a job that would be rotated annually after his death; a governmental body called the Federal Executive Council came into being, headed by a prime minister (called its 'President') and mainly concerned with economic management; a bicameral parliament with a Federal Chamber and a Chamber of Nations and Nationalities; and there remained the League of Communists of Yugoslavia as the leading force in the system, together with its shadow, the Socialist Alliance, both of which had their own presidency of which there was a president. Each segment of the federation followed a similar pattern: the most important individual was the President of the collective Presidency of the republican League of Communists; republican ('state') presidencies and executive councils had presidents of a collegiate leadership; the same structure applied to the republican socialist alliances; finally, republican parliaments were tricameral.[26]

At the centre of the arrangement was Tito and his personal authority. This web of political offices had been designed to prevent the accretion of excessive power; neither communist nor nationalist demagogues would be given the chance to control the country. Without Tito, this diffuse system left nobody with enough power or authority to act decisively and had nobody who could be held responsible for crisis, chaos and the lack of an adequate political response. After Tito's death in 1980, no individual could assume his role and the collective presidency, instituted in 1974 with a view to arrangements after his death, was composed of individuals represen-ting republican and provincial interests – which gave it little chance of swift, resolved, authoritative leadership.

Throughout the post-war period, political and economic policy debates in Yugoslavia have been conducted according to a pattern established long before the communist accession to power. The inhabitants of the generally wealthier areas historically and culturally associated with central Europe have consistently favoured greater decentralization of power, along with economic and political liberalization; politicians in the poorer Eastern and Southern parts of the country have tended to back authoritarian centralism and more conservative economic and political controls. Even throughout Tito's dominion, Croats and Slovenes argued for realization of those market measures that existed on paper, while the Serbs and Montenegrins supported the remnants of the command economy. The economically less-developed South wanted the redistribution of wealth; the Northern republics sought to secure reinvestment in their own economic infrastructure. The latter demanded greater autonomy from Belgrade; the former urged a tightening of central control.

The mosaic of geographic, political, economic, historical, cultural, linguistic, religious, ideological and international factors that forms Yugoslavia has a peculiar quality of stable instability. Centrifugal and centripetal tendencies counteract each other in a sometimes chaotic, but relatively stable way. The attempt to create a system that can integrate socialism and the market, federation and central control, and, in addition, so many other varied features, has been troubled. Yet, as Yugoslavia has stumbled from one crisis to another, there has always been scope for creative 'muddling through'. To a large extent Tito's particular abilities were responsible for this. However, whereas Tito could use his personal position to reconcile divergent republican leaderships, his successors have appeared to be increasingly feeble.

Even Tito needed to cultivate support inside the system in order to exert his authority, such as the army. In the late 1960s and the last decade of his life, the military became his most reliable ally. It was instrumental in resolving a major constitutional crisis in the early 1970s. In this period, the army became yet another facet in the 'horri-ble truth' of Yugoslav complexity.

During the ten years following Tito's death in 1980, the con-glomeration of contradictions constituting the Socialist Federative Republic of Yugoslavia slithered into a compound crisis. The military was increasingly vocal on aspects of the crisis, using its position as Tito's designated protector of the constitution to expand its role and, ultimately, contribute to the growing chaos (see Chapter 5). By the end of the decade, catalysed by the ending of Soviet hegemony and communist rule in Eastern Europe, the Titoist system was exhausted. Although in the forefront of amending the communist political system for much of the last forty years, Yugoslavia was, in many respects, overtaken by changes in other East European communist states at the end of 1989.

For Yugoslavia, the beginning of the 1990s represents the most critical phase in the country's post-war life. The withering of communist rule outside the country heralded its end within Yugoslavia and the beginning of a grail-quest for a non-communist South Slav state: six republics, two provinces, various national minorities and an army in search of a constitution. Increasingly, the republics appeared to behave as independent entities, creating the reality that Yugoslavia, to continue in any form, would have to become a community of sovereign states. The communist solution to the nationalities problem proved to be temporary. In its wake, the country was faced with the same competition between two polarized Slav conceptions of Yugoslavia passed down through history; to these, the complaints, fears and aspirations of two completely different kinds of Muslim community (in Bosnia and in Kosovo) must be added. The endemic multiple contradiction and complexity that beset the first Yugoslavia and efforts to create it, which produced a vortex of violence in the Second World War, and which suffused the second version of a South Slav state and precipitated its demise, immediately cast a doubtful shadow on efforts to constitute a third Yugoslavia and raised the spectre of another chaotic ethnic war. In this phase, an understanding of Yugoslav civil–military relations became essential.

Legitimacy and civil–military relations

Civil–military relations is concerned with the study of the interaction of the military with the civilian sociopolitical system. By military, we may understand those bodies that are responsible for the management of restrained, coercive violence to achieve a political end.[27] The term refers most often to those institutions designed to deter or combat external threat to a political community, or to act as an instrument of conquest against another political community.[28] In a 'nation-state' international system where each state desires a security it can never know because the motives and actions of other states are never certainly 'knowable' and certainly not always friendly, defence is a perceived necessity.[29] The military, a prime instrument of such defence is a given: each state has one.[30] However, military does not refer solely to bodies concerned with external activity. Although domestic matters are more commonly tackled by a civilian police force, in some cases 'paramilitary' units exist for the use of physical force in internal affairs.[31]

'Civil' refers to that which is not military. However, in terms of the sociopolitical system, this may imply numerous things. When discussing 'civil–military relations', we are usually referring to one aspect of the social–political environment. The focus of attention in the civil sphere may condition which particular aspect of the military is studied (it should never be assumed that 'the military' refers to one single, identifiable, homogenized entity – it always has divisions; military is normally used as a shorthand term for one particular part of the whole).[32] For example, we might study the relationship at levels such as government, institution (that is, for example, education or industry) or social group (by class, family or ethnicity, for example).

The field of civil–military relations has a strong record in terms of attempts to devise theoretical interpretations of events that have met with partial success. The progress made in theorizing provides a good base and makes efforts to improve easier. From previous work in the area the concept of legitimacy is prominent as a factor in explanations of civil-military relations. However, as we shall see, this has been the case only with reference to regimes – and then not wholly satisfactorily.

The present work has two goals: the first is to radically redevelop the concept of legitimacy as a *crasis*. The second is to introduce a complementary concept of military legitimacy. The conjunctive use of these two concepts will enable us to understand the dynamic of Yugoslav civil-military relations.

Three elements comprise the subject under scrutiny – civil, military and the boundary that separates them. Although any theory must consider both civil and military aspects, attempts to develop theoretical frameworks for the analysis of civil–military relations, while never entirely excluding other features, tend to concentrate either on characteristics of civilian politics or on characteristics of the military.[33] That is, we are offered either 'military' or 'civil' explanations. It seems obvious to me that neither approach can be satisfactory and we should, therefore, follow those who take a third way in which, eclectically, both civil and military explanations are used – and the 'balance of power' between them is taken into account.[34] However, for now, consideration of 'civil' explanations will introduce the concept of legitimacy.

Two types of 'civil' explanation exist. One emphasizes attitudes and values, the other is concerned with structure and organization. In my view, both types can be usefully unified and subsumed under the label legitimacy, as will be argued. To do so, as will be shown in later chapters, is significantly to benefit the theoretical study of Yugoslav civil-military relations.

The *locus classicus* of civil explanations and perhaps of the entire civil–military field is Samuel Finer's *The Man on Horseback*. A seminal work, as far as can be discerned, its author stands by it still; certainly, writing nearly thirty years after it was first published, Finer's book dominates thinking on civil-military theory.[35]

Finer begins by noting the characteristic strengths that facilitate military involvement. Such are these that he is forced to ask why military government has been the exception rather that the rule. His answer focuses on normative features. Although he notes that military strengths are offset by certain other strengths, the thrust of his work is that the degree of military involvement in politics is a function of the civilian system. Without the *opportunity* to act, military strengths are deprived of their potency; that opportunity must be civilian weakness.

Finer argues that the reason a military does not get involved in politics is what he calls the 'political formula'. By this he means 'that widespread sentiment or belief in which the title to govern is granted'.[36] Where this formula operates – that is, where 'the ruler's moral right to govern and be obeyed is generally accepted'[37] – the military has no opportunity to intervene. Finer calls this a 'mature' political culture. He has three lesser gradations: developed, low and minimal. Military intervention is most likely where there is a minimal political culture; its likelihood decreases as we move towards the mature category. Thus Finer's argument might be paraphrased: military presence in politics is an inverse correlate of political culture: where one is high, the other is low.[38]

Some criticism of Finer's model has been made. In one case, it is noted that Finer's categories are static: he offers no indication of how transition from one level of political culture to another might occur. Finer does not regard this as a difficulty – it is, for him, perfectly consistent with his objectives.[39] More frequently cited is the criticism that the analysis tends to be axiomatic: how do we know whether the level of political culture is high or low? We look at the military's role! Thus we come close to explaining military intervention *by* military intervention (or non-intervention by non-intervention). Finer, with some justice, rejects such criticism: 'This would only be so if I had anywhere stated that the *only* [original emphasis] evidence for the absence of 'wide public approval' etc., was *coups*, revolution, violence, etc.,: but this is not what was said.'[40]

Finer clearly seems stung by such criticism. The problem stems from the fact that the book is about military intervention: the overwhelming bulk of the text refers to this phenomenon. Consequently, although the author makes statements on various factors by which the level of political culture may be assessed, they are never substantially 'fleshed out' and, so, easily lost in the welter of prose on military intervention: these are trees obscured by the wood.

If Finer is misunderstood in these ways, such misunderstanding can be explained by the lacunae in his work. Wild incaution is not necessary to infer from Finer's book that military intervention indicates low or minimal political culture which, in turn, explains military intervention; neither the chapters on the 'levels of military intervention', nor others, sustain the possibility of weak political culture *without* military intervention. It is easy (albeit, perhaps, careless) to assume the argument of an internally consistent theory (that is, that military intervention and political culture are inverse correlates – see above). Criticism of Finer must focus on this. The fault is failure to give explicit, extended treatment of the possibility (or the *necessary* impossibility) of weak political culture without military interruption.

A similar conclusion to Finer's (and one endorsed by him[41]) is drawn by the proselyte Huntington. However, Huntington's analysis also improves on Finer's in that it is open to the possibility of civilian weakness without military intervention (as will be discussed). The label Huntington picks for this second type of civil explanation is 'institutionalization'. This puts less emphasis on attitudes and values and more on structures. However, in stating the 'most important distinction among countries concerns not their form of government but their degree of government',[42] he is probing similar territory to Finer. It is clear that central to any understanding of the civil-military pattern is analysis of the capacities of civilian government.

The capacities of government that concern Huntington are the 'adaptability, complexity, autonomy and coherence of its organizations and procedures'.[43] Analysis of these features will define what he calls the level of institutionalization. Where these qualities obtain, in Huntington's view, a system will have 'effective' political institutions which will command support, the scope of which is broad. But, where these institutions are 'deficient',[44] government will be weak. In such a situation, the military is likely to intervene. For it has the opportunity and (at last) the motive to improve matters. Where institutions are effective, neither of these factors apply.

Huntington derives two possible arrangements: societies can be either 'civic' or 'praetorian'.[45] Civic society possesses effective political institutions which are 'recognized and accepted as the legitimate intermediaries to moderate group conflict',[46] and the methods for resolving conflict are agreed. In contrast, the term praetorian operates not in its more common and restricted sense of the intervention of the military in politics; rather, it means 'participation not only of the military but of other social forces as well'.[47] Where there is an 'absence of effective political institutions capable of mediating, refining and moderating group action . . . [these] social forces confront each other nakedly'.[48]

The situations Huntington describes as civic and praetorian correspond to the higher and lower levels of political culture identified by Finer. If Huntington's notion of the 'scope of support' for institutions is considered, there is little distance between his version and Finer's. However, an important distinction exists. Huntington's analysis permits the identification of civil (or civic) weakness where military participation might occur. This owes to the context in which he writes. His concern is political systems as a whole and questions of their developemnt and 'modernization'. His addressing military intervention is incidental rather than essential. Whereas Finer's attention is on military *coups, per se,* Huntington approaches them *en route* to his conclusions on 'political development and political decay'.[49] This gives the Huntingtonian assessment an advantage over Finer's.

It is possible to avoid the seeming circularity of a low level of political culture explaining military intervention. Huntington widens the scope of examination. His praetorian society is characterized by the open confrontation of various social forces; it is a 'free for all' in which the military may well participate, but also may not. Thus, we are offered the *possibility* of civil (or civic) debility without military intervention.

This, in turn, brings to the surface another question: if the military may or may not intervene when suitable conditions prevail, why does it, when it does? Huntington answers that it acts as an auxiliary of the middle class. Huntington argues that it does so in two ways. Both are placed in his developmental paradigm. One is to conduct break-through *coups* in the transition from oligarchical to radical praetorianism. In this case, while only the few have power, Huntington argues, the military (drawn from 'modest social backgrounds')[50] identify with the radical middle classes and support demands for wider access to political power. The military act to catalyze the modernization of the political system, to usher in middle-class politics.

In contrast to this progressive role, the other way in which the military acts is the conservative performing of veto *coups*. The military acts to constrict a further extension of power to the mass society; it seeks to retain middle-class dominion. 'As society changes, so does the military. In the world of oligarchy, the soldier is a radical; in the middle-class world, he is a participant and arbiter; as the mass society looms on the horizon, he becomes the conservative guardian of the existing order.'[51]

Huntington's text, while offering evidence to support his thesis, implicitly opens a flaw in it. He affirms the likelihood of a sequence of *coups* following the first. Yet, if the first *coup* is on behalf of the radical middle class against oligarchy, the others must have different causes. Between ousting the oligarchy and guarding against the masses, 'there must be a whole range of cases where the military's motive for intervention is something *other* than "middle-class interest" as such [original emphasis]'.[52] If the military intervene in a 'radical' way where 'middle-class politics' hold sway, it cannot be simply in the cause of (middle)-class interest.

Although Huntington's explanation is forceful in its exploration of civic disorder, its weakness (in contradistinction with his earlier work[53]) is to explain motive *solely* in civilian terms. Clearly, class interest has motivated military intervention, but it has not been the only motive. A search for alternative reasons for military intervention, where the occasion exists, leads us to require a military explanation. For instance, it has been argued that soldiers 'cease to identify themselves in terms of their social origins but instead transfer their primary group identification to the military service itself, which has created a new style of life for them' and, so, when they act politically, it owes to 'concern for the corporate self–interest of "the institution" itself'.[54] This leads to a particular notion of 'national interest':

Luckham reports the Nigerian army's desire 'to reconstruct government and society in its own image, in accordance with the values of
which it was believed to be the unique standard bearer'.[55] Finer
summarizes these military explanations of motive thus: 'This skein of
selective induction, professional training and social code, along with
the organization and often the self-sufficiency of the military
establishment, give rise to the narrower corporate interest of the
military.'[56] In short, it is 'striking how frequently the *coup* leader's
vision of the ideal turns out to be the values and organization of the
army at large'.[57]

   This summary is notably similar to the 'military explanations offered
in Huntington's earlier work and, more particularly, in that of
Janowitz.[58] What becomes evident is that, although the opportunity
for military incursion into politics requires a civil explanation, this is
not enough; why the military uses the opportunity to intervene
where it exists needs a supplementary explanation. Neither 'civil' nor
'military' explanations are independently sufficient. Each requires the
support of the other in civil–military analysis. In some instances they
have been openly combined.

   In essence, such work follows Finer and Huntington it terms of civil
explanation. Luckham refers to both to establish the pillars of his civil
analysis.[59] By stating the strength of civil institutions as one of four
summary variables, Welch and Smith provide a direct echo of Huntington.[60] What Finer calls 'political formula', they call *legitimacy*.
Indeed, they assert: 'The legitimacy enjoyed by a government affects
the political role of the armed forces far more than any other
environmental or internal factor.'[61] This conclusion, derived from
Finer, has widespread support.[62] Regime legitimacy is essential to
the study of civil-military relations. It is by reference to a concept of
legitimacy that we shall study Yugoslav civil-military relations. As will
be argued subsequently, the concept of legitimacy used will require
modification; the traditional consensual view understood in the usage
cited is not sufficient. It must necessarily be understood to incorporate an approximation of the 'effectiveness' criterion in
Huntington's work.

Legitimacy, crisis and *crasis*

Legitimacy concerns the 'why' of power relationships. Such relationships occur wherever political activity exists – that is, the resolution
of conflicting interests by processes of authoritative resource and
value allocation through which it is decided, in Lasswell's well-used
phrase, 'who gets what, when, how'.[63] Commonly, power relationships are asymmetrical, involving the domination by one group of
another (usually, larger) group; although they are interdependent, the
capacity of one group to exact a desired response from another is
greater than its counterpart's.[64] Processes for resolving conflicts of

interest usually require an ultimate arbiter in possession of the power ultimately necessary to enforce its authoritative decisions. In a political community such as a nation–state, ultimate power resides, in theory, with the state. In this case, the power relationship is that between those who rule and those over whom such rule is exercised.

The phenomenon of widespread acceptance of information and commands emitted by a relatively small ruling group (or individual) may be labelled authority. If authority describes a division of power in which a small group's will is widely recognized because it originates with that group, legitimacy defines 'why' that will is accepted. It explains, ultimately, why the resolution of conflicting interests is authoritative; as such, it appends to Lasswell's list the question 'why?'. Therefore, we may define legitimacy as that quality in a power relationship by which the relationship may be justified; it is why those with power should and do have it and are able to act on behalf of or make demands on any or all members of the community without reference to them and why those without power should accept this situation.

The ultimate means of resolving conflict is the exercise of coercive violence. Whoever has the greatest available capacity for the exercise of coercive violence has ultimate conflict-resolving power. Yet, in the eyes of political actors, to have this ultimate power is rarely, if ever, considered enough. In most cases, it is regarded as preferable to avoid the use of violent means. Constant violence would be debilitating and wasteful.[65] So it is in the interest of those with ultimate power that their decisions should be accepted and implemented without the need to resort to coercive force. To gain this efficiency and reserve coercive capacity, it is necessary that the tenure of ultimate power should be justified with the possession of ultimate 'right'.[66] The biggest can be arbiter more successfully if it is best; might is more effective if it has right.[67]

The issue of legitimacy may be approached normatively or positively. Normative analysis of legitimacy concerns an observer's application of external criteria of moral validity to a particular division of power. Thus, if we believe that the rightful exercise of power depends on an hereditary principle, the only just rule we will identify is that of descendants of some individual (who, presumably, must have been recognised upon some other basis, such as divine choice). Alternatively, we may adopt a positive stance which involves our observing a power relationship and establishing the bases upon which the relationship is founded. That is, rather than offering our own moral standard of legitimacy, we consider the claims of legitimacy made by those with power and, in addition, the bases upon which the ruled recognise and accept their position. Instead of imposing our own standards of morality, the positive approach involves our being amoral and identifying the nature and terms of the contract between rulers and ruled in a certain case.[68] In the present argument, it is the positive sense that will be applied. Thus, our aim is to achieve a 'value-free' understanding of legitimacy. As will emerge from a review of other attempts to operate legitimacy analytically, this is not an easy task. However, as will be concluded, by seeing legitimacy as a complex of elements constituting a contract between rulers and ruled, a useful, value-free concept may be defined.

Modern discussion of legitimacy and attempts to gain a value-free understanding of it begin with Weber. Weber's aim was to establish a neutral, value-free way in which to analyse the problem of legitimacy.[69] In one view, Weber does not distinguish legitimate from illegitimate domination, but implicitly recognizes 'the plurality of legitimacies'.[70] As an analyst, Weber attempts to avoid a normative judgement by recognizing that more than one basis for legitimate rule may exist. Indeed, he identifies three 'pure types' upon which 'the validity of claims to legitimacy may be based'. These are rational, traditional and charismatic. The rational type rests on a belief 'in the legality of enacted rules' and the right in law of those in authority to make such rules and issue orders. The traditional basis depends on an 'established belief in the sanctity of immemorial traditions' and recognition that authority is exercised in accordance with such traditions. Charismatic legitimacy relies on 'devotion to the exceptional sanctity, heroism or exemplary character of an individual' and value patterns associated with that person.[71] The Weberian typology has been subject to many criticisms.[72] Chief among these, I would contend, is the submission that it is 'ruler–centric'.[73] Weber is concerned with the types of claim rulers might make; he does not ascertain 'the other, decisive, side of the experience of legitimacy: the view from below'.[74] Thus, Weber seems to assume 'a minimum of voluntary compliance, that is an interest in obedience',[75] the basis of which is belief.[76] Ergo, whatever the rulers' claim, it would seem, the ruled accept and believe. Or, from the other side, we might say, Weber assumes obedience and lays out the bases upon which such obedience will be formed.

In principle, Weber's attempt to create a descriptive rather than an evaluative legitimacy is consistent with our present cause. Incomplete in that it fails to take sufficient account of the various constituencies with an interest, its attempt to be value-free is commendable. However, as Giddens observes, to try to strip the concept of its usual evaluative moral content is substantially to redefine more common-place understandings of legitimacy. The stress placed on belief leads to a failure to practise principles; Weber only occasionally sticks to his scientific definition – otherwise he falls back into a more usual evaluative usage.[77] As we consider other attempts to create an analytically useful concept of legitimacy, we should keep in mind both Weber's attempt to be value-free and his failure to meet his goal.[78]

The Weberian understanding of legitimacy as couched in belief is the foundation stone of a school of thought prominent in Western political science. With variations, the essential notion is that a (legitimate) consensus is achieved because the dominated believe in the appropriateness of those who dominate. Lipsett writes of the need to 'engender and maintain the belief that the existing political institutions are the most appropriate ones for the society'[79] Easton concludes that to endure, a system must have 'some moderate belief in its legitimacy'.[80] Legitimacy is a matter of 'conviction', 'attitude' and 'feelings'.[81]

However, to interpret legitimacy as beliefs, feelings or attitudes is to endow it with a (potentially) transient character. Leaving aside the difficulties associated with the accurate assessment of such psychological features,[82] it is not easy to ignore the conclusion that these change – sometimes overnight. Such changeability renders a most superficial interpretation of such an important concern as legitimacy – which becomes merely the product of the shifting sands of collective mood and whim.

One solution to this problem is suggested within the belief school. This is to identify salient norms – that is the most significant features of the value patterns of both rulers and ruled.[83] Legitimacy, in this case, may be said to pertain to the degree in which 'elite' and 'mass' political culture are consonant.[84] However, as Merquior suggests, this, instead of clearing our path, offers only a 'blind alley' due to the 'difficulty of inferring value-beliefs'.[85] To some extent this problem may be handled; but any solution is fraught with imperfection. Such an analysis could only contribute to partial understanding of legitimacy; it could never amount to a whole conceptualization.

An alternative is to substitute credibility for credence. This involves an interpretation of legitimacy that incorporates the notion of power. Stinchcombe offers such an understanding.[86] In his terms, legitimacy is not a matter of pure faith or belief. Rather, power is legitimated by the ability to call upon alternative centres of power; the exercise of power is legitimate if 'the power holder can call upon sufficient other centres of power, as reserves in case of need, to make his power effective'.[87] Where such a reserve exists, it is unlikely to be called upon, as the power subject is normally aware of the probable consequence of resistance. For example, Stinchcombe cites the authority of a police officer: the officer will be effective, for the most part, because it is highly probable that various third parties (such as other officers or courts of law) will provide support if necessary.[88] Merquior objects that 'legitimacy as a power reserve scarcely deserves its name'.[89] He continues: 'Even at its strictest "empiricalness", legitimacy is a *de jure*, not a *de facto* issue.'[90] There exists, he asserts, no difference between an individual's complying with a police officer's will or that of a Mafia hireling if obedience depends on a formidable power reserve. Yet should we pronounce the latter legitimate? 'Of course not,' replies Merquior – this attitude enables us to establish our understanding of legitimacy in sharp focus.

Merquior's response is an example of an author's taking their own prejudice as self-evident fact. Even if we leave aside the cultural features of the Cosa Nostra (although we should recognize that as a social order it has its own bases of legitimacy) the individual's compliance with the mafia hireling's orders must be considered legitimate; we might even say that the individual has recognized the mafioso's 'right' to demand compliance. Within a given community, the mafiosi have authority; the reasons for that authority – if no more than reserves of coercive violence – are its bases of legitimacy. If mafiosi orders gain compliance, we must judge them to be sufficiently legitimate for the compliant. If an individual accedes to a demand because of the threat of violence, as outside observers we must identify and accept violence as the relationship's internal mode of legitimation. It is not good enough to impose our own external preferences and describe an instance of authority as illegitimate. Moreover, it is, anyway, curious to disapprove of the 'protection' methods found in a particular society such as the mafia, when the same method has been the root of all political communities since Xerxes decided that, rather than carrying out debilitating occasional raids to gain supplies, it was better to come to an agreement under which farmers would not be 'turned-over' if they gave a proportion of what they produced – in effect, paid tax – on a regular basis.[91] Today, individuals pay; they pay their dues to gain protection. In one sense, they buy the state's protection from 'foreign' powers; in another they buy protection from the state's more punitive capabilities.[92]

Merquior's criticism of power-based legitimacy is value-laden. He allows only one type of power relationship to be deemed legitimate – one where there is 'authority based on free consent'.[93] The meaning of 'free consent' invites questions. Must everyone consent? How free must they be? (For example, does he mean free from socialization, misinformation or social pressure?) Aside from these questions, there is a more weighty consideration. To allow only one kind of power relationship to be legitimate is to become a moral critic.[94] Social scientists must be aware that legitimacy is contextual, that there exists a plurality of legitimacies.[95] To be scientific, we must escape our own prejudice and recognize whatever exists, de facto. No matter how much we might prefer the idea that the sun orbits the earth, if de facto, we observe the earth's orbiting the sun, we must recognize this. Our difficulty is to identify what is there. This difficulty can only be augmented by refusal to allow all possibilities. Legitimacy is the quality that explains all power relationships. We must recognize all explanations of why one group can make demands of a larger group and gain compliant agreement. In the asymmetrical power relationship between rulers and ruled, it is the content of the agreement that concerns us; the reasons for subordinate agreement to meet the demands of superordinates are what for the latter constitute legitimacy.

In this sense, we may identify the weaknesses in Stinchcombe's model of legitimacy which Merquior's prejudice leads him to omit. First, if a ruler's legitimacy may be explained by its ability to call on the support of other centres of power, we also need to explain the reasons why those groups give their support. Secondly, unless we interpret every reason for subordinate compliance as another piece in the superordinate power reserve, the power reserve would not be helpful in a situation where we identified Merquior's completely free consent. This is to say that, as with 'authority based on free consent', authority based on power is not the only explanation of a power relationship; it is only one of the explanatory options.

Legitimacy explains why rulers rule and the ruled accept this situation. Therefore to consider legitimacy is to consider the nature of this agreement. Our need is to identify the elements of any particular social compact. As one Nobel Laureate writes: 'Ultimately, the social contract offers the only bridge between the consent of those who are governed and the legitimacy of the entity that purports to exercise the powers of governance.'[96] People usually will not have formally agreed a contract. But, in fact, their very actions constitute such a compact. Such compacts may be considered 'public goods'.[97] In particular, Buchannan argues that 'politico-legal order is a public good; disorder is a public bad'.[98] Order derives from compliance with authority. Such order is a 'public capital asset';[99] the government seeks the 'maintenance of the capital stock through time'.[100] The social compact between rulers and ruled is an asset; its continuance is a 'social capital' investment.[101]

To consider legitimacy in contractarian terms, ironically, brings to mind the originator of modern thought on legitimacy: Rousseau. However, whereas Rousseau's *The Social Contract* was the normative work of a social philosopher, the present understanding of a social compact *qua* legitimacy gives the opportunity to create a positive, analytically useful concept. Unlike Buchannan, we should not be afraid that any state activity (observed or imagined) may be interpreted as 'a conceptually possible outcome of some sort of "social contract"'.[102] Although we are unlikely to be concerned with small detail, it is nonetheless the case that to explain *anything* in terms of legitimacy is our need. Merquior repudiates the radical legal positivist position that a law may have *any* content.[103] However, a scientific, objective approach to either law or legitimacy must permit any content whatsoever. If the ruled comply with their rulers' decisions, the ruled accept those decisions; they agree to them, *de facto*: a contract has been informally agreed. Whatever the reasons for compliance, by complying they recognize the ruler's 'right' to direct and be followed. If coercive violence is the main reason for compliance, 'existentially', analytically, the ruled implicitly recognize their ruler's legitimacy for that reason. Whenever the ruled comply, they enter into a social contract; whatever constitutes the terms and conditions of that contract constitutes the ruler's legitimacy.

To state that legitimacy may have any content is one thing. There remains the problem of determining what that content is. As is evident from the foregoing discussion, the identification of legitimacy is problematic. Having surveyed various attempts to assert or affirm legitimacy, the difficulties are clear. Even to identify it in contractarian terms may lead to ambiguity and a lack of clarity. For these reasons the identification of legitimacy is difficult. Rather than try positively to identify legitimacy, it is easier to dissect its elements in its absence. 'At best,' Meyer suggests, 'we can perhaps sense the lack of legitimacy. That means we can observe *legitimacy crises* [my italics]; periods when it becomes apparent that legitimacy has broken down.'[104] It is, therefore, easier to pinpoint its absence in the presence of a legitimacy crisis than to identify its presence.[105] If we anatomize legitimacy crisis, we shall be able to identify the key components of the contract between rulers and ruled.

The foremost proponent of a theory of legitimation crisis is Jurgen Habermas. For him, a crisis signifies a 'turning point' – in medical terms, whether or not an organism is capable of recovery; in social scientific terms, 'crises arise when the structure of a social system allows fewer possibilities for problem–solving than are necessary to the continued existence of the system'.[106] Legitimacy is contingent on system integration; system failure leads to a legitimacy deficit. When faced with an economic crisis, for example, the government must negotiate that crisis successfully to relegitimate itself. If it cannot, 'it lags behind programmatic demands that it has *placed on itself*' [original emphasis]. 'The penalty for this failure is the withdrawal of legitimation.'[107] All varieties of crisis, therefore, represent a legitimation crisis: renewal of legitimacy is contingent on the need successfully to 'steer' through crises as the 'scope for actions contracts precisely at those moments in which it needs to be drastically expanded'.[108]

We may summarize a legitimacy crisis thus: support is withdrawn and consensus breaks down as social phenomena critically challenge a regime's *raisons d'etre* – its bases of legitimacy;[109] the crisis of legitimacy reflects the 'turning point' at which government *qua* living organism must adapt by effectively managing the critical situation.[110] Environmental support, effectiveness and the bases of legitimacy are the key components we must consider. Together, these areas of contract must be understood as a *crasis* – that is, a *necessary* combination of certain elements.[111] A legitimacy crisis represents a breakdown in this crasis.

Legitimacy may be identified by the non–existence of illegitimacy or legitimacy crisis. That which is not in question is legitimate.[112] However, the identification of a legitimacy *crasis* enables us to examine the elements that will constitute our explanations of power relationships. To understand legitimacy *crastically* is to recognize that it is a combination of elements each of which is necessary and works on the others in a contingent way, in which none can work independently of the others; analytically, each element might be considered individually, but any element alone cannot be understood to constitute legitimacy: legitimacy is the *crasis*.

The three elements work upon each other. Environmental support is granted where the legitimacy claims of the ruling elite are accepted. However, it is also dependent on the elite's effectively meeting the demands it places on itself in its legitimating ideology and also any demands the mass make (explicitly or implicitly) for their agreement in the social contract. The ruled may tolerate ineffectual performance if they remain attached to the legitimating ideology. However, poor performance will ultimately eat away the ideological capital.[113] Conversely, it is quite clear that effective government will reinforce an attachment to the bases of legitimacy. Equally, it is not necessarily the case that good performance will excuse permanently unacceptable claims on dominion. What is clear is that these co-relationships are so dependent upon each other that it makes no sense to regard them as separate phenomena. Analytically distinct, they are part of the *crastic* whole which is legitimacy.[114] Moreover, to view legitimacy this way enables us to satisfy a requirement made earlier. It allows us to combine Huntington's 'effectiveness' and Finer's 'sentiment' in a single concept of legitimacy.

Legitimacy and crisis: Tito's Yugoslavia

Regime legitimacy is most easily identified through analysis of crisis. Our interpretation of the post-war Yugoslav case requires examination of the critical phases in the regime's history. Before the 1980s, there were three critical moments in the regime's life: the war from which it emerged; the Soviet-Yugoslav split; and the crisis in Croatia in 1971. In each case, bases of the legitimacy *crasis* could be identified. In each case, support was generated by performance, as the regime successfully negotiated the crisis.

Inter-war Yugoslavia was poor and riven by nationalist divisions. It failed, essentially, because it was Serb-dominated and failed to persuade other groups in Yugoslavia, especially the Croats, that it was their state too. Royal Yugoslavia collapsed in 1941 as Hitler's army invaded. For the next four years there followed a many-sided and extremely bloody war in which communist revolution and national liberation occurred side by side.

The communists, led by Josip Broz Tito, won because they were the best organized fighting force in Yugoslavia and because they had the most to offer most Yugoslavs. The way in which the communists organized a National Liberation Army and used their organizational framework to establish embryonic governments in liberated territory is discussed in Chapter 2. Tito's 'Partisans' were able to appeal to Serbs because they fought more often and more convincingly than the main Serb resistance force, the Chetniks. The latter initially waited for an Allied invasion which they could support; later, they collaborated with the Axis powers to fight the Partisans, something that also cost them support. Both Partisans and Chetniks fought the Ustase, a fascistic movement installed by the Italian government in an 'Independent State of Croatia'. The Ustase had a genocidal anti-Serb policy which added to the intensity of Serb-Croat hatred. However, the Ustase were increasingly weak after the Italian collapse in 1943.

The communists, in addition to the appeal actual fighting had for the Serbs, also had appeal for other communities. The communists' slogan of 'Brotherhood and Unity' had appeal to those on all sides who were tired of the great bloodshed. They also offered Croats who opposed the Ustase a framework in which to demonstrate their opposition. Most of all, the communists offered all those who had felt ethnic injustice in the first Yugoslavia the prospect of a second version of the country in which their aspirations would be accommodated by a federation. That federation would provide a constitutional embodiment of the equality of Yugoslavia's nations within the country. The communists were able to create a broad base of support for their movement because they identified their aims with those of most of the people. They were attractive because they fought, because their aims were socially progressive, but most of all because they were not the vengeful preserve of any one particular nationality or religious group. Instead they represented a concerted liberation struggle for a federal post-war state.

During and after the war, the communists began to build a state that was federal in form, like the Soviet Union on which it was modelled. However, like that model, form and content did not match. Indeed, it was perhaps the similarity of the two countries that set them on a collision course. The regime's legitimacy, established as a result of the war, underpinned its resistance to Soviet domination in 1948, when Stalin ordered Yugoslavia's expulsion from the Cominform – the international organization in which Moscow controlled communist parties and governments around the world.

Yugoslavia was expelled from the Cominform because it demonstrated obvious signs of independence. The two leaderships were split over a variety of issues, including Tito's ambitions to include Trieste in Yugoslavia and his support for the communists in the Greek civil war – both of which made Stalin's dealings with the West more awkward. The Yugoslavs also objected to the role the Soviets seemed to be trying to take inside Yugoslavia. Whereas the Yugoslavs had expected help to do in their state what Stalin had done in the Soviet Union, particularly to develop heavy industry, it became clear that the Soviet intention was to use Yugoslavia as a bread basket which it could supply with machinery. Essentially, the Soviets were seeking to subordinate Yugoslavia. This went against the grain of Yugoslav pride in their achievements. They had fought and won the war virtually without Soviet assistance. This gave Tito and his associates the belief that they had the right to conduct their own revolution, which belief was counter to the essence of Stalinism.

Tito's regime survived because it was able to negotiate this crisis in which the very nature of the regime was challenged. It had popular support, as it had previously, against the Axis powers, in resisting external threat. However, the Yugoslav communists survived most of all because they were able to adapt to circumstances. They managed the crisis by questioning their own bases of legitimacy and developing alternative ones. The essence of the dispute with the Soviet Union was this: which of them had a correct understanding of communism? It was obvious to the Yugoslavs that either they were right or the Soviets were – and they were not prepared to let it be the Soviets. They therefore sought to establish the ways in which they were different from and better than the Soviets. They did this by returning to Marx and Lenin to devise the doctrine of 'worker self-management', in which, unlike in the Soviet model, control of production was with the workers, not the state; the state, in the Yugoslav model, would wither away.[115] In addition, it was decided to give more meaning to the forms in the constitution; therefore limited power began to be devolved to the republics; if central control from Moscow was anathema, then central control from Belgrade should be as well. The Yugoslav regime survived the deep crisis of 1948 because it was able to regenerate the support it had gained during the war by building on its bases of legitimacy and adapting them in order to negotiate the challenge successfully.

The new ideological base for the Yugoslav communist system did not emerge fully until 1952, by which time the crisis had past. As had been the case before, the new tenets existed more in principle than they did in practice. However, their existence on paper created a latency. Increasingly, people wanted the power they were told they had. This was the basis for gradual devolution of power throughout the 1950s and the basis for a reform movement that developed in the 1960s. That movement, mostly based in Slovenia and Croatia, urged economic and political decentralization. The movement made great demand for 'republicanization' – that is, for large portions of control to be given to the republics.

The thrust of the reform movement was originally economic liberalization.[116] However, much of this was lost behind a dust cloud of political liberalization that occurred after the fall of hardline Interior Minister Aleksandar Rankovic, a Serb, in 1966. Rankovic was regarded as Tito's heir apparent. However, after he was discovered to have been bugging Tito, he was ousted and found to have been responsible for a range of repressive measures. Post-Rankovic, there was considerable relaxation of political controls.

Political liberalization involved institutional change and electoral reform. Apart from Rankovic's interior ministry (UDBa), three other institutions were altered. First, the League of Communists was revamped and membership of its top bodies was broadened. Secondly, governmental and parliamentary institutions were reorganized, with changes in the executive. These included an influx of young professionals and the operation of the Chamber of Nations, one of two houses in the Federal Parliament, in which representatives began to be recalled for not accepting the guidance of republican leaderships. This last feature demonstrated that the federation had been federated; each republic was a constituency of support and mandate for its representatives in federal institutions. Lastly, the YPA was not immune to reform. The defence budget was increasingly a matter of debate; contact between the army and the people was enhanced by the full introduction of territorial defence forces. As a result of pressure from the republics, the YPA adopted the aim of seeking fully proportional national representation in its ranks and accepted the principle that 25 per cent of any national contingent in the YPA would be based on 'home' territory – in Macedonia the YPA was even encouraged to foster the use of the Macedonian language.

The growth of power in the republics was central to the legitimacy crisis that gripped Yugoslavia in the early 1970s. The extent of the republics' fiscal powers, added to both historic differences and the counterpoint of centralization and decentralization and of authoritarianism and liberalization, which characterized Tito's Yugoslavia after the split with Stalin, all created centrifugal forces. The solution to the inter-war nationalities problem, the federation, became the institutional tool of its re-emergence. Arguments for reform were delivered from national constituencies, in national interests. Those favouring decentralization were concentrated in the North-Western republics; their opponents in the Southern republics; thus the divide was not only over political and economic policy, but also of national perspective. The appearance of elections with some meaning reinforced nationalist positions; politicians with nationalist programmes appealed more to their voters in competitive elections than those with a federal agenda. The eventual outcome was a victory for the liberals, which meant centripetal forces were denied as centrifugal ones grew stronger. Those centrifugal forces seemed ready to disperse Yugoslavia to the wind.

The most significant of the national movements appeared in Croatia during 1971. The Croatian party leadership had encouraged a surge of nationalism in the hope of reaping economic benefits for Croatia. However, its political authority was undermined by alternative nationalist organizations which flourished in the more liberal environment. These exerted pressure on the Croatian authorities and created the impetus for politics with separatist overtones. There were even demands that Croatia should have membership of the United Nations. Yugoslavia appeared to be on the point of being torn apart. Devolution of power to the republics had created in the federal centre a vacuum of effective decision-making: who could pull the Croats into line?

Tito, inevitably, was the only one with enough authority to do so. However, he could only do it with army support. For several months he vacilated about how to handle the Croatian crisis. He was ambivalent about quelling Croatia's nationalist fervour. It was the YPA which seemed to make him decide what to do. YPA pressure pushed Tito into acting against Croatia. The army did not intervene openly, but it seems to have been active behind the scenes. Tito's statements and subsequent developments indicated that, in the absence of leadership from the League of Communists, the army was 'footing the bill for the party'.[117]

Afterwards, the LCY appeared to gain more central power and its 'leading role' via amendments to the constitution. However, in effect the YPA was taking a leading role within the LCY. This was evident as the army's domestic role increased. Tito asserted that 'the party, not the army was the guardian of the revolution';[118] however, the army was 'a part of the self-management system *and the party*'.[119] The party was chief guardian, but the army was a part of it. That the League was composed of parts is important: it was now a coalition of eight leagues – nine, if, as Tito implied, the army was included; the League was no longer one entity. Since the split with the Soviet Union, Yugoslavia's communist party had been looking for a real role. Along the way, devolution had produced a situation in which there had come to be eight parties in search of a role. This created a central power vacuum. The army filled that vacuum.

The regime survived with its legitimacy intact – or even enhanced by military involvement. The YPA had, essentially, lent its own legitimacy to political authority. To understand how, without overtly intervening, the YPA could fill Yugoslavia's central power vacuum in 1971, it is necessary to have an understanding of its military legitimacy.

2 The Legitimating Army

Civil-military analysis cannot rest on a 'civil' explanation alone. Although regime legitimacy must be deficient for the opportunity to exist for military incursion into the governmental domain, this does not represent a sufficient condition for the occupation of government by soldiers. Any 'civil' explanation must be supplemented by a 'military' component in the study. Thus, having outlined a concept of legitimacy to use in the assessment of civilian political institutions, we must now indicate the parallel concept of 'military legitimacy'.

There are three reasons to develop the notion of military legitimacy. First, the use of such a concept is suggested by the undefined reference to the term, *en passant*, in work on communist civil-military relations.[1] Secondly, the label is logically and lexically consistent with that applied to the other side of the civil-military divide. Thus, the hindrance of incompatible terminology found elsewhere is avoided.[2] In the third place, the use of this concept places some emphasis on both the military's links with its sociopolitical environment and any moral dimension to its role.

Although in Chapter 1 we stressed the need to play down the moral content of the term 'legitimacy', we should remain aware that this content may exist. Whereas its importance *vis-a-vis* civilian institutions is commonly exaggerated, its significance for the roles the military play is usually unnoticed. For this reason, the term is preferable to Luckham's 'military strength'.[3] The two labels address similar aims. However, Luckham's term – resting on the twin pillars of Huntington's notion of 'professionalism' and Janowitz's concept of 'organization'[4] – leaves no room for any positive moral aspect to military involvement in politics. The use of military legitimacy facilitates this; the elements of Luckham's 'strength' are, along with other notions, subsumed under the umbrella of legitimacy. This umbrella also shelters an important component entirely absent in the Luckham model: the importance of the military's links with its sociopolitical environment – that is, class groupings, political movements or 'the nation'.[5]

Finally, a further advantage over Luckham's effort is that this interpretation reduces the number of analytic components from three to two – which is consistent with the need for simplicity in good theory, while in no way detrimental.[6] This is because the need to supplement civil and military components of explanation with consideration of the boundary between them is obviated: the civil-military boundary, as will be seen, is a base of military legitimacy – and therefore contained within the concept. Our present task is to take the underused notion of military legitimacy and give it analytic definition.

Military legitimacy

With reference to the definition of legitimacy made earlier, we may qualify military legitimacy. It refers to that quality in an army's relationship with its sociopolitical environment by which the relationship may be justified; it is why the army has force and powers that are denied the rest of society; it is why the military can act on behalf of and make claims on the political community.

The legitimacy of any social or political institution must be assessed in terms of its relations to the wider political system. The legitimacy of the military as an institution is determined by its relationship to the political system. Some authors see this as a 'lower level' of legitimacy: 'The legitimacy of social institutions, organizations and social roles is a derived or reflected legitimacy.'[7] This is to say that military legitimacy depends on regime legitimacy.[8] But if the concept of military legitimacy is to have significance, it must be separated from regime legitimacy. Military legitimacy is more than a simple function of regime legitimacy. Like regime legitimacy, we may understand the military variant as a *crasis*, comprising bases of legitimacy, performance (or effectiveness) and environmental approval.

The bases of military legitimacy fall into two types: the functional and the sociopolitical. As an institution with a particular purpose – matters military, concerning the exercise of restrained coercive violence – military legitimacy must be considered in terms of that purpose: that is, its functional imperative derives from the tasks any military might be expected to fulfil – essentially, protection of the state from external physical threat. This is the military mission.

The key element, therefore, in military legitimacy is the claim that it provides the political community with the defence force it requires and does so efficiently.[9] Conversely, military legitimacy would be very much weakened if the institution were unable to perform this role. In addition, the military should provide optimal physical security. This means that security should be the means to some other end.[10] In Clausewitz's sense, the military must be an instrument of policy.[11]

The military may fulfil its functional imperative in two ways. First, it may latently perform its mission to prevent external attack without actively using its expertise. Secondly – and more obviously – it may engage in the effective use of its skills in violence to counter the similar skills of some other party. Essentially, the accomplishment of its role in either way depends on whether or not the military satisfies the criteria of being a military body. These are the ingredients of military professionalism. Thus, we might expect a legitimate military to be: expert in the management of restrained coercive violence; corporate, as a compliance based, hierarchically ordered organization with a generally coherent set of political, ethical and moral values which satisfy the 'military mind' – which implies the existence of a partially self-selective sub-culture; and, lastly, responsible – which means that it will behave in the manner expected of it by the state it serves.[12]

However, although its definitive role and its formal legal–constitutional linkage with a sponsoring political community constitute a functional base for legitimacy, the military is also governed by a sociopolitical imperative. The sociopolitical imperative is the sum of the non-functional demands made upon the military. It is quite conceivable that these may clash with functional requirements. One aspect of military legitimacy is to balance functional and sociopolitical demands. It must be able both to perform its role and, yet, not be alienated from its parent society.

The sociopolitical bases of military legitimacy may be placed in three groups: political activity; agency; and the nature of the relationship between the armed forces and society. A propos of the first heading, while all militaries participate in political life, this feature is particularly salient when studying a communist case, such as Yugoslavia. Unlike the notional 'neutrality' of armies in liberal democratic states,[13] the military is designated a political function.[14] This partially formalized political role for the military is a systemic peculiarity.

A civil-military relationship is usually characterized by integral boundaries, in which civil and military are clearly distinct elements, or fragmented boundaries, in which there is overlap between some military and some civil elements at certain points. According to the criteria by which the integrity or fragmentation of boundaries is established, the military in a communist system, judged by its structural differentiation, its functional specialization and its cohesion, is clearly distinct and has integral boundaries between it and civilian authority. This is underlined by the formal intercession between political authority and the military of the state in the form of the Ministry of Defence.[15]

Yet the extremely high incidence of party membership among officers (especially, its universality at the highest levels) would suggest considerable overlap, an absence of formality in the military-civil relationship and, so, considerable fragmentation of boundaries: there is a direct, informal link where officers constitute 'the Party in uniform'.[16] This fragmentation clashes (intellectually at least) with the integrity outlined above.

The civil-military relationship in a communist system acquires two distinct properties: it is *direct* and *formal*. First, the relationship between the military and political authority is not necessarily mediated by the state – that is the Ministry of Defence: it is *direct*. Secondly, where direct contact usually derives from association with or membership of a particular social grouping which is partial and informal, in communist systems the direct link is institutional – through the army-party organization, the military has a specific institutional role in the political process: the relationship is *formal*. (As the Central Committee is, effectively, the sovereign body of a communist system between party congresses, this formal, direct channel constitutes the approximate equivalent of the military having a formal place in the parliament of a liberal democracy.)

The importance of this peculiarity should not be exaggerated, but the direct formal link between army and party is none the less significant. It can serve as a channel that brings the military into politics. The Yugoslav constitution indicates how the scope of this formal link may be extended.[17] The Polish example demonstrates quite clearly the full implications of this formal connection: the military's participation in politics may be vastly extended to the point of implementing martial law and forming the government. But this does not take the form of a *coup d'etat*, bloody or bloodless, which normally precedes military government. It happens legitimately because the military is already a formally recognized and incorporated element in the political process. The formal link between the military and the political authority of the communist party means that as a political actor, the military is endowed with *legitimacy*.

The civil-military relationship in communist systems is distinct from that in other systems in that it is direct and formal. The existence of a direct, formal channel between the military and civilian political authority makes the military a legitimate actor in political processes – whether the scope is large or small. This legitimacy has considerable implications for the study of civil-military relations in a communist system. Whereas in non-communist societies, military involvement in politics presents a question of legitimacy, in communist states, the politicization of military activity provides a base for the armed services to act with political legitimacy.

However, while this feature distinguishes communist systems, it is not the only sociopolitical foundation of military legitimacy; there are others found in some degree in all political communities. For example, there are the various resources and activities that constitute military agency. Chief among these are the armed services' roles as a symbol of political unity; its contribution to the socioeconomic infrastructure of the state; and its operating as an instrument of education and socialization.[18]

Armies may usually be identified with a nation-state. In such cases, they may act as a symbol of national pride *vis-a-vis* military traditions and past military activity; for example, Edmonds writes of the British armed services that their 'exploits' contributed to their legitimacy.[19] There can be little doubt that the heroic achievements of the Red Army in the Great Patriotic War or the Partisans' victory in Yugoslavia (see Chapter 4) acted as bases for military legitimacy, to furnish communist examples.[20] Moreover, looking backwards at military tradition may also be a platform on which to stand the military as a symbol of present and future security. In this way the army may be used as a symbol of national unity.[21] In addition to its potential value as a symbol of unity, the armed forces may also be an 'emulative model'; for example, Bobrow cities the instance of Mao's China where the portrayal of the military's willingness to endure hardship was used in an attempt to engender a similar willingness on the part of the masses.[22]

Another way in which the army may be used as an emulative model is in the socioeconomic domain. However, the military's agency in this area is greater than its symbolic value. In many instances, it is important to be aware of 'what the military does that affects the pursuit of economic development'.[23] Often, because of what Janowitz calls the army's 'organizational format', in developing economies, the military is better suited than any other social group for the fulfilment of the demands facing a rapidly developing society.[24] With regard to communist systems, military input is considerable.

Although the armed forces' contribution in the socioeconomic sector may usually owe to military needs (present or potential[25]), its general impact cannot be overlooked. In various areas of construction and engineering work – from roads, houses, public buildings and irrigation schemes to the establishing of railway and telephone lines – communist armed forces participate in extra-military undertakings that make a big impact on a country's infrastructure and output.[26] At a more sophisticated level, in communist states, the most advanced sectors of the economy are usually related to defence and military-related production. Either as part of the military industrial sector, or as part of a wider 'military-industrial complex' (comprising scientific research and educational institutes, various planning organizations and defence-production establishments), the armed services may be identified with the most advanced levels of economic activity.[27]

The military's linkage with the highest-level scientific research educational institutions draws attention to another aspect of the armed services' agency: as the school of the nation. In all political systems, the army acts as an educator, imparting technical skill; in communist armed forces this role is augmented by politico-ideological and moral training.[28] In essence, this means a more active and overt process of socialization than that found in non-communist armies.[29]

The various ways in which the military acts as an agent of political, economical and social integration are a major base for its legitimacy in communist systems. The last of these, relating to society, leads us to the most significant of the sociopolitical bases of military legitimacy: the relationship between the armed forces and society. The core of this is the congruence of military with community.

It is assumed in many 'liberal' minds that the internal structures and functioning of the armed services should coincide with those outside them.[30] While it may be that, for liberal democracies at least, this is not necessarily the best possibility, given the competing claim of an army's functional imperative, it is certainly important than an armed force has an 'identity with a society at large'.[31] We must consider as a base of military legitimacy the extent to which the armed force, in organization and quality, is a reflection of the society it represents.[32] Army personnel in an appropriate way must embody values widely held in sectors of the political community – and the armed forces' composition must be generally representative of social and ethnic cleavages within society. 'The legitimacy of the armed forces . . . is considered suspect if significant discrepancies exist.'[33] These are the bases upon which military legitimacy may be founded. As with regime legitimacy, the bases are one element of a *crasis* in which good performance may provoke active or passive environmental support; or poor performance may engender active disapproval; or environmental support may exist in spite of low effectiveness.

Some nationalist content is inevitable where one military role is to be a national symbol, one of the 'trappings of national sovereignty'. But this is not the limit of such a role. The nationalist element is important in generating community support of the military. As stated already, the armed services' legitimacy is dependent, to some considerable extent, on their congruence with the society that spawns them. Patriotism increases the identification of the populace with the military. Even within army ranks, it is the fountain-head of political loyalties in the junior cadre. It is a key element in military socialization.

Support will be forthcoming if either the military performs effectively, in accordance with its functional and sociopolitical bases of legitimacy, or if there is some attachment to those bases that overarch poor performance.[34] But in the absence of such attachments, an ineffectual military may lose its legitimacy. For example, Edmonds cites the incipient delegitimation of the British armed forces in the years around 1970.[35] Other instances of breakdown in the social compact between soldiers and the sociopolitical community that sponsors them are the United States' Army's difficulties with regard to Vietnam and the French military's problems arising out of its engagement in that country and its politico–military activity a propos of Algerian independence.[36] Lastly, it seems likely that the Soviet Army's excursion into Afghanistan has disturbed its legitimacy.[37]

Military legitimacy must be separated from regime legitimacy. The concept refers to the *crasis* of bases, performance and environmental support with which we may explain the political role of the military. The concept is analytically purposeful as a compliment to *crastic* regime legitimacy. The relationship between civil and military institutions is a function of the interaction of these two concepts. Weak or non-existent regime legitimacy is a precondition for any significant or successful military role in executive government. Such a role is not possible where regime legitimacy is sufficient. However, where the conditions exist for military involvement in government, military participation does not necessarily occur. Only if the military organization has some legitimacy can it successfully intrude in politics. If the military does not have the legitimacy to act when circumstances are suitable, it cannot act at all.

In the early 1970s, the YPA intervened in political affairs. As will be argued, that action stemmed from the army's legitimacy. Using the concept of military legitimacy establishes the army's role in the Croatian crisis, as will be examined below. There are three bases of that military legitimacy: the creation and conduct of a communist-led army during the combined war of liberation and resolution; the fulfilment of its functional imperative in the post-war period; and the specific requirements of its sociopolitical imperative.

Formation of the NLA

Tito's Partisans won the civil war, in essence, because, in becoming the leading resistance movement, they gained the support of the majority of Yugoslavs. This gave them the power base from which to defeat their enemies and the motivation to employ whatever measures were necessary to preserve that support and the advantage it gave them. They came to power on a swell of legitimacy for their combined military-political organization. Military legitimacy came, principally, because the Partisans were in tune with the bulk of the population; victory was dependent on widespread support. Although political and military were inextricably entwined, there can be little doubt that support came mostly because the Partisans were fighting the occupation. In this sense, from the outset, the political organization and ideas of the emergent 'new' Yugoslavia borrowed military legitimacy – which was, thereby, enhanced.

Central to this was the movement's development of military organization. As the combined liberation and civil wars progressed, the Partisan's military organization passed through several stages of development, each stage representing the progress of the armed struggle and a step towards the formation of a standing army.

After the Nazi invasion of the Soviet Union, on 22 June the CPY began preparations for armed action. On 27 June, the military committee of the CPY founded a General Staff, which on July 4 issued a directive for the organization of armed formations for the conduct of action against the occupier.[38] Its aim was to harness resistance movements in order to divert German attentions from Russia. Although a full-scale uprising was not initially intended,[39] in some instances the communists had to respond to the people's initiative. Djilas indicates that although Tito ordered that only small actions should be carried out, that it was too soon for a major uprising, popular feeling was to fight: in Montenegro, 'The entire population . . . rose up against the invader.'[40]

Tito was right: an uprising at this stage was premature. This was evident in the manner of the original revolt. It lacked uniformity, varying according to place, time, intensity and available information. At the end of July it was already clear in Montenegro (where the uprising had been strongest) that 'our popular insurgent army had fallen apart' from its communist core.[41] However, for another year, in Serbia, Partisan units achieved greater success,[42] epitomizing 'organization, sacrifice and self-denial'.[43] In Bosnia, there had been a 'signal' success; in Croatia, the Partisans' weakness was the fact that it had been primarily drawn from the Serbian population; in Slovenia the Partisans had still not 'managed successfully to lead . . . the struggle', they had 'withdrawn into the forests instead of protecting the people'.[44]

This last assessment only underlines the varied forms communist-led resistance took. Certainly, it perhaps fails to acknowledge the entirely different nature of resistance in Slovenia where a coalition of parties led by the Communist Party of Slovenia had formed as early as 27 April 1941, against the Yugoslav Party's wishes. Established as the Anti-Imperialist Front, its purpose was to oppose the Axis invasion. After the Nazi attack on the Soviet Union of 22 June (when the whole Yugoslav Party began to organize resistance), it became the Liberation Front (OF).[45] Organized principally in Ljubljana, the Slovene capital, until its leadership could move to free territory at the end of May 1942, the OF had broad support. Although the Partisan movement, conducting guerilla actions outside the capital, was never so strong in Slovenia [see below]; as Djilas writes: 'the entire population was not only on the side of the Liberation Front, but participated in the resistance movement'.[46] As the war developed, however, the OF was subject to disputes and splits.[47]

The diverse elements of the resistance movement were brought together in September 1941, when a representative was sent from every area with an armed formation to a Conference at Stolice.[48] The patchwork of reports highlighted, above all else, 'considerable shortcomings as regards the links between the partisan detachments'[49] – which was only emerging as a problem as the movement grew. Indeed, this problem was also manifest below this level – Djilas reports the extreme fragmentation in Montenegro, where each town and locality of the former kingdom had its military committee attached to the pertinent section of the party.[50]

The need for greater cohesion met with several responses. The General Staff was renamed Supreme Staff and established clear organizational principles for Partisan detachments: each would have a staff composed of a commander, a political commissar and their assistants; and three or four battalions, each made up of three or four companies – a company comprising between eighty and one hundred soldiers.[51] An order was issued that 'in the shortest possible term . . . uniform dress with proper insignia on the cap' should be provided (the proper insignia was the famous five pointed red star which was also to appear on the national tricolour, under which they were to fight).[52] Later, a single set of instructions was issued, pertaining to methods for defending liberated territory, taking inhabited targets and training those without experience.[53]

The next major step came in December, when the 1st Proletarian

Shock Brigade was formed;[54] by the end of the war, there had been 295 brigades. These were elite units – service in them was 'the highest honour for every individual fighting man'[55] – specifically under communist leadership which could operate wherever necessary. Thus, while retaining a national, or territorial character (in the main), these were the first formations of an army that could be directed from the centre to perform tasks anywhere.

Prior to this, the military effort depended on local feelings but this led to low reliability, For instance, Djilas describes how Montenegrin peasants, who had been quick to rise up and take action, abandoned the cause once the Italians mounted an offensive: 'To escape artillery fire, they had abandoned the position. The peasants sped back to their homes, hoping to save their families and animals, and no force on earth could have stopped them.'[56] The territorial specificity of the early partisan detachments meant not only that members might fight only for their own village, but that they were in constant touch with their households, frequently sleeping there. This kind of attachment had awkward consequences, especially if an individual was killed.[57] To avoid these situations and create a less territorially defined, more flexible military structure, brigades were introduced.

The brigade was the main unit in Partisan military thinking. For the most part, the label referred to the three or four battalion units described at Stolice. However, the composition of the brigades did not always conform to this model. The 4th Proletarian (Montenegrin) Brigade, for example, encompassed five battalions and three platoons – one artillery support, one supplies and one medical and sanitation.[58]

The brigades' greatest attraction was mobility. The concept of mobile territorial units was, to some extent, an inheritance of the former Royal Army's thinking, a product of the incorporation of some of that army's officers in the new movement. It was also a descendant of the Serbian forces in the First Balkan War.[59] For aggressive purposes, they could be easily moved around to act alongside smaller detachments, performing a vanguard function – providing both moral and technical models. Although brigades carried the name of a particular area and mainly functioned within certain territorial limits, they were not tied to any particular place. This constituted a measure to combat nationalist or racial difficulties.[60] The aim was to create military formations with 'true military spirit'[61] In practice, only the first two brigades operated throughout the country. Otherwise, brigades were formed and operated more or less in one part of the country (Serbian brigades in Serbia, Bosnian in Bosnia and so forth) – and sometimes they were used outside their designated area. Moreover, only the first brigades to be formed were given the labels 'shock' and 'proletarian'; it was adopted later by others because it was believed to add to their moral-political and fighting quality.[62]

Perhaps more important, however, was another factor. Given the nature of the war they were fighting and the terrain on which it was being fought, it was essential that the communist-led forces were not tied down in situations – such as a pitched frontal battle – which would leave them at a disadvantage. Without evading enemy attacks and ensuring 'the preservation of one's own vital force',[63] a guerrilla army, such as the Partisans, would soon be overwhelmed by numerically and technically superior adversaries. This meant that they could only attack in suitable conditions.

The founding of the brigade system also reflected the need to seize the strategic initiative and increase offensive activity. It further constituted a notable step towards the creation of an army proper. More than an attempt to coordinate centrally the activities of local resistance groups, it was the establishment of a centrally directed combat force. As 1942 progressed, the increment of brigades (soon after the anniversary of the 1st, there would be 37 of them)[64] and strategic developments produced another logical step in November: the creation of the National Liberation Army (NLA).[65]

In many ways, the Partisans were on the back foot. Now fighting not only the Germans, Italians and the Croat nationalist Ustase, but, also, the Chetniks, they continued to seek, yet not obtain, material support from the Allies. Even in Serbia, the heartland of passionate resistance, they were experiencing difficulties.[66] However, large parts of Bosnia were liberated territory and support was widespread and growing.

At the time of the Stolice Conference, in September 1941, there were 14,000 partisans in Serbia. By the end of the year, this figure exceeded 20,000.[67] In the same period, there was an even greater increase in the number of partisans in Montenegro. Between August and the year's end the force grew from 5,000 to 20,000. By New Year 1942, there were another 20,000 partisans in Bosnia-Hercegovina and 7,000 in Croatia.[68]

In contrast, the Partisan movement was never as strong in Slovenia – throughout 1941, the total of individuals engaged in Partisan detachments in Slovenia did not exceed 700 or 800.[69] One estimate suggests that at the time of the Italian capitulation on 8 September 1943 there were no more than 2,000 Slovenes under arms – whereas the collaborationist White Guard comprised 8,000.[70] A more reasonable figure is 4,000–5,000 partisans; but this remains low and only grew significantly towards the end of the war.[71]

Between the end of 1941 and the end of 1942, the total number of partisans went from 80,000 to 150,000.[72] These troops were formed in brigades, partisan detachments and independent battalions (37, 67 and 45, respectively)[73] equipped with most types of weaponry. Their number was such that they had become 'impossible to direct'.[74]

In addition to the organizational imperative imposed by the growth in force size, other imperatives arose from the increasing need, with the changing shape of the war, for a more offensive action and a shift from the guerilla pattern to a more frontal system. The possession of substantial portions of the country – about 45,000 square km, mostly in Western Bosnia[75] – gave rise to the need to begin 'more sweeping operations, for more powerful attacks on the invaders and their Ustase and Chetnik lackeys'.[76]

To meet these new conditions, the NLA was formed into divisions and corps. In 1942, after the 1st Proletarian Division was formed on 1 November, another seven followed; by the end of 1943 there were another ten. In this period, each division comprised around 3,000 troops.[77] Petelin points out that whereas NLA divisions totalled 3,000–4,000 at this stage – and later would only be 6,000–10,000 strong, those of other armies during the Second World War averaged between 10,000 and 15,000 members.[78] The relatively small size of NLA divisions can be seen as an advantage: some of the flexibility and manoeuvrability of previous partisan units was retained in the transition to a more formal armed force.[79] By the war's end, there were 54 divisions, each containing at least 5,000–6,000 personnel; in Serbia, the 25th Serbian and 1st Proletarian divisions had around 13,000 members – several others in that region had over 10,000.[80]

A division, as a strategic operational force, brought together the following; three infantry brigades, an artillery battery, signals, reconnaissance scouts, engineers, medical and sanitation – a platoon each. By 1945, some divisions would incorporate, among other things, transport, motorized and anti-tank battalions, as well as field hospitals and construction units.[81] Its command element was small and simple in its structure, comprising a commander, a political commissar and a chief of staff.[82] Divisions were established as non-territorial, strategic entities. They were the first element of the NLA not to bear some territorial label – each division was numbered only – and not to be territorially founded. Divisions were prepared for action in all parts of Yugoslavia, although, in practice, their operations were commonly confined to the regions from which their component parts (battalions and so forth) were drawn and to neighbouring areas.[83] It is, none the less, significant that, unlike some of the previous units of the NLA, divisions were never exclusively the preserve of a particular nationality. This feature had a 'profound social meaning sense' for, in this way, the guiding principles of brotherhood and unity were fostered – indeed, made a reality.[84]

The development of the divisions was not always smooth. One example of this is the 31st Division. In the initial period, the divisional command was still organizing itself and could not give sufficient help to the component brigades. Therefore, in effect, there was no radical difference between the new arrangement and the one it succeeded. The variation in quality between the Preseren Brigade made up of widely experienced fighters and the others, established with novices, led to the retention of separate identities. A consequence of this was that each brigade kept its former capability and there was no accretion in the strategic worth of their sum.[85] Later, the differences between these brigades were reduced and eventually, after October 1944, this division was already at a level where it was ready to form part of Yugoslavia's future standing army.[86] The divisions were designed to act independently or in formation. Therefore, corps were formed in parallel with divisions to meet the need for large-scale action in a broad theatre of operation.[87] Corps were initially organized on a territorial basis. This was because of the communication difficulties experienced in the kind of guerrilla war in which the Partisans were engaged. As was the case with other units, the Supreme Command was unable to direct all operations, so this responsibility had to be devolved.

However, the territory covered by a corps was not always consistent (as had previously been the case) with administrative or operational regions. The nature of the war meant that, at the beginning at least, it never left its own territory. However, the corps did not have a permanent profile. At corps level, between two and four divisions would combine with other partisan units or groups to conduct particular offensive actions. Essentially, the corps structure enabled the coordination and direction of varying elements of the NLA towards specific tasks on the territory covered by the corps command; afterwards, divisions could be released to act independently or in other formations – or be demobilized.

The corps was a far more sophisticated organization than the division. In the early days, the corps would range in size from 5,000 to 15,000 fighters; by the end they would include 50,000. The coordination of such large numbers required a larger, more complex command than the divisions. The corps command – main staff, therefore, in addition to the commander, political commissar and chief-of-staff found at divisional level – included intelligence, supplies and medical chiefs.[88]

The final stage in the war-time organizational evolution of the NLA was the creation of four armies. The 1st, 2nd and 3rd armies were announced on 1 January 1945; the 4th followed on 2 March – the day after the NLA was renamed the Yugoslav Army.[89] These new structures provided for command of the corps. The armies were large, ranging from 40,000 to 111,000 troops and incorporated several divisions each.[90] By 15 May 1945, only two corps remained. These, the 7th and 9th, operated in Slovenia. Their essentially Slovene character probably accounts for their not being assimilated into the army structure. However, in the closing operations of the war in Western Yugoslavia, they were subordinated by the 4th army command.[91]

After the end of the war the four armies involved 28 divisions;[92] the two corps comprised another five; in all, there were 59 divisions with 261 brigades, nine regiments and three remnant partisan detachments.[93] Overall, the Yugoslav Army had around 800,000 soldiers under arms. This was already the foundation for the standing army which the post-war state would evolve, eventually to become the Yugoslav People's Army.

In considering the organizational and strategic success of Tito and his movement, one other most important factor must be noted: the formation of a fighting force was supplemented by the development of a political-economic infrastructure. Each partisan unit had a party organization. There existed parallel party and military structures.

Political work was important in the NLA – which was, after all, a creation of the CPY. Therefore, after the Stolice Conference, political sections were created. These initially operated at brigade level and below. Later, when divisions were established, they too had political sections. However, these sections did not exist above divisional level (although political commissars were attached to commanders in the corps, armies and Supreme Staff).[94]

Political sections were not merely counselling bodies. Their tasks included explaining the party line within the relevant unit of the NLA, organizing meetings and conducting courses on political matters.[95] They were also enjoined to secure the political-military integrity and morale of their unit. Moreover, their concerns were not restricted to the strength of the existing unit; these sections were also responsible for the mobilization of new adherents to the army.

Each unit had a political commissar who led the brigade's political section. Below, each battalion had a commissar who headed a cultural advisory committee of between five and seven members. The same pattern recurred at company level: the committee was made up of between three and five members.[96] These 'cultural teams' were charged with various agitprop functions, including both the dissemination of ideology and the reading of poetry.[97]

In addition to establishing the party's leading role and ensuring the internal strength of units, the political commissar at each level was responsible for liaising with the civilian communities.[98] This work could involve the securing of supplies from friendly communities,[99] acting as a link between the national or regional party committees of the CPY (or, in Slovenia, directly with the central committee of the Communist Party of Slovenia (CPS)),[100] encouraging the population in Serbian areas to fight against the Chetniks, or persuading Croatians, first, that the Partisans were not Serb Chetniks, then, that they should reject Ustase values, and, finally, that the best interests of the Croatian people lay in alliance with the other Yugoslav peoples.[101]

The political commissar's liaison role also involved dealing with the political–military authorities established to govern liberated territories. These authorities were set up on the basis of the First and Second Sessions of the Anti-Fascist Council of the people's Liberation of Yugoslavia (AVNOJ), held on November 26–27 1942 at Bihac and on November 29 1943 at Jajce.

AVNOJ was the political body in which the 'aspirations of the people's national and social liberation' were embodied.[102] The AVNOJ executive took responsibility for the setting up and counselling of governmental bodies on free territory. Through these activities, the features of a proto-state evolved. At its Second Session, AVNOJ constituted itself as the country's legislature and established a

National Liberation Committee as the first government of a new, revolutionary Yugoslavia.[103]

In addition to the partisans always forming a system of government on liberated territory, they also established an economic base to ensure the provision of material support.[104] Djilas, for example, describes the munitions factory in Uzice, where he observed all the 'virtues and all the faults of Partisan improvisation'.[105] However, armaments were not the only commodity required by the partisan army. In Slovenia for example, 1,144,000 kg. of provisions – 175,000 kg. of flour, 571,000 kg. of potatoes, 120,000 kg. of beans and 260,000 kg. of meat – were required every month.[106] Moreover, an army marches not only on its stomach but on its feet: the cobblers incorporated by one division supplied 1,706 pairs of shoes and carried out 1,098 repairs in the eight months to February 1945.[107] Otherwise, supplies were obtained from the vanquished enemy and, in the later stages of the war, from the Allies.[108]

Tito and his aides created and shaped an army. They did so initially with the purpose of diverting Axis troops from the attack on the USSR, but, mostly, of liberating Yugoslavia from occupation and conducting a revolution. That army was at all stages guided and disciplined by the political objective of military action. Tito's Partisans won the civil war, in essence, because, in becoming the leading resistance movement, they gained the support of the majority of Yugoslavs. This gave them the power base from which to defeat their enemies and the motivation to employ whatever measures were necessary to preserve that support and the advantage it gave them. They came to power on a swell of legitimacy for their combined military-political organization. Military legitimacy came, principally, because the Partisans were in tune with the majority of the population; victory was dependent on widespread support. Although political and military elements were inextricably entwined, there can be little doubt that support came mostly because the Partisans were fighting the occupation. In this sense, from the outset, the political organization and ideas of the emergent 'new' Yugoslavia borrowed military legitimacy – which was, thereby, enhanced.

Central to this was the movement's development of military organization. As the combined liberation and civil wars progressed, the Partisan's military organization passed through several stages of development, each stage representing the progress of the armed struggle and a step towards the formation of a standing army. The institutionalization of an army of this kind after the war extended from partisan legitimacy.

Military legitimacy in the post-war period: the functional imperative

Taking military doctrine as the imperative of functional legitimacy, the post-war evolution of the YPA (including the change from the Yugoslav Army to the Yugoslav People's Army) falls into three phases. In the first, the YPA was established as a conventional standing army. In the second, the army returned to its partisan roots, becoming a territorial, militia army. In the final period, the army no longer encompassed the territorial aspect of defence; instead, it became one element in a duplex defence system, the two structures being an operational army and a territorial defence force.

Official versions of the post-war development of the armed forces give the dates for the three stages as follows: 1945–58, 1958–68 and 1969 onwards.[109] These are the dates when new military doctrines were formally adopted on the basis of new defence laws. However, if account is taken of the three factors said to define military doctrine, a different picture emerges.

The military's mission is said to be defined by three factors: military–political trends in the world and Yugoslavia's position in relation to them; internal social, economic and political development; and the country's scientific and technical capability with regard to armaments.[110] If these features – including expulsion from the Cominform and the introduction of a self-management based ideology – are related to organizational developments in the army, it emerges that change occurred more incrementally through constant tinkering at various stages.

For example, one interpretation calls the period 1948-55 one of 'discovering the most adequate' organizational and doctrinal solutions to the problems faced.[111] Any consideration of what those problems were – externally, how to deal with the threat of a Soviet invasion, internally, what kind of defence force would be consistent with the new patterns of a socialist self-managing society in the process of proving itself different from and better than the USSR – and the alterations made to deal with them must arrive at one conclusion: changes in the YPA's mission have not been determined by ideological principles; they have reflected changes in the international and sociopolitical environments.

Despite Yugoslav claims that defence has been determined by ideology, matters were clearly the other way around. Moreover, the notion that defence is prime, ideology secondary, has been invoked by at least one senior officer in the YPA to justify the otherwise anomalous period of a standing army. No political movement, conscious of the realities of its situation, would 'deprive itself of a large defensive force such as Yugoslavia had at the end of the war, for the benefit of ideological orthodoxy or complete fidelity to Marxist principles', according to a former Assistant Defence Minister.[112] Essentially, the formation of a standing army met certain requirements at the end of the war; nor was its creation without profit.

The Yugoslav Army evolved from small groupings to a countrywide operational military institution. After victory in the war, it became necessary to turn the Partisans into a 'modern army'.[113] Peacetime conditions meant reductions in force levels and the creation of a permanent, standing army. As with the creation of the revolutionary army in the first place, this was something of which the communists had little experience. Again, the communists had to evolve an army to meet new requirements.

In the first post-war years, it was necessary to decide what to do with a force of 800,000. All Partisan detachments – the remnant territorial units – were disbanded and the forces in the main structure of the army greatly reduced. This left the Yugoslav Army about 400,000 strong at the end of 1947.[114] This core was 'installed' in barracks,[115] from where it was partially involved in the 'struggle' against 'traitors and quislings',[116] although perhaps only as last resort.[117] Otherwise the Yugoslav Army was concerned with its own identity as, during 1946 and 1947, several laws were adopted to institute the new army, including its being formed into three service branches – land army, navy and airforce. The organization of the army along conventional lines was deemed appropriate to the task of defending the new socialist Yugoslav state from external attack by the 'imperialist' (Western) powers and internal counter-revolution.[118]

Western support for anti-communist forces in the Greek civil war was said to be a manifestation of the 'imperialist' threat: today, Greece, tomorrow, Yugoslavia.[119] In reality, Yugoslavia was most likely to fight a local war over disputed territory with one of its neighbours – whether to defend existing borders, or, as has been suggested, to achieve an 'enlarged Yugoslavia'.[120] A centralized force, capable of rapid and decisive intervention in the event of a war with Italy over the territory around Trieste, with Austria over Carinthia, with Albania over the lands populated by ethnic Albanians, or the assimilation of Albania in a greater Yugoslavia, or with Bulgaria over Macedonia, was most appropriate to Yugoslavia's position in 1945.

Moreover, instituting a regular army met other needs. In peacetime, it was necessary to organize a military institution, the command of which was no longer co-terminous with, but would be responsible to the state and party leaderships. That, at a time when the system was new and needed stable institutions to establish itself and the country in its 'bureaucratic-statist' phase, meant the creation of a strong, centralized army.[121] This asserted the leadership's authority in a country prone to fragmentation, while eliminating the possibility of local armies forming to fight another civil war. A consequence of the shift to a regular army would be to take the partisan officer corps and train it into a professional cadre. This cadre would be in charge of a force no longer formed on a volunteer basis, but on the conscriptive military duty of all citizens.[122]

The existance of a standing army provided a framework in which a new, professionally trained, expert army could be given the knowledge and skills to meet the technical demands made on it. In the context of the 'cold war', this was held to be particularly pertinent, in order to oppose threats to the new state. The partisan army had never been equipped with state-of-the-art weaponry; now, with the expectation of Soviet aid, there was updating to be done, requiring special training.[123]

Finally, to preserve the strength of the new socialist order, in defence as in other areas, the party leadership believed the best policy was to copy the structures found in the Soviet Union. Therefore, although the initial post-war development of a regular army for open, frontal warfare may seem to be anomalous in the YPA's previous and subsequent association with guerilla types of warfare, it is consistent with Yugoslavia's 'statist' (or Stalinist) phase. The army was not an exception as the new communist state began to emulate Soviet structures.

More than the need to satisfy organizational and technical demands, it is the belief in Soviet institutions that explains the adoption of a standing army: the experience of the Red Army of the first 'socialist country' was taken to be a 'universal solution for socialist countries'. The Red Army's assistance was 'welcome' because it had emerged from the war as a 'most effective military force'. Using the Red Army as a stencil for the post-war organization of the Yugoslav Army was a 'logical consequence of these factors'.[124]

The building of a conventional army is chiefly explained by Yugoslavia's ties with the Soviet Union in this period. The use of Soviet forms and the strong cooperation between the countries had two benefits, in particular, for the CPY. First, close association gave the Yugoslav leadership 'Marxist–Leninist credentials' it sought as bases of legitimacy (even if these were later to be rejected in favour of indigenously researched ideological legitimation).[125] Secondly, the Yugoslavs really gained from Soviet experience. Not only did Soviet instructors assist in Yugoslavia, but Yugoslav Army officers were sent to military schools and academies in the Soviet Union, where technical military education was way in advance of that available in parallel institutions established by the Yugoslav Army.[126]

Partisan tradition, however, remained strong. This created crosscurrents with the conventional pattern that was being established. These 'contradictory trends' were a cause of friction between Yugoslav Army officers and their Soviet counterparts.[127] Various differences contributed to the Tito–Stalin split. These emerged after Yugoslavia's expulsion from the Cominform in 1948.

Ex-partisans, with the memory of a victorious war fresh in their minds, felt they were being 'taught to suck eggs' by Soviet advisors. It was hard for experienced Yugoslav soldiers to reconcile uncritical regard for the Red Army with complete disregard for partisan experience.[128] Whereas the Yugoslavs thought in terms of alliance, the Soviet intention was to subjugate the Yugoslav Army.[129] A further dimension was the USSR's failure to supply modern weaponry, as anticipated by Tito. Instead, obsolete equipment was provided at a high price.[130]

After the cominform expulsion, the Yugoslav Army found itself in a new position. Although for a year there was a stand-off between the two sides, each hoping the other would see the error of its ways, neither did and tension grew. Yugoslavia's erstwhile ally was now its principal enemy. The army's task shifted to deterrence of and defence against Soviet incursion. The army's attention was moved away from the Italian border and the Greek civil war to the South and focused instead on protection of the Eastern and Northern borders.

The new situation created a twofold need for a reassessment of military thought and doctrine: one strand was defensive, the other ideological. The first priority was to ensure defence against a Soviet attack. In part, international support could be invoked to deter or repel Soviet aggression. This, however, could be no 'substitute for a defence policy'.[131] It was necessary to correct military thought and doctrine.

This meant greater reliance on wartime experience in military planning. Although there remained considerable emphasis on conventional military organization, there was a limited return to Partisan thinking. The army would have to be prepared not only for frontal combat, but for Partisan action in case of aggression. To meet the new requirements, military education and training were intensified and a domestic armaments industry became a priority for rapid development.[132] Moreover, to confirm partial return to NLA practice, during 1949, 149 regiments and 20 independent brigades were formed under the direct command of the Yugoslav Army.[133]

Yugoslav theorists have explained this change by reference to developments in socialist self-managing ideology.[134] Territorial defence gave the impression of compatibility with the new theses on which the Yugoslav system was to be based. This change (and subsequent ones), it is said, have led to the 'progressive socialization' of Yugoslavia's defence capability.[135] However, in reality, as with the idea of self-management, military developments happened through necessity, not because of intellectual purity.

Both political changes and defence changes were caused by the need to counter the Soviet Union. It was serendipitous that a broadly based military structure, such as the Yugoslavs already knew from Partisan experience, was both appropriate to their blend of resources and requirements and consistent with the new principles on which the country's political life would be based. The territorial defence posture was not, however, assumed to give expression to the new ideology; it was adopted as the best means of using experience to deter or resist a Soviet attack.

Another consequence of the split was the demise of the political commissar. Although commissars had been a feature of the Partisan army, conceptually the office was a borrowing from the Soviet model. If all that was Soviet was to be rejected, political commissars had to go. From 1949 onwards, the commissar's role was diminished as the Yugoslav Army unified its command structure.[136]

In 1953, following the 6th Congress of the CPY in 1952 at which the theses of the new self-managing system were adumbrated, the political commissar was eliminated. The parallel operational and party vertebrae of command obtained a single form. Either a duplicative irrelevance where the two offices worked symbiotically or 'complex [that is, problematic] relations' where they could not, the abolition of commissars represented a more efficient form of command.[137] The commissar was replaced by an assistant to the Commanding Officer with responsibility for 'moral-political' questions.[138] Thus, party influence remained but the lines of command were simplified.

To reflect the more 'social' accent on defence and to highlight the severance with the past, on Army Day, 22 December 1951, the Yugoslav Army changed its name to the Yugoslav People's Army (YPA).[139] The alteration was more symbolic than substantial. As with other aspects of life in the years following the 6th Congress, practice lagged far behind theory in the YPA. The years until 1958 were a period for consolidation and 'discovery'.

The new doctrine of 'All People's Defence', adopted in 1958 (see below), resulted from several years gestation. After Stalin's death in 1953, relations with the Soviet Union became more relaxed, culminating in Khrushchev's visit to Yugoslavia in 1955. Thereafter, a more comprehensive form of territorial defence began to be elaborated.[140]

The further development of defence policy again performed the double role of fulfilling defence needs and being consistent with self-management. Self-managing socialism provided an ideological perspective for a 'social' system of defence.[141] Moreover, the continued construction of that system brought the YPA ever closer to its original Partisan path. In the light of this, basing defence 'exclusively' in the 1945–9 period and 'predominantly', between 1949 and 1958, on a standing army, was discontinuous with, even a negation of, the history of the Yugoslav armed forces.[142] The shift back to popular defence was consonant with ideology and tradition.

However, the greatest spur to producing the new doctrine was the formation of NATO and in 1955 the WTO. This external factor with significant practical implications prompted intensive work on organizational issues and the delineation of a new doctrine.[143] Before 1948, the USSR had been Yugoslavia's ally; after the split, because of its opposition to the Soviet Union, the country had received aid from the West – particularly the United States. The establishment of military alliances led by the United States and the Soviet Union meant that Yugoslavia's position 'in between' was made more difficult. American military aid, which had peaked in 1951 and declined thereafter as Yugoslav–Soviet tension decreased, was discontinued in 1958.[144]

Finding itself outside the main military blocs and without a clear-cut threat from any quarter, Yugoslavia required an appropriate defence policy. Since 1945, the army had reduced its force strength while strengthening its fighting capability and improving its firepower.[145] Despite force reductions, during the early 1950s Yugoslavia devoted more of its wealth to defence than did anywhere else in the world.[146] Spending levels had been sustained by US military aid. The reduction and cessation of this aid meant cutting the military cloth accordingly. The new doctrine had to recognize the realities of Yugoslavia's situation. An independent, semi-developed, relatively poor country surrounded by two large military camps, either of which, in theory, might invade had limited options. Given its rich vein of territorial experience, elaboration of All People's Defence was an obvious solution. The new doctrine satisfied the country's practical and ideological demands while utilizing its resources – knowledge, experience, technology and the economy – to effect.

The doctrine worked out over several years was assumed in 1958. By the end of 1959, the YPA had progressed well beyond preparations for frontal war, having formed 126 Partisan brigades on a wholly territorial, militia basis.[147] Until this point, although territorial units had been constituted *de facto* to meet immediate needs, they had not been embraced officially in military doctrine; now, the principle was adopted of 'combined open-partisan warfare'.[148]

The YPA was organized in strategic echelons. The first of these comprised units maintained at full war readiness. Their main purpose was to deal with a surprise attack, offering resistance that would prevent rapid, deep penetration of the country. Secondary echelons were kept on a peacetime footing, to be mobilized in case of war. Finally, Partisan units were formed across Yugoslavia for deployment at the rear and for guerrilla combat on territory that might be ceded to the invader.[149] Overall, this was the same structure with which the Partisan army had finished the war: large units for action along fixed fronts; other formations of varying size, waxing and waning according to circumstance; and smaller partisan detachments, organized locally, for guerrilla operations on occupied territory and rear support.

This major transformation took some time to complete. Frontline combat units had to be reorganized. The territorial principle had to be widened and its implementation tested. Mobilization procedures had to be brought into line with the new system. All this required practice and intensive schooling before the flexibility and strike capability of the new structures could be realized. This restructuring was not finally accomplished until 1965.[150]

Before long, there was another new military doctrine and concomitant re-organization. 'General People's Defence' (GPD) came into force in 1969. The Yugoslav armed forces were to get a radically different structure. Territorial defence was emphasized by a division of responsibility. Until this point and in other instances of armed forces based on a territorial principle, sole responsibility for defence had been with the central institution of defence; usually, territorial forces have been integrated with, or adjunct to, the army. GPD divided responsibility between the YPA and sociopolitical communities.[151]

According to the 1969 National Defence Law, the Yugoslav armed forces would comprise two equal elements: the YPA and Territorial Defence. Whereas the YPA would be the responsibility of the federal authorities, Territorial Defence would be organized by sociopolitical communities – that is, Republics, Autonomous Provinces, Communes and work organizations. This division of duty also made defence a specifically civilian affair. The new system of defence was all-embracing, as was defined in article 1 of the new law: 'Every citizen who in war, in an organized way, participates with arms in the struggle against the enemy can be a member of the armed forces of Yugoslavia.'[152] Or, as one writer has noted, the Yugoslav Constitution did not 'state the difference between a "civilian" citizen and a citizen in uniform: they are all the same in relation to basic rights, freedoms, duties and responsibilities'.[153]

The YPA was the operational force, comprised of active and reserve regular soldiers. Territorial defence units provided in-depth defence, being made up of members of work organizations and local and regional communities. The YPA was to be the best trained, best equipped, technically most advanced section of the armed forces; territorial units were to have relatively simple, light weaponry.[154] Each would perform different roles in the event of war – either separately, or together.

Yugoslav defence planners assumed two possible types of external aggression. The first of these envisaged conflict with one or both of the major military alliances; Yugoslavia would be either subject to invasion by NATO or WTO forces, or it would be involved in a war between the two pacts. Either eventuality would imply the attempted total occupation of the country.[155]

In either instance, the YPA would be charged with an initial, frontal role. Its chief task would be to delay enemy progress so that reserve and territorial forces could be mobilized. Up to half could be mobilized within six hours; complete mobilization would take perhaps two days.[156] Beyond this, its role would be to provide a lead, by example, in the resistance struggle.[157]

Territorial defence units would conduct guerrilla warfare. Although they might perform a frontal role 'independently or in co-operation' with the YPA, defending free territory from enemy attack, for the most part, they would become the main combat force on occupied territory. In particular, territorial units are excepted to be significant in resisting airborne assaults: 'on the spot', they can engage parachute troops as they land or before they have had time to re-group, whereas regular forces would take time to arrive on site.[158] These units would be expected to use all forms of resistance.

According to the Defence Secretary at the time of the introduction of GPD, anyone willing to fight 'can defeat the enemy by any means available'.[159]

The second scenario developed by Yugoslav strategists envisaged a more limited war with an individual member of NATO or the WTO. In practice, Bulgaria would be the most likely protagonist.[160] In this case, the YPA would have the principal part to play in what would be, essentially, a frontal war; territorial units would provide auxiliary back-up, but, while important, this would be secondary.[161]

The Yugoslav armed forces had one further defensive aim. Whereas an external threat was assumed to be a possibility from any source, a more specific internal mission was identified – the resistance of 'counter-revolution'. Externally, no specific enemy could ever be identified. GPD did not 'label anyone an enemy in advance. According to our concept, an enemy is everyone – irrespective of bloc or the national flag hoisted – who commits an act of aggression against the country'.[162] Internally, those who might commit an act of aggression were more readily identified: 'Cominformists' (that is those with Soviet sympathies), Albanian irredentists and Croatian 'Ustase' and similar 'nationalist' groups.[163]

The appearance of the new doctrine in 1969 can be explained in two ways – one political, the other operational. The first of these appears in semi–official Yugoslav accounts that give a political explanation. Either the changes amounted to a further step in the progressive socialization of the country's military capacity, or they were a function of budgetary necessity.

The new arrangement made possible 'the socialization of people's defence' in accordance with the principles of self-management: military organization was transformed into an armed people',[164] in which 'all factors of a socialist society based on self-management – citizens, work and other organizations from Commune to Federation . . . play a role'.[165] 'The strength of our doctrine,' Defence Secretary Bubanj boasted, 'is that it is public and belongs to the people.'[166] Indeed, the 'armed people' pattern of military force developed in Yugoslavia during and after the war was the only one consistent with Marxist-Leninist theory.[167]

As in earlier periods, however, much of the doctrine was theoretically compatible with self-management and this was a welcome but secondary feature. If 1967 offered a ten-year 'perspective' on the armed forces' progress, that which indicated a continuing need to 'work intensively' on 'the optimal solution' to problems in that quarter was not the need to produce a more social form of defence.[168] Although, in practice, GPD met civilian demands for self-managing principles to be applied to the armed forces, bringing defence into line with the decentralizing, confederative tendencies of society at that time,[169] the changes did not owe anything to theoretical argument.

The 1969 changes constituted a diminishing of the YPA's institutional status. Where previously it had sole and virtually unquestioned authority in defence matters, it had been reduced to a coequal.[170] Since the economic reforms of 1965, there had been pressure to introduce a GPD system. At the end of 1966, the military budget was questioned for the first time. If not ideological, certainly there was economic weight on the military to introduce a less costly system.[171]

The YPA was not wholly unsympathetic with regard to this matter – although there were inevitable divisions.[172] However, the system adopted was not favoured by the army. General Ivan Gosnjak, a former Secretary of Defence, offered support for a GPD system in which a limited range of functions would be taken over by, for example, communes; however, the YPA would predominate.[173] This was also the view of Gosnjak's chief-of-staff.[174]

The system introduced was not the one the YPA wanted. It was compelled to accept that system for military reasons. It was true that the concept of defence had a 'very weak point in that work organizations and sociopolitical communities were not the principal factors responsible for defence'.[175] However, that weakness was not theoretical but 'practical'.[176]

War-time experience had shown that small units operating locally could not be centrally commanded.[177] Were Yugoslavia to be attacked, it would have been highly unlikely that the YPA could achieve full mobilization before certain areas were occupied by the enemy; certainly it could not have provided anything more than specialist local leadership in the event of territory being seized.[178]

This explanation may be, more or less, teased out of some sources. It is no more sufficient than self–managing or economic interpretations. There was a real operational weakness, but this might have been dealt with along the lines suggested by Gosnjak and Hamovic, retaining military sway. It was an immediate force of circumstance that compelled the generals to put aside the 'traditional pride, prejudice and acquisitiveness of their profession':[179] the Warsaw Pact invasion of Czechoslovakia in 1968.

Curiously, Yugoslav sources absolutely ignore the invasion of Czechoslovakia in discussions of GPD. Yet it was obviously a jolt. The reaction was one of 'genuine indignation and shock'.[180] Moreover, certain aspects of the 1969 Law imply specific reference to that invasion. It was made clear that no one would have the right 'to accept and recognize the occupation of the country or any part of it'.[181] WTO troops entered Czechoslovakia to give 'fraternal assistance' at the 'invitation' of Soviet stooges in the country: no Yugoslav would legally be able to make a similar 'request' for fraternal help. This was later stated more explicitly: 'No one has the right to *invite* [my italics] the enemy's armed forces into the country.'[182]

Among various conclusions drawn, the most central was that a very real Soviet threat existed. Thus far, the likelihood of the YPA seeing action had been slim; suddenly, it appeared great. Under these circumstances, Yugoslav defence capabilities were brought into question. Although changes had been under discussion for some time,[183] the perception of an imminent possibility of attack made their rapid implementation a priority. The generals could not argue; the chance that the armed forces would have to mobilize – allied to the discovery of a weak link in the mobilization system – neutralized any opposition to the changes. The possibility of defects in the practice of territorial defence was not merely an operational concern. The first aim of any defence policy is to deter attack. It was easy to conclude that 'if the purpose is really deterrence by means of a credible threat to defend oneself with determination and effectiveness, then reliance on the regular armed forces alone would not only be inadequate but actually dysfunctional'.[184]

The need for GPD was accentuated by the Yugoslav assessment of Western responses to the invasion of Czechoslovakia. An assumption in Yugoslav defence thinking had been that external support would be available should an attack be made. Now, the notable differences between the Czechoslovak and the Yugoslav cases in mind, the defence planners had to consider directly that not only might there be an attack, but that it might have to be faced alone.[185]

Events indicated that Yugoslavia needed a defence policy which would enable the country to resist a massive attack, if necessary, without any assistance. The effectiveness of North Vietnamese contingents against US forces was not overlooked as the YPA considered its own traditions and situation at that time. A credible 'popular' defence policy was imminent. The combined demands of defence-budget reductions and the need for effective mobilization and leadership mechanisms for the territorial elements of the armed forces meant accepting a coequal role in the GPD.

The YPA was not content with this configuration. It seems that it re-established some of its esteem later. In 1974 a fresh defence law offered a pronounced modification of the 1969 Defence Law. In the latter, the operational army was the direct charge of the Supreme Command; the territorial defence units were managed by the republican defence staffs.

This was radically altered in 1974, when the Federal President became Supreme Commander of the armed forces: 'if the Supreme Commander of the armed forces – or a senior officer authorized by him – decides so, united commands for both YPA and territorial defence can be set up'.[186] Although a dual structure remained, the YPA's pre-eminence was evident – all the more so, given that the ultimate and titular leadership of the armed forces notwithstanding, de facto leadership of the YPA and, now, territorial defence units, rested with the Federal Secretary of Defence.

The re-enhancement of the YPA's position owed little to operational requirements – although it could be said that its role as the 'leading' element of the armed forces seems sensible because the defensive posture gains in credibility. The army's change of status owes even less to the further socialization of defence – rather the opposite. This must qualify arguments that characterize the shift to the GPD as a measure to assure consistency with self-managing principles in the armed forces.

The YPA's status was improved as a result of its playing a significant role in politics. Another feature thrown into relief by the invasion of Czechoslovakia was the need to aviod internal discord that might encourage an aggressor.[187] The events in Croatia in 1971 appeared for a time to threaten the continued existence of Yugoslavia. This (and perhaps a desire to get even with the Croat 'liberals' who had argued for social control of defence) prompted the YPA to involve itself.

Once again, a functional change resulted not from ideological guidance but from the influence of the external environment and domestic events. The evolutionary pattern of the armed forces evident at each juncture – from the emergence of a standing army born of the Partisans, to the bifurcation of responsibility for defensive tasks with the instituting of GPD – was confirmed. In the post-war period, the Yugoslav military was not fostered by ideological principles. Throughout it was shaped by a combination of operational, international and sociopolitical developments.

As will be seen below, the YPA's role during the 'Croatian Crisis' of 1971 was central. The army's becoming the 'more equal' partner in the Yugoslav armed forces followed this. By playing a political role, the YPA was fulfilling part of its sociopolitical role: that role rested on its sociopolitical legitimacy.

Military legitimacy in the post-war period: the sociopolitical imperative

The sociopolitical imperative of military legitimacy has three segments: the nature of the army's relationship with society; its socioeconomic agency; and its role in politics. The content of this imperative differs widely between types of political system and specific countries. In general, the distinction depends on the degree in which the army is a 'closed' institution. Should it remain in the barracks, uninvolved in political activity, or should it have full competence to engage politically?[188] Should its work be restricted to purely military spheres, or should it be expected to make regular contributions in the domain of socioeconomic development, such as construction work or medical provision?[189] Should the army be a cohesive, separate military caste, or should it mirror its parent society?

All armies have a socioeconomic role; they differ in the degree of that role. The Yugoslav military's socioeconomic activity in the post-war years was extensive. This activity fell into three areas: the development of a defence industry, the YPA contribution to the wider economy and the army's role as an agent of education and socialization.

The YPA was always involved in the building of Yugoslavia's defence industry. Although the First Five Year Plan made no provision for defence production,[190] the Tito-Stalin split made it necessary to create a domestic arms industry. Extending Partisan tradition and keeping within ideological precepts, the industry that developed was integrated with the wider economy. Thus capacity was always used for military and civilian purposes.

The war had destroyed almost all pre-war shipyards and equipment. By 1951, the capacity to produce 20,000-ton ships had been restored. For civilian use, five large ocean-going ships had been built and almost 300 smaller craft. This represented an investment of 25 billion dinars at contemporary prices. In the five years to 1965, output of military industry for the civilian market was worth 200 billion dinars at contemporary prices.[191]

Military industry's production for military purposes was subject to greater secrecy. However, in the 1970s, it was estimated to account for between 55 and 80 per cent of YPA needs. Although Yugoslavia was dependent on external sources for its most sophisticated equipment (for example, it imported MIG-21s from the Soviet Union), the domestic industry has produced, in particular, specialized light-weight armaments appropriate for guerrilla warfare.[192] Military industry also proved an export success, supplying items that included artillery, coastal-defence ships, medium-sized submarines and aircraft to non-aligned countries. At 1965 prices, this trade was worth US $30 million per annum.[193] Beyond the arms-related industry, YPA economic activity has been extensive. In the post-war period of reconstruction, the contribution of the army was vast in areas such as construction, communications, engineering, health and sanitation.

In the immediate post-war period of renewal (1946–7), YPA construction units restored 170,000 damaged edifices, built new accommodation for 25,000 people and erected 90,000 square metres of wall.[194] Between 1953 and 1964, army engineers completed 1900 km. of road construction, 254 bridges and 1,300 drains.[195] The army collaborated with the Post Telegraph and Telephone service to establish a telephone and radio relay network.[196] In the wreckage of war, medical units were formed by the army to work in the civilian community to eradicate disease, in particular, to combat typhoid and malaria.[197] Medical units made major contributions during disasters such as the one at Skopje in 1963.[198] Other parts of the army played major roles in the operations to deal with the Skopje earthquake. Between August 1 and September 10 the army built 996 flats there.[199] Military supply corps provided 50,000 meals a day at that time.[200] Indeed, supplies have been a sizeable military industry since the war. In 1980, military food production was valued at 89,884,000 dinars (contemporary prices); this rendered 28,350,000 dinars profit.[201] Immediately after the war, the army played a big role in feeding Yugoslavia.[202]

Economic activity was important not only in terms of military productive capacity, but for the employment it provided. In 1953, for example, there were 2,650 mechanics, 42,330 drivers, 2,080 electricians, 56,579 telecommunications operators, 7,727 health workers, 2,709 veterinary staff, 37,166 craftsmen and around 70,000 construction workers;[203] totalled, these figures would amount approximately to the force strength of the YPA in the 1980s.

Much of the army's role in Yugoslavia's post-war development was due to one factor; it was the best organized and technically most advanced element of Yugoslav society. By carrying out so much work, the army realized its theoretical position as 'a component part of the people' and that 'its links with them are manifold and unbreakable'.[204] 'All this confirmed the popular character of our army and the spread of brotherhood and unity between our nations and nationalities.'[205] The military's socioeconomic policy was both a basis for and reinforcement of its legitimacy.

The importance of the army's role in the community is one of the principal features of military-political education. For both this and more technical education, the army was a 'specific school of young Yugoslavs'.[206] The army's educative role dates back to the Partisans' literacy campaigns.[207] In addition to work done during military service, soldiers generally acquired skills they would take into the civilian economy. Between the end of the war and 1963, for example, 101,907 sappers and compressor-handlers, 166,270 drivers, 122,832 radio-operators, 46,857 mechanics, 7,207 sailors, 79,840 cooks and bakers and 94,673 traffic-controllers, electricians, engineers and nurses were trained by the army and later integrated into the Yugoslav economy.[208]

The military education system also created several scientific-research centres and prompted work in them that involved 3,500 individuals. Scientific research was the apex of an educational system that meant an officer corps in which 85 per cent were graduates of military academies and 14 per cent of non-military colleges.[209] As important as scientific training, the army provided 'moral-political' education. 62.61 per cent of LC-YPA committee members had attended the army's political school and a further 11.19 per cent had received political or social scientific education in faculties outside the army.[210]

The result of this education, other political work within the army and, presumably, peer-group pressure, was the nurturing of a 'brotherhood and unity' spirit and the 'Yugoslav' idea. In all its activities and in its nature, the YPA attempted to be an army of all Yugoslavs. An emblem of national unity from its creation and in its continued existence, the YPA sought and, to an extent, performed a symbolic role. A consequence of the YPA's role as everybody's army in such a patchwork society as Yugoslavia's was to make the sociopolitical imperative of being representative of society peculiarly significant.

The character of an army's principal task, defence from external threat, requires it to be cohesive. This cohesion requires large measures of dicipline, achievable only at some distance from the rest of society. The extent to which soldiers are separated from society depends on prevailing values. One country may support the idea of an army's being more effective the further it is removed from society – without becoming alienated; in other instances, it is felt that soldiers should not be a distinct caste, but a reflection of society.[211]

The YPA could be considered to have close links with 'the people'. While the demands of a total military organization were recognized, the Yugoslav army could not be closed off from society; in a self-managing, multi-ethnic country the army had to reflect society.[212] It was suspected that an army that did not attempt to mirror the complexity of Yugoslavia would pose (latently, at least) a threat to the country's unity.

In some respects, the YPA was not representative of society as a whole. No attempt was made to mirror the age or gender structure of Yugoslav society. Despite the large contribution made by women in the Partisan struggle – including combat roles – women did not feature in the post-war army.[213] They were not eligible for military service under the 1969 Conscription Law. There were some possibilities for women as reservists and after 1973 there was more scope for them in the army, although most were reported to be unenthusiastic.[214]

The age structure of the YPA cannot be said to have been a reflection of society either. However, whereas this might be expected because of the need for younger, fitter men to perform military duties, the discrepancy lies in the other direction. The YPA officer corps was relatively old; in 1964, 94 per cent of high-ranking and 75 per cent of low-ranking officers in the army-party organization were aged between 36 and 45 years (membership of the organization has consistently been put at 95 per cent or more of officers). This indicated a 'need for urgent measures' to rejuvenate the officer corps. However, at the end of 1975, about 50 per cent of the party-army cadre in one analysis were pensionable.[215] Presumably the explanation for this is that a youthful Partisan cadre remained in the army until retirement.

In Yugoslav terms, class and nationality were the most important components of its social character. As a Marxist-Leninist-inspired revolutionary movement, the partisans were keen to establish their worker-peasant credentials. Pre-war Yugoslavia had a relatively small industrial workforce, so the Partisan forces were composed mainly of peasants on whom Tito's forces were 'entirely dependent'.[216] Peasants comprised 61.1 per cent of the Partisan army; workers another 30.8 per cent,[217] and others the remainder – for the most part the leadership was drawn from this group which included intellectuals and professionals.[218] In some instances, quite detailed breakdowns can be found of unit composition.[219] However, class composition of the post-war army is not so freely documented.

Ibrahimpsic, for instance, gives figures for the war-time class structure of the army, but not for the post-war era – although he stresses the importance of 'class content' in the Yugoslav armed forces.[220]

More significant than the YPA's class character was its national composition. For analysts, Yugoslav and non-Yugoslav, and for the YPA itself, problems of nationality and nationalism are considered to be of the utmost importance.[221] The partisan army's success was, in part, due to its forging 'brotherhood and unity' among distrustful and antagonistic nations.[222] In the post-war era, it tried to maintain an officer corps composed proportionately of the various nations and nationalities.

Proportionality was important for the prevention of an unrepresentative army. Moreover, it was of practical importance. The defence system, combining regular and territorial elements, needed well-trained fighters from each ethnic group. It was necessary to have regulars with long-term training rather than just reservists who trained for a year.[223]

Nationalities were not proportionately represented in the Yugoslav army. The NLA was dominated by Serbs and Montenegrins, who made up 75 to 80 per cent of the NLA; 15 to 20 per cent of the NLA was Croat and 3.8 per cent Slovenes;[224] Serbs were the majority nation in Partisan staffs, followed by 'Jews and some Croats and Slovenes'.[225] Efforts to maintain a national 'key' in the officer corps were not greatly rewarded. Serbs and Montenegrins continued to figure disproportionately in the officer corps; other nationalities tended to be underrepresented. The percentages of various nationalities in the political organ of the YPA pro rata their level in the population demonstrated this: Serbs 64.3 (39 per cent of the population); Montenegrins, 13.2 (2.5); Croats 11.7 (22); Slovenes 3.2 (8.3); Hungarians 0.3 (2.3); Albanians, 0 (6.4).[226] Another set of figures for the full-officer corps (including non-party members) gave similar percentages. Serbs 60.5 (41.7); Croats 14 (23); Slovenes 5.0 (8.5); Montenegrins 8.0 (3.0); Macedonians 6 (7); Muslims 3.5 (6.5); Albanians 2.0 (6.0); others 1.0 (4.3).[227]

In addition, breakdowns of generals and the High Command were given. For generals, the figures were: Serbs 46 per cent, Croats 19 per cent, Slovenes 6 per cent, Montenegrins 19 per cent, Macedonians 5 per cent, Muslims 4 per cent, Albanians 0.5 per cent and others 0.5 per cent. These figures, while indicating greater alignment of nationalities in the higher ranks of the YPA with Yugoslav society as a whole, also provided further evidence of discrepancies – notably the vast magnification of Montenegrins in the ranks of generals.

Figures for the High Command showed a more even distribution of jobs between nationalities. Serbs were under-represented in the High Command (33 per cent) and Croats over-represented (38 per cent). Slovenes (8.3) and Macedonians (8.3) were more or less proportionate to their numbers in the population. Montenegrins were 8.3 per cent – again well over their contingent in Yugoslavia's ethnic fabric.

Muslims (4.1 per cent) were fewer than their standing in the Yugoslav community would make appropriate. Albanians and Hungarians are not represented.[228] The High Command figures signal efforts in the YPA to ensure that the higher levels were, as far as possible, a reflection of Yugoslavia's national composition. The relatively small number of officers in the High Command – perhaps 20 to 30 – would almost certainly produce distorted figures at any time; these figures seem a reasonable mark of an attempt to maintain the 'key'. This point is borne out by Denitch's fleshing out of the above figures.[229] Other figures confirmed the national imbalance in the officer corps.[230] All demonstrated an uneven spread of nationalities. This was a big concern for the army leadership which began campaigns and programmes to increase the number of the nationalities with low representation.

One comprehensive set of figures established the severity of this situation.[231] In 1973, Slovenes comprised 8.2 per cent of the total population. Yet only 3.8 per cent of total YPA personnel. 4.3 per cent of officers and 2.8 per cent of NCOs were Slovenes. In addition, only 5.8 per cent of the YPA's non-military employees were Slovenian. It was suggested that 'if the number of Slovene officers continues to decline, Slovenes will soon have almost no cadres at the command level'.

The decline was evident in the enrolment figures at military educational establishments. With the exception of the Marshal Tito Airforce school at Mostar, only 10 per cent of the requirement was satisfied by registration at Intermediate Military Schools; there was only a 20 per cent take-up of places at military academies. In one case, for 60 places there were only 68 applicants – of whom only 23 were physically and mentally acceptable. There were no candidates whatsoever from 18 Slovenian *opstine*. In sum, where there should have been 200 students in military education, there were only 101. Moreover, the position was worsening. In 1969 scholarships were established to attract young people to military schools. At first, there were 200 applicants; by 1973 there were only three – despite the bursary's value being 40 per cent greater than elsewhere.[232] Difficulties included tradition, pay and conditions. Problems recruiting Albanians have been said to stem from language and educational difficulties.[233] Equal representation of nationalities was (and would remain) paramount for the YPA. To sustain its tradition of 'brotherhood and unity' and maintain itself as a symbol of 'Yugoslavness', it had to be seen to be the army of all Yugoslavs.

The aversion of nationality discrepancies and divisions was of greatest moment because of the YPA's position in the Yugoslav political system. This extended beyond its symbolic role concerning 'national unity'. As with other communist militaries (the more so because of Yugoslavia's self-managing ideology) the YPA was not excluded from politics. Soldiers were always an integrated part of the political community. In 1965, 21 active-service commanding officers were deputies in Federal or Republican assemblies and in 1957 there were representatives in the leading bodies of the socialist alliance.[234] However, the military did not engage in politics with a high profile for most of the post-war period. Instead, the YPA concentrated on its functional and professional development described above. In the mid-1960s, the army began to play a discrete political role in the ouster of Internal Affairs chief Aleksandar Rankovic and later in the resolution of the 1971 Croatian crisis.[235]

The legitimating army

The essential thing to bear in mind when analysing the party-army relationship in Yugoslavia is that it was never one of discrete, rival institutions: the Yugoslav army was created by the Communist Party to conduct the simultaneous war of national liberation and revolution which began in 1941. The army and the party share the same roots. After 1945, the Partisan Army was transformed into the YPA. It became a 'professional' army, preoccupied with external threat. Initially, that threat was perceived to originate in the West. So the Yugoslavs turned to the USSR for assistance. Soviet military advisers were posted to Belgrade; Yugoslav officers went to the USSR for training. The Yugoslavs wanted Russia to help them modernize their military capability.

But Soviet 'assistance' turned out to be more a question of domination. The Soviets sought to control the YPA and through it, Yugoslavia. This was one of the main causes of the split in 1948 – the first to surface in the dispute. Soviet advisers went back to Russia. The Yugoslavs had wanted advice not incorporation: the Soviets wanted 'to encourage the transformation of the YPA into a conventional fighting force modelled on the Red Army and, in the process, subordinate it to Soviet control'.[236]

Open conflict with Moscow meant a real and imminent threat of external invasion: Yugoslavia was under the shadow of a Soviet invasion. A domestic arms industry was set up. By 1952, the YPA had 500,000 men under arms; 25 per cent of national income went towards defence.[237] YPA organization emphasized conventional defence rather than the Partisan tradition.

There was, to some extent, a divorce of party and army. This *de facto* divorce was emphasized in the wake of the 6th Party Congress in 1952. In redefining the party's role in society, its role in the YPA was redefined. Consequently, party influence was reduced and the YPA became increasingly autonomous and conventional – and, throughout the 1950s, more 'professional'.[238]

After the Soviet-Yugoslav rapprochement of 1955, defence expenditure was gradually reduced and 200,000 men were demobilized.[239] By the time of the reforms of the mid-1960s, the army had become mostly autonomous. It 'remained something of an institutional anomaly – monolithic, hierarchical, centralized – immured against reforms associated with "self-management"'.[240] It had become a 'supranational' institution hermetically sealed off from society, because the characteristics peculiar to military bodies – organization, hierarchy, discipline, responsiveness to command – meant it could more easily transcend or submerge political or ethnic differences. It had largely been forgotten in the processes of self-management and devolution.

However, in 1968 efforts were made to 'republicanize' the YPA: it was called 'opening to society'.[241] It was encouraged to participate in local communities. Under pressure from the Republics, the YPA adopted the aim of securing fully proportional national representation in the officers corps.[242] Also, the principle that 25 per cent of any national contingent should be based on 'home' territory was assumed – the Macedonian YPA command even fostered its own language, where Serbo-Croat had been the army's standard language. Contact between the army and the people was increased by the introduction of Territorial Defence Forces (TDFs) under the new 'General Peoples Defence' (GPD) policy.

This was brought in after the Soviet-led invasion of Czechoslovakia in 1968. For many years the YPA had resisted such a move. In 1969, the liberal tide, together with Czechoslovakia meant that it could do so no longer. Moreover, its independence – not to say its pride – was further diminished as 'coequal' and joint command structures were set up. Despite 'republicanization', the YPA remained an 'all-Yugoslav' institution.[243] Because of the GPD policy and the 'opening to society', the YPA was brought closer to its roots: the Yugoslav revolution – from the development of which it had been previously isolated.

The so-called 'opening to society', proved a plank of legitimacy.[244] Contact between the YPA and the people was encouraged, especially by the introduction of the All-People's Defence System.[245] The 'opening to society' processes brought the military on to the political stage; 'opening to society' was itself a base of the YPA's legitimacy as a political actor. When, in 1971, a legitimacy crisis occurred at the centre of the Yugoslav Federation, the army was still a cohesive, supranational institution. But it had been brought into the heart of socioeconomic and political life. It was placed in a position where it was called upon to assume responsibility for the preservation of the Yugoslav system from domestic threat. In assuming this responsibility it was fulfilling a *legitimate* role.

Croatian nationalism had taken on separatist tones with demands that Croatia should have its own army and membership of the United Nations. Yugoslavia was on the point of being torn apart: what was to be done? Devolution of power to the Republics had created a vacuum of effective decision-making in the centre: who would pull the Croats back into line? Tito inevitably was the only person with enough authority to bring the Croats to heel. In April 1971, he publicly denounced Croatian nationalism. Eight months later – after much indecision – he instigated the replacement of the Croatian Party leaders. An 'anti-nationalist' campaign was begun. But still no move was made to halt or reverse the past ten years trend towards national affirmation. However, by September 1972 there was a call for heightened 'ideological and political unity – of action' in the LCY.[246] In effect, this meant a reassertion of central control; the Party was to take again its 'leading' role: it would fill the power vacuum.

The LCY was unable to fill the vacuum: it was populated with the very people who had forced and supported the reforms that led to the crisis.[247] Tito's actions suggest that although, ultimately, his authority counted, it was not he who filled the gap. His hesitation and ambivalence during 1971 were 'enough to confuse the Republican leadership'.[248] It required Tito's authority to quell Croatia, but he was not confident about doing so.

It would seem that the YPA made him confident, eventually – either by persuasion or support. Chronology suggests the former. In April, when Tito first denounced Croatian nationalism, there was already a suggestion of military involvement.[249] By July, he was threatening to 'step in and make order with *our* army'.[250] However, Tito's September visit to Croatia seemed an 'apparent endorsement' of what was happening there.[251] It seems that Tito was finally persuaded to act after YPA leaders showed him suppressed television footage at Bugojno in November of the Croatian League's meetings, with only Croatian flags and with nationalist songs and anti-Tito slogans.[252] The army did not intervene overtly but it seems to have been activity behind the scenes that prompted Tito to resolve the crisis. Tito's statements and subsequent developments suggest that the army was 'footing the bill for the party'.[253]

Although, formally, the LCY was to gain more central power via amendments to the Constitution in 1971 (embodied in the 1974 Constitution) and, in effect, regain its leading role, the YPA was adopting a leading role within the LCY itself. The army 'was a part of the self-management system and the party'.[254] Although, according to Tito, 'the Party not the army' was 'guardian of the revolution',[255] the army was a *part of it*.

That the League was composed of parts is important. It had become a coalition of eight Leagues – nine if (as Tito implied) we count the YPA – and no longer one entity. Throughout the 1950s and 1960s the party had been searching for a role as the Yugoslav system adopted self-management. Devolution intensified its problems. Now there were eight parties in search of a role and no one at the centre with the mettle to provide order – except, perhaps, the YPA.

Fulfilment of a legitimate political role in these circumstances brought the army back to its roots – the revolution from which, for some time, it had been isolated, but with which it had common origins. That revolution had evolved. In 1952, the YPA had been disconnected from a centralized, unified LCY. That party was now a coalition of eight parties. In 1971, as the coalition seemed to be falling apart, the army joined course again with the revolution. The revolution's legitimacy was weak; the YPA provided the necessary backbone to redress that frailty. It was able to do so not only because it was formally involved in politics and shared roots with the revolution, but because it was a pan-Yugoslav institution. Its loyalty was not to any one Republic but to the Yugoslav Federation. Its own legitimacy – indeed, its own survival – depended on the Federation's continuation.

The Constitutional amendments of 1971, fixed in the 1974 Constitution, suggest not only that the YPA was dependent on the Federal State, but the Yugoslav Federation was dependent on its ninth partner – the military. That the military's role in politics was necessary, integral and legitimate was made perfectly clear in the early 1970s as that role was formalized. The YPA was accorded equal status with the autonomous provinces in the new 166-member Central Committee of the LCY. Thus it had 15 representatives in the Central Committee.[256] It was clearly a ninth partner.

The regime had negotiated the crisis with its legitimacy restored – even enhanced – by military involvement. The YPA was an *instrument* of that regime legitimacy of which it was also a *function*. It was a function in that its existence was dependent on the regime's continuation – no regime, no military. Yet the regime required YPA participation as a binding agent and an instrument of stability and cohesion to ensure continued legitimacy. It was evident that the YPA was an integral part of the Yugoslav political system: once its begetter, it was now, it seemed, its saviour.

The Yugoslav Army was not 'a classical military organization'.[257] It was, in the Huntingtonian sense, 'professional': it was expert, corporate and responsible. However, contrary to the assumptions made by Huntingdon and others, it was fully prepared to take its allotted place in the socioeconomic system, to participate – indeed, this was one of its 'responsibilities', as Tito affirmed: 'it is no longer sufficient for our army to be familiar with military affairs. It must also be familiar with political affairs and development. It must participate.'[258] It was not a discrete aspect of the social and political systems, and it knew it.

Nor, in spite of its prominence in domestic politics, was the YPA praetorian. In a praetorian regime, the military from time to time intervene in government – usually imposing or supporting a chief executive who is the military's choice. The Yugoslav army did not insinuate itself: in a most 'professional', responsible way it was doing its duty as a legitimate participant in the Yugoslav polity. It was a *necessary*, integral element of the Yugoslav system. This was made perfectly clear in the early 1970s as the YPA's role as a ninth partner in the Federation was formalized.

Between 1971 and 1974 the military's role as the ninth partner in the Federation was recognized: its informal role was formalized in the new Constitution of 1974, drawn up on the basis of decisions taken at the 20th Congress of the LCY in May of that year. A new 166-member Central Committee replaced the old LCY Conference of 280 members. The former comprised 20 members from each of the six republican parties, together with members from each of the two provincial parties and the YPA party organization. Thus the YPA was made the ninth partner by its being accorded the status of an autonomous province.

As five other members of the army were included in the republican and provincial delegations, the total military representation on the Central Committee was 20 – that is, 12 per cent.[259] Furthermore, two generals, Nikola Ljubicic (Defence Minister) and Dzermil Sarac (Army-Party Organization Secretary), were members of the Presidium of the Central Committee (the latter, notably, was an *ex officio* member, so guaranteeing army representation). Finally, at the highest level of government, in the Executive Office, Ivan Kucoc, an active duty general, was named as one of the 12 members. Quite clearly, the YPA's role was significant.

Its role was, though, essentially one within the Federation, as the ninth partner, rather than within the wider system in general. Its representation at republican level was considerably less than at federal level. The Autonomous Province of Kosovo, with 3 per cent of its Central Committee members from the military, had the highest level of YPA participation.[260] The military was not to be incorporated as it had with the 'opening to society' of 1968; rather, it was being coopted on the premise that it would impart a measure of its own cohesion, stability and strength to the Federation.[261]

As a result of its being accorded recognition as an 'all Yugoslav' ninth partner, the military regained some of the autonomy it had lost with the introduction of GPD. In the new 'unified' defence system, the YPA emerged in a preeminent position: 'The shift in the Yugoslav political centre of gravity enabled the YPA to lobby for a redefinition of territorial defence that would restore its authority and central role.'[262] The YPA came to the coalition which was the Yugoslav Federation as a member with both the right and the duty to participate in all discussions of major social and political issues. It was wholly appropriate for the YPA to put forward its (usually conservative) views on any topic.[263]

YPA involvement was as a member of the system, not as an opponent or usurper. The YPA had the might with which to make a physical intervention, but it declined to use it. It was prepared to prod the civilian leadership on the Croatian issue, but it was also well aware of the liabilities in 'assuming a more overt political role'.[264] It was drawn into the political process because its leadership essentially remained unified while 'the party leadership passed through various stages of disarray'.[265] But the YPA never overstepped its welcome: the military had a clear sense of its own role within the system and therefore of its own inadequacies. Seemingly, the YPA was aware of the nature of civil-military relations in Yugoslavia.

The YPA was not a discrete institution; it was not in conflict with the Yugoslav regime; it did not want to be excluded from, nor intervene in and control domestic politics. It could not allow itself to extend its role too far on two counts: first, the existence of territorial defence units meant that to overreach its legitimate participation could end in civil war with a 'people's army'; secondly, it could not intervene, because to do so would threaten its own future survival and that of the system to which it owed allegiance.

In the early 1970s, the YPA (or at least its leadership) became, to some extent, essential in maintaining the stability, cohesion and, most importantly, the authority of civilian political institutions, above all, the LCY. The YPA was well aware of this in assuming the role it did to conserve the Yugoslav system. It had a vested interest in ensuring the Yugoslav state's survival: it was dependent on it. Recognition of this fact served to ensure that the military would not intervene physically, or, indeed, overtly beyond its allotted role in the system. The YPA recognized the reciprocal, symbiotic nature of Yugoslav civil-military relations.

The nature of Yugoslav civil-military relations was *necessarily* symbiotic. The YPA was both an *instrument* and a *function* of regime legitimacy. Its existence was dependent on regime continuation; the regime, to continue, had to preserve its legitimacy. The YPA was an instrument because the regime's legitimacy was dependent on its continuing to play the role it played after 1971.

The military was dependent on the regime: no regime, no military. In Yugoslavia, civil authority and political institutions rested on the principles of self-management and participatory democracy – the symbols of legitimacy; without them, the regime's legitimacy would 'wither'. For the military to usurp civilian power would have been contrary to those principles; they would have been shattered. So the military had to remain subordinate; it had to have an appropriate sense of role. But that sense of role was dependent on the regime's continuing legitimacy. Above all, to ensure the YPA's subordination and loyalty, there had to be a cohesive leadership.

Ironically, the YPA was the binding agent used to generate some measure of leadership cohesion. Its legitimate presence in civilian politics was based on the conscious premise that the military imparted some of its own stability, strength and cohesion. The regime depended on YPA participation as an instrument of cohesion with which to ensure continued legitimacy. Yet, the YPA's existence was dependent on continuing regime legitimacy; the YPA's role was a function of that legitimacy. In Yugoslav domestic politics, the YPA's strengths were harnessed and yet its involvement was constrained so as not to reveal its inadequacies: the Yugoslav regime could both have its cake and eat it, it seemed. However, after 1980, Yugoslavia lurched into a polygenous crisis of legitimacy and YPA efforts to perform its political role of restoring systemic equilibrium and imparting legitimacy only served to reveal those inadequacies.

3 The Multiple Crises of the 1980s: Politics and the Military

There were grounds for optimism *vis-a-vis* Yugoslavia's future after Tito's death in May 1980. Although many problems were known to be latent – particularly nationalism – other features since the resolution of the Croatian crisis had fostered regime legitimacy. Among these factors was the codification of decentralizing reforms in the 1974 Constitution – which appeared to satisfy national interests by severely limiting central, federal power. Another element contributing to confidence in the regime was the relative material prosperity gained during the 1960s and 1970s. Economically and socially, most Yugoslavs had 'never had it so good!'.[1] The initial transition from the individual presidency of Tito to his successors' collective presidency appeared to be untroubled. This was a further boost to Yugoslavia's viability.[2] However, the auspicious omens for the post-Tito era disguised the gathering of dark clouds. These stored up economic, nationalist and political difficulties. After 1980, the atmosphere became inclement: a multi-faceted crisis of legitimacy was unleashed.

The economic quagmire

After an economic boom between 1976 and 1979, Yugoslavia became locked into an economic crisis. An 'artificial prosperity' had been achieved by a combination of rapid modernization and readily available foreign credits.[3] Western lending peaked in 1978. By 1980, the IMF's terms for granting loans to Yugoslavia had become far more rigorous. A consequence of these measures was contraction of the economy. This was the onset of crisis.

The following decade saw a series of 'stabilization' plans but the economy was too rocky for these. In each case, the chief aim was sustained reduction of domestic demand in order to lower imports and release output from domestic consumption for export.[4] However, acute balance-of-payments and debt-repayment difficulties were not alleviated. The IMF applied pressure for a big devaluation of the dinar.

This was fiercely opposed by some regional leaders; Bosnia, for example, disproportionately reliant on hard-currency imports for its productive capacity while having little corresponding significance in exports, was against exchange-rate adjustment. Further dissent on devaluation focused on the inflationary pressures it created.[5] Inflation-related fears were not ill-founded. By the end of the 1980s Yugoslavia was experiencing hyper-inflation – facing the prospect of a rate in excess of 1,000 per cent.[6]

IMF pressure increased in 1982. Private lendings to the country had fallen sharply, imports had reduced acutely, yet hard-currency reserves were only US $1.7 billion. This amounted to one month's worth of imports requiring convertible currency. The IMF organized a series of meetings involving itself, the Yugoslavs and various other parties. These produced a *de facto* rescheduling of the Yugoslav debt in the form of an emergency package. This package ensured a further US $6.5 billion of loan to support the agreement between the Yugoslavs and the IMF.[7]

That agreement was to accept the proposals of the Kraigher Commission. These recommended liberalization of the economy; its harsh measures included raising interest rates to realistic levels, allowing the dinar to float and making real wage cuts as the effects of inflation were not redressed.[8] These measures were only partially implemented, however.

One effect of the limited implementation of a market mechanism was diminishing domestic demand which fell 12 per cent between 1980 and 1983.[9] Decreased demand, not surprisingly, provoked reductions in output growth rate. Gross Material Product (GMP) dropped form 7.5 per cent annually in 1978–9 to 0.9 per cent in 1982; then −1.3 per cent in 1982 and −1.3 per cent in 1983.[10] Average annual growth between 1981 and 1985 was 0.6 per cent.[11] Although the 1985–6 period promised reasons for hope (the economy grew 3 per cent), this was not sustained.

The reason for this was the replacement of the government led by Milka Planinc which had been biting the bullet of economic reform by a new Federal Executive Council (FEC) led by Branko Mikulic. Planinc's ouster was interpreted as a victory for conservative forces; her programme of liberalization (albeit with harsh consequences) was arrested and replaced by a policy of *ad hoc* responses – which achieved little.[12] Under the Planinc government, the dinar's depreciation had been restricted – in 1982 the annual rate was 75 per cent, but the following year it fell only 50 per cent. Between the Decembers of 1986 and 1987 annual inflation leapt from 100 per cent to 170 per cent.[13]

Eventually, in 1988, Mikulic's government was compelled to introduce the measures advocated by the IMF almost a decade earlier: dinar devaluation, real interest rates and the free movement of prices as a precursor to the lifting of all price controls. These measures were, however, unsuccessful. Towards the end of 1988, unemployment was approaching 20 per cent, the foreign debt had risen from US $19 billion in 1983 to US $23 billion and inflation was soaring.[14]

The IMF observed in 'disbelief and despair'.[15] The FEC could not control price or wage inflation; each fuelled the other. As prices rose, living standards fell and disquiet in the population emerged; an epidemic of strikes erupted in the country. In 1982 there had been 174 strikes in Yugoslavia. In March 1987 alone, there were 168, embracing 20,000 workers. Although most were short-lived, some were not; strikes by mostly Bosnian coal miners at Labin in Slovenia lasted over a month.[16] An anti-inflation policy resting on the need for pay restraint floundered.

The Mikulic government was swallowed in the swamp of economic crisis; on 30 December 1988 the government resigned *en masse*.[17] Mikulic's successor, Ante Markovic, arrived with a strong, liberal, reformist record.[18] Markovic's first speech held at least one ray of promise – certainly for those at the IMF: he abandoned the rhetoric of self-management.[19] Yet whatever the new Prime Minister's attitude to the past and the measures necessary for resolving the crisis, he faced the same impediment as his predecessors – lack of support.

Yugoslavia was undergoing a profound crisis of legitimacy. There had been little faith in or support for the authorities' attempts to rescue the economy. Polls found a general decay in popular support. Confidence in the party fell from 49.8 per cent in 1980 to 22.9 per cent in 1982.[20] Of only 46 per cent of Slovenes familiar with the 1983 economic stabilization plan, 46 per cent disagreed with it.[21] Finally, a 1983 poll had discovered that, to Milka Planinc's alarm, there was little confidence in Yugoslavia's ability to overcome its difficulties and small hope for the future.[22] These findings were underlined again in 1986.[23]

Dissensual dissipation of support for the pan-Yugoslav regime was evident in national and republican divisions. These were manifest in outbursts of nationalism and the inability of the various leaderships, including, ultimately, the federal leadership, to demonstrate commitment to a united Yugoslavia and resolve the country's grave economic crisis.

Albanian unrest in Kosovo and after: nationalist preserves and systemic paralysis

Yugoslavia was precipitated into a critical phase by the outbreak of Albanian nationalism in Kosovo in 1981. In March and April of that year strikes, demonstrations and riots by the Autonomous Province's majority ethnic Albanian population shocked the country. Arising from student protests resulting in 21 arrests and 35 injuries (12 of which were police officers), the riots became an uprising involving tens or hundreds of thousands of people.[24] Official figures recorded nine deaths and 257 injuries, whereas other sources estimated mortalities to have been up to 1,600.[25] The figure of 1,600, suggested by US Senator Jesse Helms, must be judged a gross exaggeration. As Kosovo was closed to journalists and other observers at the time, no reliable independent assessment can be made. When similar disturbances occured in 1989, reporters were present; there were sizeable discrepancies between official and press figures for casualties (see below). Between the first protests and the end of 1983, thousands of people had been arrested summarily and sentenced, in the main, to 60 days in prison;[26] 658 Albanians 'received sentences ranging from 1 to 15 years for "counter-revolutionary" crimes'.[27]

The nationalist outburst in Kosovo was allowed because of a blend of ignorance and disinformation. The sum of this was failure to recognize and defuse the problems that were the causes of the Albanian explosion. Even in the wake of rioting, Stane Dolanc impressed on foreign journalists that there was no problem in Kosovo because the problems concerning the Albanian nationality had been solved during the war.[28] In part, this ignorance may have been because of the provincial leadership's persistent refusal to inform Belgrade about the extent of nationalist feeling and organization. The Kosovan leadership, regarded as 'Yugoslav' – that is, 'non-Albanian' – by the population, but, ethnically, Albanian, for the most part, was aware that it might lose its limited powers if it was thought that a problem existed. Even Serbs in Kosovo were not well informed – the Serbian and Albanian language party dailies carried different coverage, only the latter recognizing Albanian discontent. The content of party dailies reflected what the provincial leadership knew; district committees were regularly witholding information from the Kosovan leaders.[29]

Whatever the impediments to a free flow of information, the 'Albanian question' had clearly not been resolved in 1945. Superficial harmony during the 1950s and 1960s made possible the suggestion that the Albanians did not realize they had a problem until they were told so at the time of the Rankovic purge in 1966.[30] Even if underlying tensions are ignored, the articulation of aspirations to greater self-determination and republican status as early as 1966 and a series of demonstrations between 1968 and the 1981 riots were signs of an unresolved difficulty.[31]

The Kosovo problem had (and continues to have) two mainsprings. One was Serbian-Albanian rivalry over several centuries; the other was the post-war socioeconomic development of the province. Serbs and Albanians have important historical stakes in Kosovo. For Serbs it is the bosom of their orthodox Christian church; the seat of the Serbian Orthodox patriarch was at Pec in Kosovo in medieval times. Kosovo Polje is the plain on which Serbs fought Ottoman invaders, thereby standing for Christendom against the Muslim horde. According to Serbian mythology, it was only their battle on St Vitus' Day, 1389, that saved Europe; the Turkish onslaught was so much reduced that it lacked the momentum to take Vienna. The Serbs were defeated at Kosovo Polje, but the nobility of having faced up to the overwhelming Ottoman forces and done battle when defeat was certain passed into Serbian self-image and consciousness throughout subsequent centuries. Another dimension of this pride in defeat was revanchism. After Kosovo Polje, the Turkish army crushed the Serbian Empire. Serbian pride required vengeance.

As the Serbian centre of gravity moved to the North, Kosovo became increasingly populated by Albanians who were islamicized by the Turks. This process fuelled Serbian lust to regain what they considered to be theirs by right and to evict the newcomers. Animosity towards Muslim Albanians throughout six centuries has remained intense, whereas the Serbs' close cousins, the Montenegrins, have, at times, shown themselves open to integration with ethnic Albanians.[32]

Most accounts of the Albanian colonization of Kosovo stem from a Serbian perspective. The increase in numbers of Albanians inhabiting Kosovo after the Serb exodus is undeniable; however, a more Albanian-oriented history would recognize that Kosovo was not a purely Serbian preserve; Albanians claim to be direct descendants of the ancient Illyrians, meaning they predate South Slavs on the territory.[33] More poignantly, if the Serb claim to Kosovo rests on its being the cradle of Serbian culture in the middle-ages, a similar Albanian case is found in modern times. After the Serbs' five-century absence, Kosovo again became the nucleus for a national culture. The Albanian national awakening in the latter part of the nineteenth century began in Kosovo. The first Albanian nationalist political movement was formed there in Prizren in 1878; another group, this time from Pristina, successfully secured autonomy from the Ottoman empire for Kosovan lands in 1912.

The Serbian authorities believed these territories should belong to Serbia. Some Serbs, notably the Social Democratic Party, supported the Albanians, seeing no reason not to help them build an independent state and arguing that failure to assist might quickly lead to Serbia's new neighbour becoming an enemy.[34] The Serbian government, however, sent its army to occupy Kosovan lands. Since 1913, with the brief exception of inclusion in Mussollini's 'Greater Albania' during the war, Kosovo has belonged to Belgrade.

The Serbian occupation was violent and repressive. The Serbs committed large-scale atrocities against the Albanians and made other attempts to 'dismantle the fabric of their culture and society'.[35] These included the denial of Albanian ethnicity and the use of the Albanian language; they also included a 'most brutal' colonization policy,[36] in which Albanians were stripped of their farms, and Serbs and Montenegrins were given great incentives to migrate to Kosovo. Armed resistance continued into the 1920s.[37]

Partisan annexation of Kosovo during 1944 and 1945 brought an end to Kosovo's short spell as part of 'Greater Albania'. In line with the tenets of 'brotherhood and unity', Albanians were recognized as a distinct ethnic group. However, they were not allowed self-determination, nor to make much contribution to discussions about the new political system that would incorporate them. Indeed, the Partisan army repeated the actions of the Serbian military a quarter of a century before; thousands of Albanians perished as a revolt formed against Partisan terrorization.[38]

The long-simmering antagonisms in Kosovan history constituted fuel ignited by sparks of socioeconomic development in communist Yugoslavia. The 1981 crisis was a direct product of the Tito regime. There were four major components of the crisis.

The first was repression, the absence of political freedoms and a consequent lack of information and public political debate. Although Tito's regime had, theoretically, given the ethnic Albanians national cultural rights they had not known in pre-war Yugoslavia, in practice these did not amount to much. With few exceptions, such as Albanian language schools, these rights meant little. Until the fall of Rankovic in 1966, the province functioned as a Serb colony, run as a police state.[39]

The teaching of specifically Albanian aspects of history and culture was tightly constrained by the Serbs – especially that which pertained to former unity with Albania proper. Many Albanians, particularly those living outside Kosovo in Macedonia, Montenegro and narrow Serbia, were intimidated into defining themselves as other than Albanian – 'Yugoslav', 'Muslim' or 'Turk', for example. In some cases they were made to adopt their names with a Slavic ending to give an impression that they were Slavs; this increased their chances of employment.[40]

This situation engendered underground opposition groups. In 1964 an illegal organization promoting the idea of an Albanian republic was revealed. The political trial following its discovery ended with 57 people, including the movement's leader, Adem Demaci, being imprisoned for terms of 3 to 15 years.[41] Subsequently there would be more pro-Albanian groups organizing themselves illegally. In 1975 the 'National Movement for the Liberation of Kosovo' was uncovered. Formed by Demaci's supporters, it was accused of conspiracy against 'the people and the state'.[42] Sentences for those involved ranged from 4 to 12 years.

Groups seeking enhanced status for Kosovo and improvement in conditions there have continued to develop. In extreme cases they have demanded union with Albania, in others republican status for Kosovo within Yugoslavia, and in still others simply jobs. Such groups reflect the strength of Albanian disenchantment. As one eminent Yugoslav scholar has commented, 'in a healthy political system there is no need for illegal political organizations'.[43]

Illegal opposition groups continued, in spite of the limited realization, post-Rankovic, of some rights. Indeed, much of this added to the difficulties. The loosening of controls allowed the Albanians in general to discover how much was wrong with their situation and permitted them to express their discontent. Thus, demonstrations demanded various ameliorations of the position in Kosovo. Often, these were suppressed by the authorities; this gave rise to stronger feelings and more subversive groups making bigger demands. In the three years before 1981, the security services were reported to have found (and dealt with) two separatist organizations.[44]

An important addition to any assessment of the repressive nature of Yugoslavia, especially Serb politics in Kosovo, is consideration of information policy. As already indicated, channels of communication between the various levels of the various authorities and output in newspapers left many gaps in information. This became a hot topic at the time of the 1981 riots.[45] Too often, both before and since the riots, reliable information on Kosovo has been thin. Often 'stereotypical' jargon is substituted for usable data.[46]

However much repression and restrictions on information and political activity created and reinforced ignorance, prejudice and antagonism, the economic standing of Kosovo was an unmistakable cause of the 1981 unrest. Always Yugoslavia's poorest region, it had become proportionately poorer *vis-a-vis* the country's richer areas. In 1947, the level of economic development in Kosovo was half the Yugoslav average; in 1980, this had become one quarter.[47] Between 1952 and 1984 a 4.1 to 1 ratio between Slovenia and Kosovo for wealth grew to 6.1 to 1; the gap widened particularly rapidly after 1965. Horvat emphasizes this disparity and its exponential character: if there were a 6 per cent growth rate, it would take Kosovo 24 years to catch up; a growth rate of only 2 per cent would require 91 years; in both cases, there would also need to be a zero rate of growth in Slovenia throughout the period involved. However, if constant prices from 1972 are used, in 1984, Slovenian *per capita* social product was 7.67 times larger than in Kosovo.[48]

Massive investment did not help the situation. In the period 1971–5, Kosovo received US $685 million of aid from Federal funds. It received, on top of monies from Belgrade, a further US $240 million worth of assistance from World Bank credit to Yugoslavia between 1975 and 1980 – almost one quarter of what the country received.[49] Yet Kosovo's economic condition worsened. The province's economic predicament combined with demographic changes, the third element in the Kosovan crisis, each in some way amplifying the other.

By 1981, particularly in the light of the region's wealth, Kosovo was overpopulated. Always poor, the area had none the less sustained a pre-war population of 716,000. In 1981, this figure had more than doubled to 1,555,000.[50] Even with considerable injections of aid, Kosovo had difficulty supporting a population of this size.

Parallel with the overall expansion of the population was a big shift in Kosovo's ethnic texture. From 1961 to 1981, the actual number of Albanians leapt from 646,000 to 1,227,000. This doubling meant an increase in the proportion of Albanians in the region's inhabitants from 67.1 per cent in 1961 to 77.5 per cent 20 years later. The increase in Albanians corresponded with a decrease in Serbs. Serbs have widely claimed that Albanian hostility has been the cause of an exodus.[51] However, it is notable that whereas up to a quarter of a million Albanians emigrated to Turkey for political and economic reasons before 1966, the exit of Serbs from Kosovo began only after the mid-1960s.[52]

The exodus of Serbs from Kosovo coincided with the increase in Albanian expressions of discontentment. More pertinently, this migration corresponded with rapidly decreasing living standards in the region. Horvat maintains that the underlying cause of immigration was economic backwardness; he also urges that the process could not be arrested without economic development.[53] The violence in 1981 might have influenced Serbs leaving Kosovo, but it could not be judged a sufficient explanation. An official statement in October 1988 put the number of Serbs and Montenegrins to have left Kosovo since the riots at 25,661. This would make the claim of Serbian LC Secretary, Zoran Sokolovic, that 31,000 had left in this period an exaggeration. This figure might be a reasonable estimate for the 15-year period in which a German institute reported that 250,000 Albanians had left Kosovo for other parts of Yugoslavia and other parts of Europe for political and economic reasons.[54]

Large numbers of both Slavs and Albanians certainly left Kosovo to look for work. Unemployment in Kosovo was 3.33 times the Yugoslav average; whereas 210,000 people worked in the social sector, 114,000 were unemployed. Unemployment heightened tensions a propos job distribution. Whereas per thousand Kosovo inhabitants 258 Montenegrins and 228 Serbs were in employment, only 109 Albanians had jobs.[55] In the mid-1960s, when Kosovo's problems began to be revealed, one in 17 Albanians had a social-sector job, whereas one in four Serbs and one in three Montenegrins were in such work.[56] In 1982, although over three quarters of the Kosovan population, Albanians made up only 60 per cent of the work force; the combined total for Serbs and Montenegrins, with only 15 per cent of the total population, was 33 per cent. This situation was even more ethnically disproportionate vis-a-vis positions of responsibility, particularly in the administrative agencies of Kosovo's sociopolitical organizations where only 54 per cent of the 251 presidents were Albanian and about 38 per cent were Slavs.[57]

The fourth factor contributing to the crisis was the expansion of education for Albanians. Before the war there were 19 Albanians among the 17,734 Yugoslav students at university; in 1981 there were 26,000 regular students and 37,000 in all attending university in Pristina.[58] This meant there was a large pool of educated young people with high expectations. The patterns of employment detailed above meant that they could not be absorbed into the Kosovan economy;[59] leaving aside any language problems, their aspirations could not be met outside the province as other Yugoslavs often failed to recognize their qualifications. The ill feeling often found in educated, but unemployable, groups was augmented by the over representation of Serbs in good jobs in the provincial administration and economic hardship as inflation bit into already low living standards.

The Kosovan conflagration began with student protests. Quickly, sizeable segments of the Albanian population joined in what became riots. The combination of a new, large, educated Albanian group, demographic patterns of employment, unemployment and ethnic composition in Kosovo, economic backwardness in an ever-receding economy, and the absence of free, open discussion of grievances precipitated violent outbursts.

Following the revolt, Kosovo was subject to martial law. Militia and YPA units were moved in to control the province. This was expensive. Armed units remained in Kosovo long after the riots; on their first anniversary, the cost of the Reserve Militia's continuing presence in Kosovo was put at five million dinars per individual per month (at contemporary prices).[60] The martial forces were unwelcome, often being jeered, booed and spat upon by local inhabitants.[61] The armed presence increased hostility.

So, too, did mass arrests and heavy prison sentences. Even outside Albanian confines, these caused disquiet. Mitja Ribicic, a Slovene, and a war-time party elder, wondered if 'education' rather than 12 years in jail might be a better way to deal with 18-year-old protesters.[62] Moreover, he added, Kosovo's problems would only be solved by finding political and economic solutions and by the Kosovans' own hard work. Instead of the ameliorative measure Ribicic intended, the political solution found was one well tested in communist systems – a purge. A process of 'differentiation' was initiated to weed out the 'unhealthy' forces in the party and in society. The Kosovan LC leadership was changed and over 1,000 members were expelled from it; sometimes whole branches of the party organization were closed down.[63] Many individuals were also forced out of their jobs, including teachers and university lecturers.[64]

The problems in Kosovo did not go away during the remainder of the decade. Indeed, they flared again in 1989 (see below). In addition to the sometimes violent and separatist variant among Kosovo's majority ethnic Albanian population, nationalism has had other manifestations. Serbian nationalism has been a backlash to Kosovo.[65] An otherwise liberally oriented Serbian Academy produced a 'Memorandum' in 1985, outlining Serbia's anomalous position in the Socialist Federative Republic of Yugoslavia and calling into question the 1974 Constitution, dubbing it anti-Serb.[66] A group of ethnic Serbs from Kosovo told the Federal Assembly that if it could find no solution, they would solve the problems themselves. Unlike their brethren who had left Kosovo, they were determined to stay and fight – with arms if necessary.[67] Serbian nationalist fervour supported the rise of Slobodan Milosevic to leadership of the Serbian LC and, then, the Republican presidency. His unabashed nationalist policies saw changes in the Serbian, Vojvodina and Kosovan

Constitutions, taking away the force of the two provinces' autonomy. These stimulated more riots by the Albanian community and a constitutional crisis throughout Yugoslavia.[68] A 'Muslim' consciousness had developed in Bosnia[69] and Slovene nationalism had emerged prominently.[70] Interacting with strong democratic and liberalizing trends, Slovene nationalist sentiment became particularly vibrant in response to the growth of Serb nationalism. In response to the 'Memorandum' of the Serbian Academy, the Slovene journal *Nova Revija* produced a Slovene National Programme.[71] This was suppressed, although its authors were not prosecuted. Slovene feelings were then further amplified by Serb activity in Kosovo.[72]

The centrifugal forces of nationalism amounted to a lack of faith in the SFRY. The lack of commitment to a united Yugoslavia was demonstrated in the inability of the various leaderships, including, ultimately, the federal leadership, to resolve the country's grave economic crisis. Indeed, these republican and national divisions were, in a viciously circular way, the cause and effect of the economic problems. Each regional leadership protected its own interests at the expense of all-Yugoslav requirements.[73] Even where the leaderships could agree on a remedy for economic ills, there was 'little real commitment to making it work, because that would have meant the sacrificing of republican interests deemed important by the republican elites'.[74]

National and economic difficulties stem from the political system. Faced with various crises, this system seems unable to function adequately. The regime seems unable to operate appropriate 'steering' mechanisms (to recall Habermas); it is unable to 'manage' the crisis. According to Schopflin, the regime has 'neither the instrumentality nor agreement on the criteria for the resolution of conflicts'.[75]

It could even be argued that this system caused the crisis. The US $ three billion deficit in 1979 was a function of the financial decentralization of control on foreign payments. It came as a surprise and was allowed to happen because there was no central view on what was happening. When the first post-Tito financial crisis occured, the system's complexity and inertia were not understood.

When a Zagreb bank could not repay its $500,000,000 debt, the system was incapable of action. The central bank, because of decentralization (and without Tito to take short-cuts), could not act without agreement to save the bank. In the wake of rescheduling the Polish debt, Western banks thought the Yugoslav coffers were empty (they were not) and lost confidence in Yugoslavia. As a result, under conditions of increasing internal chaos and external fiscal pressure the economy plummeted.[76] The multi-faceted crisis had its root in the political system.

The interlinked crises as a whole constituted a crisis of legitimacy. Discussions on a new constitution began in 1986. Whenever (if ever) this eventually appeared, in establishing a new basis for the regime's legitimacy, it would have to be the instrument of reform and, if effectively achieved, relegitimation. However, with Slovenes and Croatians favouring multi-party reforms and Serbians opposing them, the prospects were not bright.[77] Meanwhile, the multi-faceted legitimacy crisis had worsened and the YPA's voice in the political arena had grown louder.

The YPA and politics in the 1980s: military legitimacy circumscribed

The Yugoslav crisis of legitimacy and the Polish precedent for martial rule in a communist system led to speculation that a 'Yugoslav Jaruzelski' might appear. In one Slovene's view such a phenomenon was the 'only factor able to stop the creeping chaos'.[78] The possibility of military rule seems to have been behind Milka Planinc's statement that if her plans were not accepted 'a different government' might step in.[79]

Milovan Djilas noted such speculation and the military's greatly increased role, but concluded that it is 'not likely that the military will take power'.[80] An earlier rejection came from a member of the Croatian Republican Presidency who said that such speculation was made 'by people who knew nothing at all about our system' and therefore did not understand that the army is 'an integral part of the people'.[81] This view was echoed by Defence Secretary Branko Mamula. He rejected 'certain speculations' (presumably, a propos of a coup) on the grounds that the military role, as a part of the system, was 'laid down by the Constitution'.[82]

The Constitution was central to the military's role in the political system. In 1971, General Ivan Miskovic said that 'only in cases where the constitutional order was threatened would the army become an instrument for solving internal difficulties'.[83] This seems consistent with YPA activity in Kosovo in 1981. It is also consistent with other military behaviour. The army would only act constitutionally. This meant that it would only usurp the political processes if no civil element remained to protect the Constitution. As long as some central civil authority remained, the army would constitutionally be the coercively instrumental partner in an alliance. Were Kosovo to erupt again (or similar disquiet emerge in another region) it would be part of the YPA's constitutional role to repress the disturbance and preserve the political order. Only if no 'pro-Constitutional' civil authority remained to lead a 'pro-Constitutional' alliance would military rule become a possibility. If some central authority remained, the army would be its ally in securing the Constitution. While constitutional order prevailed, the YPA's legitimacy as a political actor would remain intact. It would use its coercive might, where necessary, to support party leaders in protecting the Constitution or to supplant them if they failed to maintain constitutional priorities. In the light of this understanding, it is

instructive to note Milan Daljevic's reminder to the 13th Congress of
the LCY in 1986 that the YPA's political activity was a constitutional
role.[84]

This formalized, legitimate political role was based on the notion
that the YPA would ensure a 'pan-Yugoslav' voice in politics,
inheriting Tito's mantle when he died. Tito emphasized this:
'Brotherhood and Unity are inseparably linked with our army . . . I
believe that our army is still playing such a role today . . . our army
must not merely watch vigilantly over our borders, but also be
present inside the country . . . there are those who write that one day
Yugoslavia will disintegrate. Nothing like that will happen because
our army ensures that we will continue to move in the direction we
have chosen for the socialist construction of our country.'[85] This role
was given substance by the appointment of generals to key posts and
their *de facto* presence in the party leadership.[86]

Although there had been some suggestion that Tito did not see the
army's role this way,[87] it seems unlikely to have been accurate.
Certainly, the military believed that it acted in accordance with
'constitutional orientations and Tito's views on the social role of the
Yugoslav People's Army'.[88] The YPA was conscious of its 'responsibility', a feeling that 'developed during Tito's time, especially
during periods when the country experienced problems'. Moreover,
'this sentiment continued to grow after Tito's death'.[89]

At the heart of the army's role was its all-Yugoslav character; it was
'the army of all the nations and nationalities of the country'.[90] Its
pan-Yugoslav outlook was inherited from the YPA's Partisan roots.[91]
It was a continuation of war-time traditions that the military was
involved in politics. The Yugoslav military was 'always at the centre
of the revolutionary process, neither separated from society nor
closed to it'.[92] The embodiment of 'brotherhood and unity' or
'togetherness' the YPA had remained essentially the same through
the rejuvenation of its officer cadre.[93] 'There are no differences
between the war-time generations, only small numbers of which
remain in the YPA, and the post-war generations', it was asserted,
which fact assured 'the continuation of the most positive
achievements of the national liberation struggle'.[94]

Its pan-Yugoslav character was the basis for the YPA's role as an
'integral part of the LCY'.[95] In broader terms, both civilians and
soldiers recognized its role as an 'integral part of our society'.[96] That
role was to bind the various elements of the Yugoslav political mosaic
as best they could; the YPA was a cohesive element amid disarray.
The army had been, was and would remain 'a strong factor of
stability in our socialist self-managing system and one of the cohesive
factors of Yugoslav society'.[97] Milanko Renovica underlined this in
his address to the LCY's 13th Congress. In his passage on the armed
forces, the president of the LCY Presidium stressed the 'integrity' of
the army.[98]

That 'integrity' was the 'firm moral-political unity and national and revolutionary character of the Armed Forces and the Army', which had 'reaffirmed itself at all critical moments, whenever we [had been] passing through difficulties in our development'.[99] Yet it also entailed the understanding that the army wished 'neither to impose nor to remain in the barracks, nor above or beyond society, [for] it [was] already an integral part of the political system'.[100] The YPA had an important, legitimate role to play. In Renovica's words, the armed forces were 'not a quiet island on which there is no sensitivity to the troubles stirred up in Yugoslavia. They guard the destiny of this society.'[101]

As guardians of society, the generals could not be a quiet island. They had 'resolutely' rejected 'any attempt – no matter by whom and where it may be made – to diminish this [i.e. political] role'.[102] Indeed, in some ways the role may have been augmented.[103] Certainly the army has not remained silent. The generals were quick to voice their criticisms.

Understandably, the YPA was worried about 'harmful trends, especially the trends emerging from the holes of the vampire like resuscitated nationalism'.[104] One senior figure has expressed surprise at the numbers of young people who came into the army imbued with nationalist ideas; he wonders 'how young people, born and educated in this society can succumb to such phenomena'.[105] The economy, too, was an area of concern.[106] While the YPA has keenly supported the economic stabilization programme, Mamula has found it 'difficult to understand inconsistencies in implementing the agreed policy as well as the pronounced subjectivity of the League of Communists and other organized socialist forces of society. Members of the armed forces react most to the slowness and certain inconsistencies in implementing the agreed policy and the the widely spread phenomena of giving preference to partial interests at the expense of common, general Yugoslav ones.'[107]

Essentially, such criticism was of the party itself. Notably, 'members of the army, primarily Communists', reacted to the 'behaviour of certain subjects in society, particularly those who should take measures against various violators of working and moral norms, of enrichment without work, favouring someone in the cadre policy and so forth. The current economic and political situation in the country [did not] suffer any compromises in the implementation of the stabilization programme.'[108] The YPA's worry was the League's waning legitimacy through its failures to provide good leadership; it was seen to be losing the trust and confidence of the people.[109] In brief, The League of Communists had to 'transform itself and be capable . . . of justifying its leading social role also in the new stage of our development'.[110]

Despite YPA chiding, however, there was little improvement. The YPA was not noticeably effective in performing its political role. It tried, but achieved little. It hectored, yet was unable to catalyze decision-making processes and effect the unity of political will for which it aimed. The YPA was not very effective because its role had been circumscribed by weaknesses emerging in its legitimacy. The 1980s were marked by growing legitimacy problems in Yugoslavia. But the deepening legitimacy difficulties did not necessarily indicate a yet greater amplification of the YPA's role, such as, perhaps, a military government. Such an extension of the army's role would be unlikely because of certain weaknesses that emerged in the YPA's legitimacy. These weaknesses mean a martial solution is unlikely to be the answer to Yugoslavia's difficulties in the 1990s. Although the YPA's voice grows louder, raising the volume is all it can do. As the growing weaknesses identified in Yugoslavia as a whole impinge on its legitimacy, military action in domestic politics becomes increasingly circumscribed. Moreover, as we shall see, frailties in regime and military-political legitimacy affect the YPA's functional legitimacy; Yugoslavia's defence capability is increasingly circumscribed by these weaknesses.

These weaknesses may be focused in four areas: the incremental weakness of the pan-Yugoslav principle; the diminished power of the national liberation struggle as a legitimating doctrine; the YPA's inability to be socially representative in terms of national proportionality; and a growing anti-military posture among some young people.

YPA legitimacy became constrained, in the first place, because to be all-Yugoslav was not in the 1980s what it was in 1971. Although the YPA tried to carry Tito's mantle, the role proved too great for it; the army lacked Tito's full, all-Yugoslav authority. Whereas Tito, especially with the generals' support, was more than all the others, the YPA was merely 'another', an equal. The force of its pan-Yugoslav position had been weakened by the fissive tendencies of the Yugoslav Federal order. The YPA represented 'Yugoslavism' as eight other units represent partial interests.

The army was, indeed, a part of the system, not above it; it could only influence as a ninth element, it could not dominate. Where it exerted itself, it was decried as 'unitarist' – that is, as advocating something between Serb hegemony and quasi-Stalinist centralism. The army could only be effective if it was in coalition with other centres of political power. This was the case in 1971 with Tito. In the 1980s there was no comparable all-Yugoslav force with which the YPA might ally itself. Without some alliance, the army remains weak. The YPA's voice in the Yugoslav nonet was not a strong one; its plea for harmony was rejected amid nationalist discord.

As the pan-Yugoslav notion seemed less attractive, so, too, the national liberation war and concomitant revolutionary struggle were less effective as legitimating principles. As Schopflin argued, they may still have engendered respect among young people for whom they represented the 'historic' foundations of the system; but they had no direct, legitimating appeal.[111] Thus, the much valued 'links with the people', an 'historic' feature of the YPA were weakened.[112]

One indication of this weakening is the phenomenon of physical attacks on YPA members, such as that at the Split naval school.[113] During 1986 there were at least 30 such attacks.[114]

To some extent these attacks represented nationalist sentiments. Nationalism was also a problem in that proportionality was more important to military legitimacy than it might be elsewhere. For however much Yugoslav soldiers identified themselves as Yugoslavs,[115] the YPA had to appear to have national proportionality. Although this had been achieved in the High Command, where one analysis yields 38 per cent Croats, 33 per cent Serbs and 8.3 per cent Slovenes,[116] the YPA was predominantly composed of Serbs and Montenegrins.[117] The army was perceived, therefore, as a Serb institution.

The issue of national proportionality could not be easily resolved. This was reflected in the YPA's great concern about difficulties in youth recruitment. Mamula recognized the detriment this might be to the YPA's all-Yugoslav character.[118] He stressed the need to preserve the 'officer corps' integrity' by attracting sufficient numbers of Slovenes, Croats, Albanians and Hungarians, of which groups, insufficient numbers registered at military schools.[119] 'Reduced interest among young people in the military profession' – especially 'a poor response from the developed regions of the country' (i.e. Slovenia, in particular) – meant 'an equal national representation could be jeopardized'.[120]

Deficiencies a propos the Slovenes remained acute. Although they were well represented at the highest levels, Slovenes were markedly under-represented in the YPA as a whole. Figures for 1973 were presented in Chapter 2. Subsequent figures could not have made the YPA leadership more optimistic. Only 3.51 per cent of applications to military academies in 1982 came from Slovenia.[121] Later figures offered consistent findings. Between 1980 and 1985 the percentage of Slovene officers fell from 3.8 per cent to 2.55 per cent. 'The situation could only get worse', it was reported, as only 60 per cent of the number of Slovenes needed were attending military schools; only 4.5 per cent of those in military academies were Slovenes.[122]

Explanations for the under-representation of Slovenes in the army included 'the unfavourable material position of military officers, the lack of motivation towards a military profession among young Slovenes, and the fact that young people in Slovenia have fewer problems finding employment than in any other part of the country'.[123] To some extent, material explanations are, however, inadequate. Although not without relevance, such explanations must accompany an awareness of anti-military sentiment seemingly prevalent among Slovene youths.

Aside from objections to the conditions of military service,[124] criticisms of the YPA included the emphasis on drill, alcoholism, disregard for human individuality, exploitative conditions and corruption.[125] Further criticism argued for the YPA to be 'depoliticized'.[126]

'Depoliticization' might be expected to have meant the increased 'socialization' of the army,[127] by which we should understand that there were calls for it to be brought into line with self-management practices.[128] Although there was some encouragement to 'make it possible for the greatest number of people to be involved in the collegiate form of work',[129] self-management could not be extended practically; it was inimical to the direct command, hierarchically structured army. An obvious implication of the YPA's moving towards self-management norms, were that to happen, would have been 'republicanization' – the creation of a separate army in each unit of the Federation to match their political and economic identities. Such notions had been firmly rejected in YPA quarters.[130]

Other issues concerned linguistic practice within the YPA,[131] and the YPA's criticism of the Slovene Youth Organization on matters such as its adaptation of the 'Third Reich' poster for 'Youth Day'.[132] But the major issue of contention between Slovene youths and the YPA was over conscientious objection and the possibility of performing military service in a civilian capacity.

A proposal made by the Slovene Youth Organization to permit 'conscientious objection', although initially thoroughly rejected at various organizational levels, would not fade away. It was an 'initiative' that struck at the core of Yugoslav defence principles which derive from the Partisan tradition that everyone has an equal duty to fight; this is a constitutional obligation; moreover, no one has the right to surrender.[133]

Although the 'initiative' received some support from the Slovene party leadership, where it and similar demands were regarded as legitimate,[134] the YPA, not surprisingly, found them 'unacceptable'.[135] The army argued for equality: it could not be right that 'some families' sons and daughters laid down their lives in defence of the country and not others'.[136] To allow this would be to 'legalize privilege' and would be 'incompatible with the principles of a self-managing society'.[137] It would be contrary to the principle of equality under which military service is a 'constitutional and legal duty for all psychophysically healthy and capable young men'.[138] The YPA argued in detail, as well as in principle. One foundation of the Youth proposal was conscientious objection on religious grounds. This had been rejected as insignificant: in the previous 15 years, only 152 people had been convicted for conscientious objection for religious reasons.[139] Indeed, as far as conscience was concerned, for Daljevic, 'the most honourable and most noble conscience is the patriotic conscience'.[140]

Perhaps, as Milanko Renovica stated, the publicity made the initiative seem a 'key problem' for relations, which 'undoubtedly' was 'not true'.[141] Certainly, although the generals could have won a debate which, in truth, should never have contained a viable challenge, their sensitivity (like a bear with a thorn) led them to make a blundering attempt to 'deal' with their persistent critics from

Slovenia. The outcome was concession on the issue of conscientious objection and a further weakening of military legitimacy.[142]

The deterioration of civil-military relations in Slovenia

During 1988, an unhappy civil-military relationship became wretched. Civil-military relations may be analysed at various levels, of which two are relevant here: one is the relationship between the armed forces and society; the other is that between the military and political elites. I would argue that civil-military relations in Slovenia deteriorated in 1988 not only because the chasm between large sections of Slovene society, particularly the young and the Yugoslav Peoples Army (YPA), increased, but because in the course of events, the Slovene political leadership was antagonized and brought into greater harmony with Slovene youth. The catalyst in this process was the trial, in July 1988, of three journalists and a non-commissioned officer for contravening military secrecy. With regard to the army, the decision to prosecute and the way in which it was done must be judged as bad politics, bad public relations and bad for defence.

The YPA's handling of that trial (which will be discussed below) eased the mutual distrust and criticism that characterized the relationship between the Slovene leadership and its youth. That relationship had developed in the 'liberal' political atmosphere created in Slovenia, in particular, by party leader Milan Kucan. Kucan had promoted the notions of a 'legal state' and 'pluralism' of interests, both of which represented experiments in the rule of a communist party. Under the guardian eye of the party (LCS) and the umbrella of the Socialist Alliance (SAWP), various 'informal' social movements were allowed to develop. These included religious groups, a Green movement and a re-invented Young Peasants Alliance – which reserved the right to become a party proper if it was not satisfied.[143]

Prime among these buds of pluralism was the Slovene Youth Organization and, in particular, its weekly publication *Mladina*. *Mladina* became the forum for the expression of the most radical ideas available. It frequently criticized Republican and state institutions and the political leadership that allowed it to flourish.[144] Prominent among *Mladina*'s targets was the YPA and its position in Yugoslav society. It was the linchpin of the fracture in the YPA's relationship with young Slovenes.

Between 1986 and 1988, the YPA was often offended by *Mladina*. In April 1988, General Milan Daljevic explained that over a five-year period, the Ljubljana Military District Command had kept a file on articles in certain Slovene publications. Of the 407 texts in the file sent to the SAWP the previous month, 267 had appeared in *Mladina* during 1987 – and of these, only one was considered acceptable. Moreover, Daljevic had counted 80 texts in the first three months of 1988 alone, and suggested that *Mladina* had almost become a military magazine.[145] Although the editor-in-chief of *Mladina* suggested a much lower figure,[146] it is undeniable that, over a number of years, *Mladina* had issued various challenges to the YPA. Throughout 1987 and 1988 a dialogue persisted without any love lost between the magazine and the army's newspaper *Narodna Armija*.[147]

For much of the time, debate focused on the initiative of the Slovene Youth Organization to permit concientious objections and the performance of military service in a civilian capacity. The proposal seemed to reflect the lack of interest among Slovenes in military occupations, not to say an anti-military sentiment. However, the concept was anathema to the YPA.[148]

The relationship between *Mladina* and the military declined logarithmically in the early months of 1988. The editors' sights were firmly trained on the Federal Secretary of Defence, Branko Mamula. First, a strongly adverse editorial dealt with Mamula's visit to Ethiopia, characterizing him as a salesman of death for (they presumed) concluding arms deals with a regime that spent money on arms while half its population suffered famine.[149] Then, over a four-week period, *Mladina*, equally provocatively, revealed how conscripts had been used to build Mamula a 'villa' at Opatija.[150] *Narodna Armija* called it a 'flat' and said it was not for Mamula personally, but for the Federal Secretary of Defence.[151] The YPA was clearly annoyed. In May, Mamula resigned, seven months before his already announced retirement date, with little explanation; it seems reasonable to judge that the cause was the fallout from *Mladina*'s broadsides.[152] He was replaced by General Veljko Kadijevic.

Other articles on the military constantly appeared in *Mladina*, as did a regular flow of anti-military cartoons. During this period, the managing editor of *Mladina*, Franci Zavrl, and another journalist were indicted for allegedly libelling the YPA in an article in the weekly *Teleks* on the differences between young people and the generals.[153] There was even a report that a member of the Slovene Constitutional Commision was proposing, *de facto*, an independent Slovene Army, which would remain part of a federated Yugoslav Army.[154] The divorce between major currents of Slovene opinion and the YPA was strained to its extreme. However, the army's relationship with the Slovenes became much worse in the following months.

On 31 May, Janez Jansa was arrested on suspicion of betraying a military secret. Jansa had become a particular irritant for the YPA. Writing on military matters in *Mladina* over 15 years, his articles had become increasingly critical. At the time of his arrest, Jansa was a candidate for the Presidency of the Slovene Youth Organization (this candidature was maintained until he became ineligible).[155] Subsequently, another journalist, David Tasic, and a non-commissioned officer in the YPA, Ivan Borstner, were also arrested; lastly, shortly before the trial, Zavrl was again indicted.

These arrests caused considerable concern among the Slovenes. A large protest rally in support of the accused was organized for 21

June, coinciding by accident or design with the opening of the League of Communists in the YPA (LC-YPA) conference. Called a 'cultural meeting', the event was 'dignified' according to Kucan, who was astounded at reportage of the meeting elsewhere in the country – particularly that by Belgrade TV which described escalating nationalism and counter-revolution.[156] This reaction from outside Slovenia increased concern there – concern that was already heightened by the arrests, the lack of information surrounding them and the rumours that circulated in the absence of detail. In this nervous atmosphere, the Presidency of the LCS demanded that 'consistent respect be given to the law and that the public – and thus also the LC – be familiarized with all the facts and the legal basis for the initiation of the proceedings [against Jansa, Borstner and Tasic]'.[157] The Presidency also called, at this juncture, for the founding of a Committee for Human Rights to work within the SAWP. Two days later, the Republican Presidency reported that although there had been no irregularity in the investigation, 'concern is caused by the fact that the Slovene public is alarmed, that the feeling of distrust in the institutions of the political system is growing'. The Republican Presidency also called for full information and the observance of constitutional and legal provisions, particularly with regard to rights and freedom of action. It also specifically urged the SFRY Presidency, as the supreme command of the YPA, to ensure that the military court's proceedings would be consistent with the law.[158] The political leadership remained ambivalent about the *Mladina* – YPA question. Kucan, at the June LCS Plenum, stressed the importance of legitimate discussion of issues concerning the YPA and defence and set himself apart from *Mladina*.[159]

The breakwater was the trial itself. Jansa, Borstner, Tasic and Zavrl (JBTZ) were charged under Article 224 of the Yugoslav legal code, relating to the disclosure of secret military documents.[160] Although Borstner admitted the offence, the others had at best only possessed the document. As some lawyers pointed out, Article 224 referred to the disclosure, not possession, of a military secret.[161] Neither this, nor other questions involving legal niceties and 'human rights' matters influenced the trial. Borstner was sentenced to four years imprisonment, Jansa to 18 months and Tasic and Zavrl to six months each. On appeal, Zavrl's sentence was increased to 18 months.[162]

The JBTZ trial had two significant aspects: it was heard in camera and in Serbo-Croat. To a Slovene public convinced that the trial was an army 'frame-up' to get even with Jansa, in particular, and some other *Mladina* journalists, these aspects of the trial were as provocative as any anti-YPA text in *Mladina* could have been. Moreover, it was these features that precipitated the qualitative shift in the deteriorating civil-military relationship – that is, it is these two matters that stirred the Slovene authorities. Both moves fuelled the idea that the whole action was anti-Slovene: an impression that brought youth and leadership into greater alignment. In this respect, they were mutually reinforcing bad moves – unless the YPA expressly wanted to provoke. That a military secrets trial should be heard behind closed doors seems clear – as indeed it did in some parts of Yugoslavia.[163] However, the nature of the document in question was of considerable concern to many in Slovenia. The political leadership suggested that the contents of the document be made known.[164] This request was denied by the military court on the grounds that to do so would be to commit the crime of which the four were accused – disclosure of a military secret.[165]

The document was not, technically, a secret. Tomaz Ertl, Republican Secretary for Internal Affairs (RSNZ), admitted that the document – Ljubljana Military District Command Order 5044-3 (from 8 January 1988) – had not been marked 'secret'. However, his opinion was that the document would obviously be secret to anyone with knowledge of military affairs.[166] This only fuelled public questions about the document itself. Borstner admitted passing Order 5044-3 to journalists whom he thought might be sympathetic. He also stated that he did so because the document constituted a 'grave threat' to the Slovene people and their sovereignty.[167]

It was widely rumoured that the document was a plan to destabilize Slovenia, create a state of emergency, clamp down on the liberal Slovene press and replace the liberal Slovene leadership either with Slovenes sympathetic to the more conservative YPA, or with outsiders. This was denied. It was suggested that no such interpretation could be put on the document. Stane Dolanc, perceived by Slovenes as pro-Federation, rather than pro-Slovene, said similar orders to 5044-3 had been made in all republics and provinces and were merely routine.[168]

Mladina alleged that the leadership must have known about the document and the arrests beforehand. This claim was made on the basis of a set of shorthand notes, apparently taken at a meeting in March by Milan Kucan, on which *Mladina* based a report. That article claimed that these matters were discussed at such a meeting.[169] This was denied – although it was admitted that Kucan and Dolanc had attended a meeting with the Republican security services at which a question from the Ljubljana Army District Command had been discussed.[170] *Mladina* and other Slovene leaders asked that the notes of that meeting be made public. That request was refused.[171]

However, what was discussed at that meeting became an open secret as the copy of Kucan's shorthand notes from the meeting circulated in Ljubljana was admitted to be authentic. The notes apparently made it clear that the Military Command had raised the issue of whether the Slovene authorities could contain the situation if arrests of journalists were to provoke public unrest. The notes also showed that Kucan and even Dolanc were opposed to the suggestions made, believing that they were unnecessary.[172]

Kucan made a statement on the leaked notes, in which he

condemned their leaking and said that the interpretations put upon them were incorrect.[173] His rejection of the broad understanding gained from the notes and condemnation of the leak are open to question, but seem purely formal. Despite his denial of any knowledge concerning the leaking of the notes, suspicion must be that Kucan himself was the most likely source of the leak. If this is so, the purpose of the leak would have to be his desire to make public what, in fact, was popularly understood, thereby confirming it. Certainly, Kucan's assertion that Order 5044-3 was not discussed at that meeting was true. Ertl admitted that it had not been felt necessary to discuss the imminent arrests and their possible repercussions with Kucan or others, because it was a routine security matter between the military and the RSNZ which did not concern the political leadership.[174]

The leaking of Kucan's notes from the March meeting appears to have had two purposes. One was to demonstrate Kucan's 'innocence', giving the impression that 'others' (that is, 'outsiders', whether Serbs or soldiers, with their base in Belgrade) were 'attacking' Slovene interests. Moreover, in light of the wide belief that Order 5044-3 contained provision for replacing the Slovene leadership during a state of emergency, Kucan's leaking of the notes should be seen as an act of self-protection. In this sense, the second role the notes had was as a device with which to manipulate the Slovene public. By at least implying that he was threatened because he was on 'the Slovene people's side' and making clear that he had rejected the ideas of arrests and a state of emergency, Kucan was able to strengthen his popular support.

The solidifying of popular support was a beneficial result of the arrests and the leaking of the notes. Kucan was a remarkably able politician, who manipulated circumstances in his own interest. However, I would argue that his position was, none the less, 'honest'. Two things lead to this conclusion. The first is the fact that neither Kucan nor other Slovene leaders were consulted about the arrests. Given the opposition shown in March to what appears to have been a similar proposition, and the absence of an obligation to do so, it seems likely that the military and the security services decided to proceed without consulting the leadership. This action also implies that Kucan's opposition in March was firm and, presumably, unexpected.

The second reason to infer Kucan's honesty is his repeated calls for those outraged at the arrests to protest peacefully and avoid anything that would create the conditions for a state of emergency. These calls were echoed by others – particularly the Committee for Human Rights, newly formed with Kucan's blessing (and maybe at his suggestion) as another strand within the pluralism of the Socialist Alliance.[175] The Committee organized a big 'cultural meeting' attended by at least 50,000 in Ljubljana. The 'meeting' – effectively a demonstration of solidarity with Jansa and the others and a protest against their arrest – was restrained and peaceful. It contrasted strongly with contemporaneous protests in Serbia in which noisy crowds marched through the streets chanting, and, even more so, with later Serb protests which besieged the local assemblies in Novi Sad and Belgrade and the Federal Parliament. Descriptions of the cultural meeting as 'subversive' and 'counter-revolutionary' in the Serb news media, while the less pacific Serb protests were labelled 'democracy', caused consternation among the Slovenes.[176]

We may supplement the foregoing assessment of Kucan's position with reference to events in Kosovo in the early months of 1989. Parallels may be drawn, albeit with some caution, between what was widely understood to have been planned *vis-a-vis* Slovenia and what occurred in Kosovo. There, Serbian-imposed changes to the largely Albanian-populated province's autonomy – pushed through without any measure of moderation – led to popular protest and, subsequently, the declaring of a state of emergency, after which the provincial leadership was purged (see below). In noting the similarity between the alleged plan for Slovenia and events in Kosovo, it should be recognized that events in Kosovo were the outcome of Serbian designs and actions; the YPA was used as a repressive force at the behest of political leaders. This contrasts with the idea that it was the army itself that was trying to destabilize Slovenia.

The Kosovan events, none the less, showed what might have happened. They also affirmed the existence of contingency plans for the imposition of states of emergency (it is not unreasonable to suppose that every army in the world has such plans). This would be supported by Dolanc's statement that orders similar to 5044-3 existed in all republics and provinces. If this was so, it would be possible to suspect Kucan of using the existence of such contingency plans to manipulate Slovene sentiments and engender popular support for his leadership. However, the stand he clearly seems to have taken in March, the fact that he was not consulted by the Military Council or, even, the RSNZ, in May, and his subsequent behaviour indicate that there was some real threat to his own position and to the Slovene republic. Later reports in the Italian press confirmed the threat; in accordance with international protocol on military manoeuvres close to their borders, the YPA command had alerted the Italian Chief of General Staff of the possibility of the use of force in Slovenia.[177]

The honesty of Kucan's position does not alter the fact that he manipulated the situation to his own benefit and that of the rest of the Slovene leadership. The holding of the trial in camera, in spite of the admission that the document had not been marked secret, enabled the Slovene leadership to align itself with the public. However, the other significant aspect of the trial – its being held in Serbo-Croat – was an even more potent issue around which leaders and public could rally.

The homogenization of Slovene politics

If the inferences drawn from rumours and leaks gave credibility to Borstner's assertion that the Slovene nation was gravely threatened, nothing appeared a more concrete piece of evidence that this was the case than the decision to hold the trial in Serbo-Croat. Language is a principal focus of cultural identity. The Slovenes, proud of their language and cultural identity, were shocked by this decision.

The issue is an important one. Article 212 of the Slovene Constitution states that all official business on the territory of the republic of Slovenia should be conducted in Slovene.[178] This was taken to be consistent with Article 3 on 'the sovereignty of the people' in each of the socialist republics, and Article 246 on the equality of languages, of the Federal Constitution. The JBTZ four, in particular, Franci Zavrl, protested against this.[179] The military court rejected the protest. The military prosecution referred to the rules of procedure on military courts, arguing that according to Article 21 there, the language used in a military court was at the discretion of the court itself, as long as those whose native tongue was not that of the court were given an interpreter; he added that JBTZ were given interpreters.[180]

The Slovene Presidency took up this protest. It requested the SFRY Presidency, responsible for military courts, to rule on the matter.[181] The Federal Presidency ruled that the court was in order: this verdict was made on the basis of 'well qualified opinion'.[182] It is not unreasonable to suppose that the opinion was military, given the tendency to leave military matters to the military. Joze Smole, leader of the SAWP, asked how any book of rules could take precedence over constitutional provisions.[183] Certainly it is hard to understand how an incongruence between a particular legal code, on one side, and the Federal and Slovene Constitutions, on the other, could be resolved in this way. A constitution is, theoretically, the ultimate legal document in any political administrative territory; it supersedes all other legal matters.[184] To the Slovenes – and to the independent observer – it seems clear that the trials were unconstitutional. This becomes ironic if the YPA's constitutional duty to defend and uphold the constitution is borne in mind[185] By breaching the constitution (seemingly) in its conduct of the trial, the army was twice in dereliction of its duty.

Janez Stanovnik, President of the Slovene Presidency, set up a group of delegates from the Slovene Parliament to investigate the circumstances of the trial and its constitutionality. The group concluded that the trial had been improper. Its report was twice accepted by two of the three chambers of the Slovene Parliament. On both occasions, it was rejected by the Chamber of Sociopolitical Organizations – largely because of the role played there by YPA members. This partly contributed to Mladina's exaggeration after the second presentation of the report before the Parliament that part of a definition of a military dictatorship was having soldiers in

Parliament.[186] Eventually, all chambers accepted the report. For a long time JBTZ did not begin their prison sentences; Kucan and the party leadership, Stanovnik and the Republican leadership and the various elements of the Socialist Alliance – particularly the Committee – all called for pardons in view of the unconstitutionality of the trial.[187]

The languages issue homogenized Slovene politics more than anything else. Kucan (again manipulating the public from a justified position) asked how any territory in which Slovene was not used in all official areas could be regarded as sovereign.[188] Franc Setinc, who had hitherto made his speeches in Federal bodies using Serbo-Croat, ended his statement at a Central Committee meeting in Slovene. He later ended an interview, conducted in Serbo-Croat on Zagreb TV – in which he was explaining his behaviour at the Central Committee meeting – by reverting to Slovene. In both cases, he was making the point that Slovene is an official language of the SFRY. He stressed that there were some things he could only satisfactorily explain in his own language.[189]

The language issue also raised an old question concerning the use of languages in the YPA.[190] According to Article 243 of the SFRY Constitution the equality of languages in the army 'shall be ensured', but the reality is that Serbo-Croat is the command language, used in almost all circumstances (reflecting the preponderance of Serbs and Montenegrins among junior officers).[191] Action had been promised on past Slovene demands for the use of Slovene on Slovene territory. The trial, and the questions of language and constitution arising from it, re-fuelled such debate.

In the eyes of the leadership and the population, the trial was an attack on Slovenes and Slovenia.[192] The anti-Slovene impression homogenized around the language question. It crystallized the image of the YPA as a Serb institution and reinforced the notion among many Slovenes that 'they' (that is, those from the Southern Republics, in particular, Serbia) were not only a drain on Slovene prosperity, but also intent on gaining centralized control over Slovene affairs and depriving Slovenes of their 'freedoms'. The relatively new phenomenon of Slovene nationalism was hardening in the face of what was perceived to be an attack by the agents of an ever more vigorous Serb nationalism.[193]

The perceived proximity of the YPA to that which is Serb was important in the process that unified the elements of Slovene political life. It was, however, mistaken as later developments showed (these will be discussed below) when some amelioration of the civil-military relationship was evident at the elite level. For a period, at least, however, the Slovene leadership was antagonized.

In evaluating these events, it is hard to avoid three conclusions: for the YPA, the trial was bad politics, bad public relations and bad for defence. In only one respect can it be judged a success. That is, the YPA, stung by *Mladina*'s criticisms over a few years and behaving like a bear with a thorn – Jansa – in its foot, wanted to get its own back. This is clear from the sentence given to Jansa – 18 months in a maximum security prison for dangerous offenders (Borstner, given four years, was directed to an open prison). If this is what was intended, it must be seen as a pyrrhic victory in the light of the adverse effects of the trial and the ten-month delay before Jansa went to prison. Then, like the others, he served his sentence with little constraint: he served only five months, going home at weekends.[194]

It is impossible to say whether the decision to hold the trial in Serbo-Croat was intentionally provocative or crass. The outcome indicates the latter; but provocation would be consonant with the evidence suggesting a desire to create conditions in which to declare a state of emergency and impose martial law. What is clear is that the trial was a bad move politically. It antagonized the Slovene leadership which had previously defended the YPA against the Slovene youth. This brought the youth and leadership into alignment. Political solidarity set around the combined ideas of Slovene nationalism and 'pluralist' politics. The events in the summer of 1988 emboldened Slovene politicians in their advocacy of more 'liberal' politics, of 'socialism on a human scale',[195] of pluralism. In particular, the initiation of the Committee for Human Rights was significant. Operating within the Socialist Alliance, it paved the way for the formation of the Social Democratic Alliance towards the end of 1988. In effect, this was a proto-Party and a clear focus of organized opposition to the Communists. Its existence, however, also strengthened the Communist leadership.[196]

The trial – in particular the language question – politicized a majority of Slovenes and encouraged a rise in nationalism. At such an important juncture in Yugoslav history, heightening the polarity of Slovenia and Serbia, this was not conducive to the agreements required to solve Yugoslavia's problems. Most of all it ensured that – albeit in the guise of the liberal policies it advocated – the Slovene leadership was encouraged to take firm stands in the Federal arena.

With regard to the YPA, this meant Slovene obstruction in October and December, first a propos of constitutional amendments on YPA financing and, secondly, on YPA funding in the budget. At the October Conference of the LCY, agreement was delayed by Slovene refusal to agree to certain amendments. Prime among these was a provision for emergency funding of the YPA which had failed to gain adequate resources in previous years owing to the effects of inflation (see Chapter 4). The proposal was to make extraordinary funds available between budgets, the money to be raised by a Federal tax on income. This was rejected by the Slovenes. Eventually they agreed a compromise in which provision for emergency funding was made constitutionally possible, but by an increase in purchase tax – which would be a Republican, not a Federal matter. Thus, the YPA could ask for funding – but such funding would have to be agreed, first in the Republican and Provincial Parliaments and then in the Chamber of Republics and Provinces (not in the Federal Parliament).[197]

The problems this would probably engender were evident in December when the Federal budget could not be agreed (leading to the demise of the Mikulic government). An extraordinary decision was taken to ensure YPA funding. Perhaps this indicates that the apparent Slovene victory in October (albeit resting on a degree of ambiguity) meant little. Milan Potrc, leader of the Slovene Parliament, immediately wrote a strong letter to the Federal leaderships, stating that the Slovenes had only voted for this in the Federal Assembly because the army would otherwise have been without money and rapidly in a state of chaos; however, he strongly pressed the point that this was improper and that it should have been a matter for the Chamber of Republics and Nationalities.[198] He was fully supported by a detailed statement from the LCS CC Presidium.[199] The issue was not further tested.

Slovene acceptance of the vote on emergency funding in the Federal Chamber was symptomatic of the measured accommodation of the YPA and Slovene politicians since the October Conference. At the Conference, the LC-YPA had sided with the Slovenes and others in opposing the power-plays of the Serb leader Milosevic.[200] In doing so, the YPA demonstrated that, contrary to beliefs in some quarters, particularly in Slovenia, it was not a crude Serb agency. On the contrary, its 'Yugoslavness' was apparent.

All this may be evidence that the trial had chastened the army. It may also reflect the effects of the change from Mamula to Kadijevic (it is likely that the JBTZ affair sprang from the Mamula era – it is difficult to see how Kadijevic, if he were so inclined, might have intervened successfully to save YPA face). It is also possible that Kadijevic's hailing from the same village as Stipe Suvar, the LC Federal Secretary, presumably with the inevitable connections of village life, might have played some part. Whatever the reasons for the army's behaviour at the conference, the YPA was clearly chastened by its experience. This emerged in attempts at better 'public relations' with the Slovenes.

For an organization with severe difficulties in recruiting Slovenes – who were already largely 'anti-military' and uninterested in military service – to be seemingly so openly hostile to the Slovene nation in the Slovene capital was not a good public relations exercise. Showing its recognition of this (and its contrition for clumsy political behaviour) Kadijevic visited Ljubljana to announce that, from Army Day (22 December), in addition to Serbo-Croat, the army newspaper *Narodna Armija* would be published in the other official Yugoslav languages – Macedonian and Slovene. Moreover, all signs and notices at military installations in the Slovene Republic would be in Slovene, as well as Serbo-Croat. Finally, steps were to be taken to encourage non-Slovene officers serving in Slovenia to learn the language.[201] For all this, it is hard to conclude that the publishing of *Narodna Armija* in Slovene after 45 years was enough to combat the damage done by the trial.[202]

The YPA decision to proceed against JBTZ in the manner it did was bad politics, bad public relations and, from its point of view, most importantly, bad for defence. Ultimately, bad politics and bad public relations are bad for defence. The territorial defence system, in which the YPA is the leading element of the Yugoslav Armed Forces, rests on cohension. Splits of any kind, especially along national lines, are bad news in this regard.[203] Whatever the army may have hoped to gain, it would be hard to conclude it was successful. Any success was achieved at a high price, in terms of Slovene relations with the military – particularly with regard to the question of ethnic tensions within the armed forces and the adverse effect this had on defence capability. Bad relations were exacerbated at both popular and elite levels. The Slovene public became increasingly estranged: the divorce between young Slovenes and the YPA widened further. However, the political leadership, while continuing to pursue the matters of Slovene sovereignty and the constitutionality of the trial, showed signs of being able to work with the military, if necessary, at the CC conference in October.

In terms of Republican politics, the homogenization of Slovene opinion was a direct result of the YPA's actions. Party and youth leaderships finally came together on the same platform in March 1989 in response to Serb policies and behaviour in Kosovo. However, their alignment with each other was always uneasy – there were soon signs that the two were again becoming more antagonistic. The non-party elements in Slovenia had the scent of success. The events of 1988 pushed the Slovene leadership to make its liberal, pluralistic philosophy more of a reality. The substance of this was the formation of first the Committee for Human Rights and later the Social Democratic Alliance. These foci of opposition to the Communists continued to push for the existence of a multi-party system. Politics in Slovenia continued to be characterized as 'politics on a human scale', not politics on the people's scale. This was not the case for long, however. In the second half of 1989, the Slovene leadership chose to expand its interpretation of 'pluralism' and to favour a multi-party system.

As Slovenes led the push towards pluralism, the YPA's position became increasingly awkward. The army's sensitivity to difficulties with Slovenia showed the effect of anti-military challenges on military legitimacy. Weaknesses in military legitimacy inhibited any greater political activity. Only in the most desperate circumstances might the YPA use force. The generals have persistently said they would only use force to preserve the constitutional order. What this means became less and less clear as the debate on a new constitution progressed through 1989.

On amending constitutions in Serbia, Kosovo and Slovenia: towards multi-party pluralism

For an organization determined to preserve the constitutional order and 'resolute on Tito's path',[204] the question must be: is the new constitution a continuation of Tito's path or a deviation from it? The question grows in interest if we note the opinion of one military mind that 'there is no need to raise the question of the Constitution. There is no dispute about the Constitution.'[205] Curiosity is amplified if we consider the logic of arguments that the solution to economic problems lies in political pluralism while remembering Mamula's opposition to political pluralism.[206] As late as April 1989, YPA views adamantly opposed 'pluralism'.[207] Later in the year, however, the concept had become more acceptable to the army.

The YPA opposed 'pluralism', believing that it would necessarily mean the undermining of defence preparations. The 'non-communist' stances emerging in Slovenia, it was thought, intended the depoliticization of the army and its exclusion 'from policy in all its aspects'. The logical conclusion of this would be a 'single-nation army'.[208]

The debate sped on with the Serbs under Milosevic wanting to retain and strengthen single-party rule, while Kucan's Slovenes prepared for multi-party elections in their republic in 1990.[209] In both cases, republican constitutions were amended to progress the relevant leadership's programme.

In contrast to Slovene pluralist realities and ambitions for themselves and the rest of Yugoslavia, the Serbians, led by Republican President, Slobodan Milosevic, while recognizing the need for a market economy, also wanted a greater concentration of political power in central hands. This meant a re-assertion of the party's leading role and of democratic centralism. In effect, because the Serbs were the most numerous of Yugoslavia's ethnic groups, this would mean giving power to the Serbian Party: thus the aim of the Federal Constitution, as supervized by Tito, to limit Serb hegemonism would be thwarted – and the reason for its being needed in the first place exemplified.[210]

The 1974 Federal and Republican Constitutions were neither fish nor fowl with regard to Serbia. The establishing within the Republic of Serbia of two Autonomous Provinces, Kosovo and Vojvodina, impaired the authority and sovereignty of all concerned. This was undoubtedly an anomalous constitutional situation. The dual intention was to limit Serbian dominion and to recognize the rights of the majority ethnic Albanian and Hungarian communities in those provinces as per constitutional principles derived (notionally, at least) from AVNOJ.[211] The autonomous provinces were established within the territory of Serbia, recognizing that the areas, although encompassed by the old Serbia, were not necessarily Serbian in character; a large ethnic Hungarian population in Vojvodina and a dominant

Albanian community in Kosovo were recognized and given limited, non-sovereign rights to self-determination. The ethnic homogeneity of Kosovo, in particular, should have meant it had republican status along the same lines as other republics.[212] However, the enormous psychological importance of Kosovo to the Serbs made this unacceptable. The compromise proved to be unsatisfactory.

The indigenous Albanian population wanted complete independence from Serbian authority: the indigenous Serb population did not like the changes which altered their old 'colonial' status in the region. Their complaints became the foundation of a swell of nationalism, both harnessed and encouraged by 'Slobo' Milosevic, and led to the Serbian constitutional amendments in 1989. The result of these alterations was a 're-unification' of Serbia.

In March 1989, Serbia amended its own constitution. In doing so, it aggregated important responsibilities of its two 'autonomous' provinces – Vojvodina and Kosovo. In this process, control of the mainstays of the provinces' autonomy – including the police, the militia, defence and the judicial system – was transferred to the Serbian authorities in Belgrade. Reactions to the Serbian changes were opposite. Received without significant protest in Vojvodina, where ethnic Hungarians are not a dominant group, the amendments met with great hostility in Kosovo. Resistance by the Kosovan leadership, supported by strikes and mass protests, was brutally suppressed.

Albanian 'irrendentists' and 'counter-revolutionaries' constituted the pretext for Serbia to force the Federal Government to impose martial law in the province. A state of emergency was declared and executed in a way that matched the reported content of the document in the Ljubljana trial. Local leaders were arrested and replaced with Milosevic supporters.

Protest was brutally quashed. In an incident that bears similarities with later, more widely publicized events in China – the principal difference being the absence of verifying Western television crews in Kosovo – the militia shot protesters. Although eye-witnesses from the hospital in the Republic's capital, Pristina, estimated between 140 and 180 dead, the official figure was 24. It is alleged that the bodies of the dead were only returned once the families, after considerable intimidation, undertook not to speak about the matter to anyone.[213]

In the Western regions of Yugoslavia, the repressive acts of the Federal and Republican security institutions caused concern. In Ljubljana, between one and two thousand people attended a rally at the Cankarajev Dom, opposing the state of emergency in Kosovo. Live radio and television relay gave the meeting an even wider audience as Communist leaders, including Kucan and Smole, appeared for the first time on a public platform with representatives of the opposition, such as Ivan Oman (leader of the Peasant's Alliance) and Dimitrij Rupel (President of the Social Democratic Alliance). One effect of this was the signing of a petition against the imposition of a state of emergency in Kosovo by 450,000 people in Slovenia within a day.[214] Criticism of Serbian actions did not come from within the country alone. The abuses of 'human rights' in Kosovo (from the removal of political rights through the constitutional amendments, to the violent suppression of peaceful protest and the process of 'isolation' of ethnic Albanians arrested, under which prisoners could be held indefinitely without being charged and were tortured and kept in conditions of degradation) were condemned. International critics included Helsinki Watch, Amnesty International, the European Parliament and the US House of Representatives, all of which sent delegations to Kosovo.[215]

In the wake of the JBTZ trial and the subjugation of a people equal in size to the Slovenes – albeit much poorer – the Slovene leaders, overwhelmingly supported by the population, drafted amendments to the Republican Constitution. The purpose of this was to make clear the nature of their membership in the Federation and assert their rights. At one stage, the homogenized constituency of Slovene political life appeared to be separating out again. Indeed, the whole Republican leadership was attacked for its weakness in not opposing, first, the Serbian amendments through Federal organs and, secondly, the declaration of martial law in Kosovo.[216]

In particular, Republican President, Janez Stanovnik, was widely criticized for attending the Serbs' celebration of the 600th anniversary of the battle of Kosovo-Polje. That battle, which the Serbs lost to the Turks, is the single most powerful historical symbol for Serbs; in a sense, the Serbs had just 'won back' their ancient prize, the founding place of the Serbian Orthodox church. Stanovnik's presence, therefore, lent a veneer of approval to Milosevic and his actions.[217] The publication of the amendments brought the Slovene strands together again. This unity was in the face of criticism emanating from Belgrade, the capital of both Serbia and the Federation, fuelled by Milosevic and his allies and voiced in the Milosevic-controlled press in Belgrade.[218]

The most controversial amendments can be seen to stem directly from the circumstances of the trial and Serb efforts to recentralize. Prime among them was an unequivocal statement of the condition of Slovenia's membership of the Federation – on a voluntary basis with the right to self-determination and, therefore, secession. Although this was clear in Yugoslavia's original post-war Constitution, it was not spelled out in the 1974 version, which spoke only of the Republics' 'sovereignty'. Although, in most cases, the concept of sovereignty can only mean one thing – that the sovereign is the inalienable ultimate authority – it appears that, for certain Yugoslavs, the implications of this, enclosed in the Slovene amendment, needed to be spelled out.[219] As even a leading element in the more independence-oriented opposition made clear, 'the amendment on self-determination is merely a threat and part of the psychological war Slovenia is waging against the conservatives in Belgrade'.[220] One marital partner, having assumed that certain things were, perhaps, self-evident and to be taken on trust, finding their faith betrayed, decided to issue a reminder that it had entered the union of its own accord and, if abused, can walk out of it in the same way.

Other amendments stemmed from this: a delineation of economic sovereignty; that Federal organs active in the Republic (the YPA included) should respect the equal-rights status of the languages of the Yugoslav nations and nationalities, in accordance with the Federal Constitution – in effect, use Slovene, not Serbo-Croat; the proposal of a mechanism for dealing with federal breaches of the Slovene Constitution; and a provision that the declaration of a state of emergency and the deployment of military forces on the Republic's territory could only be decided upon by Slovene authorities.[221]

One controversial amendment emerged for slightly different reasons. When the Slovene Parliament voted overwhelmingly to accept the amendments, there was one notable feature which had not been reported, only two weeks before, in references to discussions on the changes between Ljubljana and Belgrade. This was the removal of the party's leading role from the newly amended Constitution.[222]

The late appearance of this clause indicates that, following heavy criticism from Serbia and hyperbolic reports in the Milosevic press that Slovenia was about to secede, the Slovenes wanted to make a stand. It was an assertion of the pluralist, 'liberal' direction in which the Slovenes believed they and other Yugoslavs should travel together. Moreover, it amounted to a broadside against the Milosevic tendency, which was advocating a stronger role for the party in a more centralized Yugoslavia – the implication of this was a type of neo-Stalinism.

Fundamentally, the amendments were a statement of the future Slovenia wished to share with other Yugoslavs, not a declaration of intent to secede. Indeed, the situation recalls Ivan Cankar's *Bailiff Yerney*. The metaphor created by the greatest Slovene writer for his country and his people under the Austro-Hungarian empire retained relevance for their position within Yugoslavia in 1989.[223]

The Slovene-led push for multi-party pluralism was not only popular at home,[224] but garnered support in other republics.[225] In response, both Serbia and the YPA shifted stance. Both now favoured the erstwhile Slovene programme of single-party pluralism under the Socialist Alliance. However, the Serb position on pluralism seemed little more than 'a lot of words' behind which the reality was a significant 'strengthening of the "leading role" of the LC' and 'differentiation' (that is, an ideological purge).[226]

The YPA, on the other hand, seemed to move (somewhat reluctantly at times) towards a credible stance on pluralism. Although Brovet could get confused addressing Zagreb reservists in July 1989 by declaring the army in favour of pluralism and a strengthening of democratic centralism,[227] other statements made it clear that there was distance between the Army and 'narrow interests' which called on the YPA to protect them – that is, Serbians.[228] Indeed, the

Slovene misjudgement of the YPA as a purely Serb enclave continued to be countered by its criticism of Serb and Montenegrin nationalism.[229] Although military attitudes to consitutional amendments in Serbia and Slovenia were poles apart, the different nature of the sets of changes makes this understandable.

Whereas the unifying element in the Serbian amendments made some of the YPA's defence preparation tasks more straightforward,[230] the Slovene changes by making military activity in Slovenia subject to approval by republican authorities were clearly impediments to the army's doing its job. Nonetheless, the army's reaction was excessive and in some respects misplaced.[231] As more enlightened opinions in Slovenia acknowledged, in the last two years of the decade, the YPA was caught between two 'devils': the Slovenes and Milosevic.[232] Although the predominantly Serb and Montenegrin YPA officer corps cannot have been completely immune from the nationalist feelings abroad, especially given the greater proximity of the Serbian leadership's desire for and the general military receptiveness to greater central authority, the generals moved quite quickly towards accepting the advent of pluralism.

The YPA no longer objected to pluralism although it still maintained that a multi-party variant was anathema and would be a regressive step.[233] Moreover, another senior military figure seemed clearly to acknowledge that reforms were unavoidable, including a move towards pluralism; furthermore, YPA opposition to a multi-party system was, not unreasonably, based on the fear that 'that road would lead to further national, and even nationalistic, divisions in Yugoslavia'.[234]

This was a more weighty difficulty than another objection advanced by one of Kadijevic's deputies, Stane Brovet.[235] His objection was that a multi-party system would require a complete restructuring of the army. In the event of war, under the provisions of the laws on GPD, political sections would be expected to play a role similar to that taken by commissars in the Partisan years, acting as local agents of the political authority using the instrument of military force – in effect, directing the military command. The LCY-YPA sections would act with the authority of the LCY-CC.[236] Evidently the authority of the Communist party could not remain in this way under a multi-party system. It was not difficult, however, to conceive of an non-party agent of the Presidency performing a similar role, or even purely military units acting without local representation of political authority. Certainly, as was pointed out, there had been no great difficulty in other parts of the world.[237] It could not be considered as a serious barrier to the development of a multi-party system.

The YPA, while clinging to some of the old dogmas on which its leadership was nurtured and retaining grave doubts about the consequences of pluralism, clearly altered its position. As described earlier in this chapter, the volume of statements by army leaders may have increased, but their impact has decreased; the YPA's capacity to act was restricted because its legitimacy as a sociopolitical actor became increasingly circumscribed. When the army did act in the JBTZ case, this was outside direct political processes – and, above all, counter productive. One article in *Narodna Armija* made it clear that pluralism eventually had to generate multiple parties.[238] The YPA's edging towards the acceptance of pluralism signalled the weakness in its political legitimacy. The YPA had to be prepared to accept what came. It was most unlikely, therefore, to seize power.

Given the way in which weaknesses in military legitimacy have impeded the YPA's political role, it is appropriate to ask if those same weaknesses and the more general socioeconomic frailties of Yugoslavia had implications for defence. Did they have any impact on functional legitimacy? This is the topic to which we must turn in Chapter 4.

4 Crisis and Military Legitimacy: the Social Matrix of Defence

Did the causes and conditions of the YPA's political debility, those features that defined the Yugoslav crisis, impose on its functional legitimacy? As will emerge in this chapter, the answer is 'yes'. Not only this, but the examination of the topic will show that it was concern for defence in the context of crisis which underlay the generals' intervening in politics. The YPA's functional legitimacy was undermined by those factors that characterized the general societal crisis in Yugoslavia and weakened the military's political legitimacy. The economic crisis affected its first two roles: reductions in funding meant it was less able to maintain technical modernization and training; national divisions and criticisms of the YPA inhibited its 'leading role' in the defence system.

The premise of the YPA's role, indeed, the validity of the Yugoslav defence posture, rested on cohesive action on the part of all Yugoslavs. The YPA, via TDF, required the support of the people. For the defence system to work, the YPA had to have good links with the people. Those features such as national divisions, anti-military attitudes and inadequate national proportionality, which weakened the military politically, in this instance impaired its functional legitimacy.

This effect was augmented by the adverse effect of botched entries into the sociopolitical arena. In particular, army-society bonds were even further broken down in Slovenia by the trial of Jansa et al. Indeed, the restructuring of the YPA was interpreted as a reaction to damage caused to military legitimacy by the trial. Robert F. Miller, for example, linked the closure of the Ljubljana Army District at the end of 1988 to the 'corrosive effects of nationalism'.[1] Our exploration of the impact of the Yugoslav crisis on YPA functional legitimacy may begin therefore with this point. Was the closure of the Ljubljana Army District at the end of 1988 connected with earlier political events in Slovenia, notably the military secrets trial?

Abolition of the Ljubljana Army District: YPA restructuring

On 25 December 1988, the Ljubljana Army District (LAD) ceased working. All its responsibilities were transferred to a new authority, the Zagreb Military District (ZMD). From both a Slovene and a non-military perspective, this appeared suspicious, not only in fact, but in the way it was accomplished.

The change arrived with no ceremony and little warning. One of the first public signs of change was on Ljubljana TV three days before. A report on a session of the Ljubljana army-party organization used the nomenclature 'military post 3553' instead of the LAD's number, 2050.[2] The LAD Commanding Officer, Major-General Svetozar Visnjic, made the new arrangements known in a traditional Army-day interview with Slovene journalists which appeared on 22 December. He said that full details would be issued by the SFRY Presidency.[3]

The SFRY Presidency issued its brief announcement on the eve of a national holiday. The official notice was not expansive. The changes, it explained, were because of improvements in and the rationalization of command and control via technical modernization in the armed forces and reductions in the size of the YPA.[4] Indeed, the changes even merited no more than two column inches, purely referential, in the army newspaper.[5]

The 1988 reorganization differed from earlier YPA changes (see Chapter 3). Whereas previous major alterations had been widely discussed, the latest changes slipped in almost silently and unnoticed. Detailed information was not forthcoming. Enquiries by a Slovene journalist floundered not because the Republican Secretariat for People's Defence was closed around the New Year holiday, when the official decree was made, but because of considerable reluctance by the press office there to explain the changes.[6]

The manner of this notice gave rise to great doubts in Slovenia.[7] Issued on the eve of a holiday (and, coincidentally, at the same time as the Mikulic government resignation) and outstandingly meagre in its content, it caused unease among Slovenes. Not surprisingly, rumours spread that the LAD had been abolished because of events earlier in 1988. Speculation linked these changes to the trial; it was pointed out that any similar trial in the future would escape the problems experienced with the trial of Jansa et al. as it would be held in Zagreb.[8] Clarification of the causes and consequences of the changes, and the implications for political and military thinking, were sought.[9]

Did the debilitating impact of the trial on YPA-Slovene relations cause a crisis of military legitimacy profound enough to warrant reorganization? The reorganization was clearly not a response to events in Slovenia, however much a non-military Slovene perception might find it so. Evidence of long-term planning and the pan-Yugoslav character of the alterations attest to this.

Slovene reaction focused on the effects of reorganization in Slovenia and stemmed from a false assumption. The changes meant that instead of the LAD for the whole of the Republic (and slightly beyond), there would be two corps, one based in Ljubljana under the command of Major-General Dane Popovic, the other based in Maribor under the command of Major-General Vukasin Vilotic.[10] These corps would be under the direct command of the ZMD.

Much of the Slovene reaction was based on a false assumption of contiguity between the former army districts and political-administrative regions throughout the country and, therefore, that the Slovenes were being 'stripped' of their republican command. Previously, however, only the Ljubljana and Skopje Army Districts had been more or less identical with the Slovene and Macedonian Republics. Otherwise the erstwhile army districts did not follow republican-provincial contours.

In addition, the reorganization was not limited to Slovenia. Eight former entities (six army districts with headquarters in Ljubljana, Zagreb, Sarajevo, Belgrade, Nis and Skopje, together with a regional command in Titograd and the Naval Command in Split) were reduced to four: Zagreb, Belgrade, Skopje and Split (the latter military district was the Naval Command again). Restructuring removed any vestigial contiguity of political-administrative region and military command borders.[11]

It emerged that the Slovene Presidency had initially thought the changes were not in line with constitutional arrangements on defence.[12] This was based on their presumed effect on the role of republics and provinces in the GPD system. According to the Constitution, sociopolitical organizations – communes, autonomous provinces and republics – along the other groups in society have the 'right and duty' to organize defence in their domain.[13] The Presidency feared that the role of the republics in organizing and leading GPD in the event of war would be changed.

In particular, the Slovene leadership foresaw problems of coordination it the YPA command for the Slovene region was now in Zagreb: that is, in a neighbouring republic, Croatia. Along with this, it was thought that reorganization would diminish the political authority of republics and provinces a propos the condition of the YPA. Nonetheless, the Slovene leadership was persuaded of the army's case. On the latter issue, the YPA was under the authority of the Federal Presidency; the republics were responsible for territorial defence. As to the question of coordination, they were assured that all agreements on common action would take place only in Slovenia; direct contact with Zagreb would not be necessary. As Soban has commented, practice was likely to show that this would sometimes be unavoidable.[14] The Slovene leadership was, however, mollified. Kucan told his fellow Slovenes that the reorganization was purely strategic.[15]

Another question arising from the new military configuration in Slovenia concerned the commanding officers. The new system corresponded with that operating at the close of the war, there being two corps in Slovenia. It differed in that the wartime corps were led by Slovenes; those in 1989 were not.[16] The reason for this was not a complete lack of suitable high-ranking Slovene officers. For example, General Milan Zorc, a Slovene, was in charge of the Sarajevo Command. A colonel, Milan Gorjanc, was acting Commanding Officer in Titovo Uzice (therefore filling a general's position). There was, however, some suspicion of a lack of confidence a propos Slovene generals.[17]

The Slovene corps in the latter stages of the war had Slovene generals for one particular reason. The Slovene liberation movement was at least semi-detached from the Partisan movement. The Liberation Front (OF) was specific to Slovenia and forged bonds with Tito's movement; the OF organized a military force in Slovenia.[18] For a period after the war there appeared to be a tradition of appointing a Slovene to the highest YPA office in the region. As Jansa had observed, this tradition had ceased some years before.[19]

It is not clear why that tradition was ended. What is clear is a trend towards centralization in the YPA and in the Armed Forces as a whole. Already by 1974, the coequality of the two elements of the armed forces in the five-year-old GPD system had become imbalanced, the YPA, de facto, having become the senior element.[20] Gradual erosion of regional authority in the Territorial Defence Force (TDF) was completed in 1980 with the establishment of a Council for Territorial Defence. Answerable only to the Federal Secretariat for National Defence, which was staffed by soldiers, and of which the minister was always the most senior YPA officer, the council's foundation meant a concentration of YPA control; the TDF became an 'integral part of the YPA itself'.[21] Creeping centralization within the YPA, culminating with the changes which included the LAD's abolition, was signalled at the end of 1987. At that time the ZMD which assumed the responsibilities of the LAD and its equivalent in Zagreb, was formed. The year 1988 would appear to have been one of transition.[22]

Certainly the restructuring had been in the pipeline for a long time. One source had predicted YPA centralization, believing there would be a tripartite structure.[23] Jansa, the arch YPA watcher, had reported secret plans to disestablish the LAD in February 1988.[24] The Slovene leadership had agreed to the changes in principle, a month later.[25] At that time, they had expressed doubts. Above all, Kucan had wanted the public to be informed about the discussions.[26]

It is possible that the speech by Admiral Branko Mamula, then Secretary for Defence, at the Political School in Kumrovec on 18 April 1988 was a response to Slovene doubts.[27] The timing suggests some connection. Whether as a public elucidation of YPA concerns for the benefit of Slovene politicians, or as a veiled, partial response to their suggestion of public debate, or both at once, Mamula signposted military reorganization. For the first time, he announced changes. Already achieved was the adoption of a new operational and tactical system of (respectively) corps and brigades; others which would give a 'new quality' to YPA ability to fulfil its role were to follow.[28]

Otherwise, Mamula had covered most of the same material before: in a speech in Zagreb in February 1986 about his book, *Savremini Svijet i Nasa Odbrana*, and in that book itself.[29] Implicit references to his 1985 book indicate that restructuring had been planned for at least three years. The 'unfinished tactical exercise', 'Autumn '87', the first of its kind in Slovenia for 13 years, was almost certainly a test of working plans.[30]

Mamula was presumably addressing his Slovene critics in the section of his speech devoted to the role of republics and autonomous provinces in the defence system, declaring that the 'defence of Yugoslavia is indivisible'.[31] Each force involved in defence from whatever part of Yugoslavia, he continued, had to be considered an integral part of the armed forces of the country as a whole and of its constituent elements.

Mamula addressed the question of republican-provincial boundaries. Referring to war-time experience, he pointed out that combat could not be contained within these; this had been so in the past and would be so in any future war. Accordingly, in military exercises, units would move from one region to another, There was, Mamula suggested, a need to consider all the parts of the armed forces as a unified whole. (The significance of this is discussed below.)

'Unity' was a central feature in Mamula's thinking. The entire territory of Yugoslavia was one sphere of 'united operations'. The defence chief detailed what he described as four unities: unity of the whole country as a theatre of operations; unity of the armed forces in that theatre; unity of the armed struggle; and unity of command and control in the armed forces.[32] More centralization and greater unification of the components of Yugoslav defence is a logical extension of these unities. Why did Mamula think greater unity was of such note?

Centralization of the YPA was based on three things: strategic-doctrinal perception; operational-technical complexity; and the external conditions of the Yugoslav crisis. First was the Yugoslav calculation of the threat it might face. Mamula's analysis of contemporary developments in military technology and strategy concluded that in the event of war, the country would be subject to a 'unified' attack. Military applications of information technology, new capabilities *vis-a-vis* conventional arms and the advent of systems such as electromagnetic pulse (EMP) weapons created new trends in military thinking and therefore presented new questions for countries such as Yugoslavia whose defence doctrines and strategies were framed on the premise that they 'cannot keep up with top achievements in the technological race'.[33]

Those trends included the merging of the elements of military operations – fire-power, mobility, the various arms of military organization – and a merging of numerous operations in time and space into a single 'unified strategic operation';[34] the trends also embraced the quickening of the war process modern technology facilitated, the major implication of which was that the opening period of a war would also be its closing period: the war would be concluded after, perhaps, only one battle. Yugoslavia, it was envisaged, would face a new form of 'super-blitzkrieg' in which 'the entire area of a limited theatre of operation, such as ours, [could] be subjected to a simultaneous strike'.[35] Mamula's successor, Kadijevic, emphasized these points in a speech to the Federal Chamber of the SFRY Parliament only a month before the restructuring. A synthesis of doctrines (of 'in-depth strike', 'combined ground-air attack' and 'rapid deep penetration') formed a radical 'strategic blitzkrieg doctrine'.[36]

Yugoslav defence planning envisaged a threat in which a unified theatre was central. The potential enemy, therefore, would impose 'unity of theatre' on Yugoslavia's armed forces. The need to respond to attack in a unified theatre explains, in part, the increased centralization of the YPA. However, this YPA analysis of the implications of modern technology did not provide a sufficient explanation. It was arguable that in many cases, new technological developments perhaps favoured 'decentralized forces, dispersed in a guerrilla fashion'.[37]

The second reason for increased centralization was a clear need to simplify the GPD system. As Mamula had indicated in his 1985 book, the 'duplexity of the armed forces' could produce 'structural and functional dualism'; indeed, practical inadequacies had 'led to the question of the unity of the armed struggle in the whole theatre of operations'.[38] Both the YPA and TDF had horizontal and vertical structures.[39] This created problems of coordination.[40] The 'first essential characteristic of the system of General People's Defence and Social Self-Protection which most of all creates command and control problems is its *complexity*'. [Original emphasis][41] Experience showed, said Mamula, that 'duplication and parallelism' were too often found in the system.[42] This only diminished the effectiveness of command and control.

On exercises, the YPA had found units from two different army districts in one battle zone; in addition TD units had been operational in the same zone. Each of these had had its own command – which, in turn, had been part of a separate hierarchy of command. This stemmed, in part, from the lack of conformity between political-administrative and army district borders; for instance, Ilirska Bistrica (Slovenia) came under the Zagreb AD; Osijek (Croatia) was in the Sarajevo AD. Two armies could be operational in one republic; the naval command spread through the four republics with access to the sea. As ADs tried to fulfil their responsibilities, they inevitably 'encroached' on territory that was not perceived as theirs; sometimes this could cause discontent.[43]

Geographic inconsistencies also affected the composition of zones of military action. In one divisional zone, there could be anything between a few thousand people and over 100,000. Alternatively, these zones could cover the area of two separate communes (and in some instances more).[44] The complex of relationships in the previous arrangement involved mobilization difficulties (albeit ones largely caused by the earlier shifts of authority from local bodies to the YPA). Doctrine required the mobilization of TD units; the number of actors meant complications arose in exercises. It was, therefore, desirable that areas of mobilization should correspond to units' areas of operation.[45]

Mamula and his colleagues sought to rectify these various discrepancies. The new system would enable faster, more effective reaction at each level of command and control – above all, in the case of an unexpected situation.[46] The YPA's quick-response role was thought to be facilitated by the introduction of new operational (corps) and tactical (brigade) organizations. The YPA could now better fulfil its 'strike' function in the event of attack; this improvement strengthened its position as the 'basic factor in the prevention of surprise attack'.[47] A simplified system would improve Yugoslav defence capability.

It is difficult to judge if command and control actually became less complicated and better put into action. Only time and practice could reveal if the new format would reduce the incidence of overlapping jurisdictions, duplicated functions and contingent headaches. At the highest levels, there was unlikely to be difficulty between the military districts. Within each district, it has been suggested, problems were possible. The military districts created new administrative demands; there had to be a new network of 'systems and sub-systems'.[48] Each district would have more subordinate units; more units implied more linkage between them – both horizontal and vertical. This aspect of the reorganization has been connected with a general Yugoslav pattern: 'Centralization in Yugoslavia has never reduced, rather increased, the administrative and technocratic apparat.'[49]

Considerable complexity remained. As we saw in Chapter 3, the YPA had been constantly tinkered with in an effort to optimize defence capability. One major omission in the restructuring was the air force and air-defence force; during 1989, a fifth military district appeared to meet the need for an air command. Further amendments to iron out other kinks could be anticipated.

Evident complexity remained vis-a-vis terminology. Whether the label 'military district' was enough to ensure that the new system was differentiated from the old with its 'army districts' could be questioned; terminological inconsistency was likely to create confusion.[50] At the strategic-doctrinal level, Mamula's conceptualization did not translate well into Slovene: the Serbian words 'ratiste' (theatre) and 'vojiste' (battlefield) were both rendered by 'bojisce' in Slovene and required 'broad' or 'narrow' meanings to be appended. A measure of this problem was one Slovene discutant's addressing this topic, but getting the Serbian words muddled up.[51] Indeed, language issues in general gained in importance from reorganization (see below).

Strategic and technical explanations of reorganization, if not wholly satisfactory, were consistent with the official statement that it owed to reductions in force size and rationalization. Several questions remained. The YPA's secret plans, according to a leak, envisaged the application of the new organization in July 1989;[52] if so, why were changes initiated six months early? Was this merely because arrangements were accomplished ahead of schedule? Or was it a response to other pressures – such as the events in Slovenia? The fact that, after such long-term planning, implementation of the changes was somewhat botched, suggests that it was not a matter of early completion, The rushed introduction was probably caused by external events; if Slovenes were wrong to think that the LAD disappeared because of circumstances surrounding the trial, it was not impossible that the timing of its exit was connected with that trial.

Critical aspects of functional legitimacy: the economy

The economic crisis made it difficult for the YPA to maintain its standards and modernization. Reductions in funding struck three areas: arms and equipment; force levels and their nature; and the living standards of the YPA cadre. In effect, during the 1980s, the military had to trim its coat according to its cloth.

The YPA received reduced funding from 1976. Effectively, this meant cutbacks and some changes. For the period 1976–80, the YPA's budget allocation was set at 6.17 per cent of the social plan. In practice, it received only 5.39 per cent. In 1980, the new five-year plan foresaw funding at 5.8 per cent of national income. Yet in the first two years of that period, funding reached only 4.79 per cent.[53] In 1983, military spending was put at 150.58 billion dinars – at 5.09 per cent of social product, 20.9 billion dinars below the planned 5.8 per cent and 3.2 billion dinars below the planned 5.8 per cent which, in 1981, was judged to be the 'lower limit' at which the YPA could be funded.[54] After 1983, funding was initially-planned annually at that 'lower limit'. In 1984, spending fell well short of that figure.[55] Later, both 5.2 and then 4.94 were set as percentages of GDP below which defence expenditure could not be allowed to fall; however, in 1988, Kadijevic put the percentage of GDP actually spent at 3.85.[56]

Of course, a declining defence/GDP ratio 'need not signal a declining capacity for defence'.[57] Indeed, in hard-currency terms, per capita spending, although not as high as in 1981, was greater in 1988 than in 1983. Per capita, military spending fell from US $129 in 1981 to US $72 in 1983 and US $69 in 1984.[58] These reductions in funding were compounded by the adverse effects of foreign exchange trends and inflation.[59] However, in 1988, per capita spending was US $85.[60]

Moreover, it was clear that, irrespective of the impact on defence capability, there were consequences for economic activity. Domestic cutbacks, in association with global economic conditions, created problems for the defence industry. The defence sector, which employed about 77,000 people in 1988, was structured to produce for 'Armed Forces development plans and programs when 6.17 per cent of the national income was set aside to finance the YPA'.[61] Reduced expenditure meant reduced production, leading to problems of 'inadequate use of capacities'.[62] New economic circumstances, including the liberalization of a 'unified' market, weakened the defence industry – which had previously out-performed other parts of the economy. There were reports that the army was not the business partner it once was – in one instance, orders were down 40 per cent on the previous year.[63]

Funding difficulties generated problems in military planning. It became very hard to obtain goods and services in some parts of the country.[64] 'The demands of the development and modernization of the YPA call for stable, even and long-term financing,' asserted the Generals.[65] Quite clearly, the financing system had 'serious short-comings in the regular payment of approved budgetary funds'.[66] However, in spite of 'reduced resources' the military was determined not to 'economize in attaining the essential aims of training and a high degree of preparedness, but that we must carry out training and education at a considerably higher level'.[67] Despite this determination, certain changes became necessary.

'Rebalancing' the budget seemed to have had some effect on the Air Force and Air Defence, in particular, restraining its planned modernization and expansion.[68] It also focused the army's attention on its domestic arms industry. Although by 1983, 80 per cent of Yugoslavia's arms requirement was developed and produced domestically,[69] it was decided that the country should be self-sufficient in this regard by the end of the decade.[70] Although consistent with the Yugoslav concept of general or total defence, the attempted move towards self-sufficiency seemed to be a response to funding problems and, especially, to the question of foreign currency transactions. On the one hand, developing a domestic industry (which is, anyway, YPA controlled) ensured that less precious hard currency would have to be spent.

On the other hand, a concentration on this industry also meant foreign currency *earnings* for the YPA to offset some of the budget cuts. In 1989, 50 enterprises, employing 70,000 people (1.09 per cent of all Yugoslavs in employment) were involved in Yugoslavia's production of military equipment for export.[71] The export performance of military industry was strong in the 1980s, enabling the YPA to assert that 'The Yugoslav People's Army does not owe a single dollar abroad, nor does our country's overall indebtedness have any connection with the armed forces.'[72] Between 1981 and 1985 these were worth US $7.5 billion; exports exceeded imports by 3.5 or 4 times.[73] In 1982 the ratio had been only 2.5 to one.[74] Amid the chaos of the Yugoslav economy, this would seem, therefore, a notable success.

A large part of the success in foreign-currency earnings was due to 'services' supplied – particularly engineering. Otherwise, innovations such as the burst-firing stream corrector to improve automatic rifle precision[75] were an exception to the production of mostly outdated, Soviet-designed armaments. However, advances made in technological areas left the Yugoslavs as equals in cooperative partnerships, rather than merely licensee assemblers as they had been formerly.[76] In the 1980s, 10 per cent of Yugoslav military needs were produced under licence, with a further 10 per cent imported.[77]

Despite these difficulties, the Yugoslav defence industry tried to continue its advancement and expansion; it was, perhaps, less likely that Yugoslavia would be self-sufficient in defence needs in the 1990s. Certainly, in terms of actual defence, self-sufficiency was a chimera. Although 'the preparation of all economic and other potential for use in war is of special importance'.[78] if Yugoslavia had been subjected to attack, it would, perforce, have had to look for external assistance.[79]

Domestically, the army continued to play a major role in constructing and renewing the country's infrastructure. Contributions were still made in all the fields outlined in Chapter 2 that formed the YPA's sociopolitical legitimacy.[80] In particular, construction and engineering work remained important, including the building of roads and bridges.[81] The YPA's past activity in these areas was also used in efforts presumably intended to underline its sociopolitical role.[82]

Despite the relative success of the defence industry, the cuts had a considerable effect on force levels and the nature of the YPA. A rationalization programme in 'high and higher commands' reduced numbers while (it was claimed) increasing efficiency.[83] In absolute terms the YPA was reduced form 252,000 soldiers in 1981 to 210,000 at the end of 1986.[84] At the end of 1988, a further cut of 13 per cent in force levels was announced.[85]

As well as shrinking, the YPA began to change. A protean institution, it saw reduction of the period of military service and creeping 'professionalization'. Although he was against the reduction of the term of conscription for 15 months to 12 months,[86] Mamula initially welcomed some reforms.[87] However, the cut in serving time was not welcome; allied to insufficient funds for reserve officers the change, forced by fiscal constraint, meant a lowering of standards.[88]

Another change has been the decision partially to 'professionalize' the YPA.[89] In direct opposition to then Chief-of-Staff, Petar Gracanin's assertion that 'recruiting professionals . . . is not a solution for us'[90] the process of recruiting those with needed special skills for fixed terms began in 1987.[91] One commentator has argued that the creation of a professional army espousing 'Yugoslavism' was the YPA leadership's aim.[92] Whether or not this is so, it is evident that the initial impetus was a necessity: there was a need for the YPA to 'tighten its belt'.[93]

'Tightening one's belt' meant personal denial for army members. In one sense, this meant turning their savings into stabilization funds.[94] In another it meant enduring living standards which at various stages have been said to be 'at a level below which we could not go'.[95] Nonetheless, in 1986, Mamula was able to tell them that the standard of living of the regulars had fallen at least 1.5 per cent.[96] The standard of living has clearly been an affair of great worry to Yugoslav soldiers. It can have been no great comfort to have been informed that soldiers' living standards were keeping pace with the societal average.[97] In 1989, a series of changes included facilitating promotion to the rank of captain and beginning new pay structures, including enhancements for extra duties and overtime payments.[98] However, it seemed unlikely that the material conditions of life in the YPA would ever match former standards.

Apart from the material falls in personal and institutional standards, there was the question of morale. It is feasible that poorly kept and equipped troops would lose their confidence; poor funding 'in addition to material and financial damage . . . leads to the moral-political problem of broader social importance for the reputation of the army and the Yugoslav community's attitude towards it'.[99] In other words, this represents the possible alienation of the army from society and a weakening of its legitimacy. Reports constantly iterated the high level of moral-political readiness of the YPA. It was doubtful that such levels could be maintained indefinitely without some improvements.

Morale must have been affected by the debate surrounding YPA finances and its economic activity. With two-thirds of the federal budget devoted to the army,[100] in times of fiscal restraint YPA economic activity came under scrutiny. Annually, the YPA budget was the subject of longer and more difficult debates in the federal parliament, culminating in the near failure to reach agreement at the end of 1988 referred to in Chapter 3. An argument flared in 1989 about the Generals' case. Teodor Gersak, a defence analyst, questioned, among other things, Kadijevic's assertion that Yugoslavia's military spending was the smallest in Europe.[101] Gersak used SIPRI figures to demonstrate that of Yugoslavia's neighbours only Greece spent a higher proportion of its GDP on defence.[102] *Narodna Armija* assumed Gersak (a Slovene) to be a cohort of Jansa et al. and was amazed that a reputable, responsible defence journal could publish his article.[103] Gersak defended himself and continued his criticism.[104]

There was opinion-research support for those who questioned the YPA budget in print and in parliament. In Slovenia, 43.7 per cent thought the army received too much money; nearly 82 per cent believed completely or mostly that the YPA should be financed like education and health only in line with the country's economic level.[105] There was also strong support for the extensive criticism of the YPA's role in the 'worldwide selling of death'.[106] In one opinion poll, in spite of the benefit to the economy, 49.6 per cent thought arms sales should be stopped.[107] However, while opinion in these areas undermined military legitimacy, there was support for some of the army's other socioeconomic activity. For example, 97.5 per cent backed the YPA helping during 'catastrophes' and 88 per cent supported its role in building roads and so forth.[108]

The economic crisis forced the YPA to reduce its size, slow down its modernization plans and personally affected individual soldiers. This meant its leading role in the defence system was weakened by technical inadequacies and diminished morale. Its leading role was also damaged by the clamour of particularist national voices.

Critical aspects of functional legitimacy: nationalism

It is significant that the special 'thematic' edition of *Vojno Delo* in the first part of 1989 concluded its collection of essays with an article on nationalism in the YPA.[109] This indicates that the issue was the most important in military minds. Nationalism, above all else, was deleteriously affecting the army.

The article by Vuk Obradovic focused on two separate manifestations of nationalism in relation to the YPA. The first was Slovene, embracing the mixture of nationalist-liberal criticism of the army originating in Slovenia; the second was the damage caused by Albanian nationalism within YPA ranks. This article, following one on 'interpersonal relations' in the YPA,[110] indicated that in its efforts to secure Yugoslav defence preparedness the army was having considerable difficulties with morale and cohesion.

Concern about Slovene nationalism centred on the idea of forming Republican-based armies.[111] This idea, present in the Croatian demands in 1971, was now found in Slovenia – which had lost its 'national' army in 1945. According to Janez Jansa, the most prominent Slovene thorn in the YPA's side, 'none of us ever took a stand for a Republican army'.[112] What Jansa had advocated during his candidature for the presidency of the Slovene Youth Organization was that each nationality should be able to serve in nationally homogenous units where their own language was spoken.[113] Slovenes would serve with Slovenes, Macedonians with Macedonians and so forth. Obradovic challenged this conception for its failure to explain how it might be realized in a 'nationally heterogeneous milieu'.[114] The only option would involve reducing the role of the Federation to one of merely coordinating the activities of republican armies.

The YPA's opposition to this idea was not further detailed (although inferences may be drawn from the subsequent discussion of Albanian nationalism – see below). There had been some military openness to the issue. The Commanding Officer of the erstwhile LAD, General Svetozar Visnjic, while 'not an advocate of republican armies' thought there was a need to 'consider the multi-national aspect of our country' and 'clarify' some matters.[115] Another officer, explaining why it was necessary to have a nationally proportionate officer cadre, made the following case: 'In the event of aggression, let us say we mobilize a division of Slovenes and appoint as commanding officer a Croat, for example, or a Serb, or a Macedonian. That would not make sense!'[116] This clearly indicated the possibility of an ethnically homogenous unit (division).

The notion of ethnically homogenous units was not without merit. Partisan experience of more or less nationally pure units attests to this – although it could be maintained that TD, not the army, fulfilled this role. More importantly, such a system could have had benefits in terms of unit cohesion.

Cohesion is an ineluctable trait of military success. This is particularly so in cases such as the Yugoslav. As Mamula said at Kumrovec, 'Only . . . our human factor can play a decisive role in conditions of technical inferiority.'[117] In another variant of 'people's defence', the 'Swiss command has always argued that it is the "unit cohesion" their system achieves that makes their army too tough a nut for stronger neighbours to crack'.[118] Morale is especially important in systems of 'nations in arms'.

Military experience demonstrates that soldiers fight for their fellows.[119] The regiment, regionally based, where it has been used, has played a major part in this. One author emphasizes the totality of the regimental system.[120] Tactical unity in combat is believed to be in a ratio with soldiers' knowledge and 'sympathetic understanding' of one another.[121] The regiment's organic texture seems to give it strength; it is a focus for loyalty that non-regimented systems lack.[122] Even where a soldier may not know his colonel's name, he will know all about his 'buddies', his comrades-in-arms, and they will fight for each other.[123] Certainly, the 'unit cohesion' generated by the regimental system has enabled survival and reformation 'with phenomenal speed and effectiveness' even 'under brutal casualties';[124] regiments provide resilience.

The effectiveness of regiments is well established.[125] The regiment is a place where 'an ethnic group's primary (and very real) affiliations can be represented and made to feel more at home'.[126] It has been argued that ethnic regiments significantly benefit unit morale.[127] National units enable 'a sense of *esprit de corps* to be maintained'.[128] It seems self-evident that an ethnically homogenous, regimental system could have improved YPA effectiveness.

In particular, such a system would have resolved the language question to which the YPA was 'devoting special attention' in 1989.[129] This included speeding-up the implementation of a decision to place bilingual signs in barracks, according to LC-YPA chief Admiral Petar Simic.[130] It also meant publication of *Narodna Armija* and *Front* in Slovene and Macedonian, as of Army Day, 1988, and the appearance of *Narodna Armija* in a mixture of Latin and Cyrillic scripts from 9 February 1989 (presumably to meet Serbian needs). This seems to have been a response to the demands at the time of the Ljubljana trial (see Chapter 3) that the constitutional principle of the equality of languages be respected. The introduction of Slovene and Macedonian editions of military periodicals appears to have been agreed when Kadijevic visited Slovenia in November 1988 in an attempt to improve YPA-Slovene relations; at that time there was 'discussion about aspects of the implementation of the constitutional principles on equality of languages within the YPA'.[131] After a wait of 44 years, the production of non-Serbo-Croat editions of *Narodna Armija* was swift. As *Nasa Vojska* (since 1945, the paper of the Ljubljana Army District, published in Serbo-Croat) enthused, 'only a month after the idea came its realization, without regard for the problems found in that time by the editors of CGP Delo who will publish *Narodna Armija* and *Front* in Slovene'.[132]

Despite these efforts to improve the language situation, the issue remained. There was a necessary conflict between the constitutional theory of the equality of languages and greater centralization.[133] The constitutional provision (Article 243) stated that one of the languages of the nations may be used for command in the YPA. This 'flexible formulation' in practice meant that, although Serbo-Croat was no longer the single, official command language it had once been, the working language in the army was still Serbo-Croat; in the YPA, the principle of equality of languages was to a large extent 'relative'.[134] The restructuring reduced the number of occasions where Serbo-Croat might not be used, reducing the chance of finding 'practical solutions to questions of language equality'.[135]

The language issue principally underlay the Slovene opinion that the YPA was disdainful of Slovenes; according to the *Slovensko Javno Mnenje* (*Slovene Public Opinion*, a mass survey of 2,000 Slovenes conducted annually), 49.5 per cent completely agreed that this was the case, with another 26.8 per cent mostly in agreement.[136] Even more than the discontent the language issue provoked among Slovenes, it also created very practical problems, particularly, it has been suggested, a propos Albanians. Albanian army students in Belgrade were required to spend a preliminary year studying Serbo-Croat to overcome language impediments.[137]

Given the advantages that would seem to have been likely to accrue should the YPA have adopted ethnically homogenous regiments, why was its resistance so adamant? Any explanation must bear in mind the comparative experience of that other multi-national communist military, the Soviet Union's. Between the wars and during the 'Great Patriotic War', the Red Army had ethnic units.[138] Before the war, such units were being disbanded because of the 'severe challenge' of Muslim minorities.[139] Yet national regiments were quickly revived after 1941. These were successful in fairly limited roles; their creation had been necessary to ensure the military effectiveness of non-Slav soldiers by avoiding 'linguistic and cultural problems'.[140] In the main, there was a 'high level of concern for minority liability'.[141] A propos both the Soviet Armed Forces (SAF) and the Warsaw Pact allies, the Soviets opted for integrated military structures. A multinational force 'clearly generates immense difficulties in command, control, communications and logistics, but such an army circumvents the problem of political reliability'.[142] The YPA, like its Soviet counterpart, opted to solve the complex of technical difficulties rather than deal with an army composed of national units.

For the Yugoslav generals, concern about unreliable national elements was aroused by Albanian nationalism. Obradovic, after discussing Slovene nationalism and notions of a republican-based army, turned to the presence of Albanian 'terrorism' within the YPA. The worst case of this occurred on 3 September 1987, when an Albanian soldier, stationed in Paracin, opened fire in the barracks, killing four colleagues and wounding a further five.[143] This act was generally interpreted as a manifestation of the 'counter-revolution' in Kosovo.

At the 17th Central Committee session, in October 1988, Chief-of-Staff, General Stevan Mirkovic, warned against 'soldiers associating on the basis of nationality'. He stated that 'so far' it had been Albanians who had done this and in extreme cases were 'oriented towards terrorism'.[144] The number of reported cases of Albanian nationalism and separatism grew 22-fold between 1981 and 1988.[145] Although 220 'illegal groups' were identified during the 1980s,[146] only 7 per cent of Albanians in the YPA, associated with such groups, were tried. The YPA favoured 'work on education'; socialization was better than prosecution. Only this could ultimately rectify a situation in which 'extreme nationalist groups' could 'disturb unity in the army'.[147]

Albanian and Slovene attitudes to the YPA, in their different ways, had an immeasurable, but telling, impact of it. Albanian disruptions of units induced YPA commanders to concur in the 'universal recognition by military professionals that deviants . . . can undermine a group's cultivated definition of the situation and thereby threaten morale'; 'severe unit morale degradation' can result from the acts of a few individuals; and 'alienated people bring their social distance with them when they enter military service, and this is not necessarily eradicated'.[148]

Both Slovenes and Albanians may be considered to have become 'alienated' from the army in significant numbers. They exhibited characteristics of alienation such as 'isolation' (holding a set of values different from those of the army) and 'cynicism' (the individual's willingness to participate in collective undertakings and to sacrifice for the general good – key components of the military ethic – are substantially weakened).[149] One Yugoslav military source understood that 'nationalism is the result of personal impotence, frustration and doubt',[150] all alienating traits. Alienated individuals, lacking morale and debilitating *esprit de corps*, impair fighting capability. As an eminent British general has affirmed: 'History shows, over and over again, that large numbers, good organization, up-to-date equipment and sophisticated tactical doctrine are all useless if the soldiers are demoralized.'[151]

These problems were manifest in YPA recruitment frustrations. It seems to have been impossible to attract an adequate ethnic intake to officer school; in addition to Slovenes and Albanians, Croats and Hungarians were under-represented.[152] But Slovenes and Albanians posed the biggest problems.

In order to maintain the ethnic 'key', standards for Slovenes, Croats and Albanians were dropped to a level where 'people are accepted even if they [did] not satisfy the conditions of competition', whereas, 'excellent candidates' from other areas were rejected.[153] This had been the case particularly with regard to Albanians. In addition to the language question already touched upon, other educational deficiencies were found in Albanian candidates for officer school. They had to study 'everything' the army had concluded they did not 'know as well as students from other primary [basic] schools', such as maths, physics and chemistry.[154] Further problems arose: either students failed their preliminary year, or they just passed but then could not fit in. In an implicit reference to Kosovans, one military voice said, 'Were we to draw up a single list, then we would not have a single candidate from certain communities'.[155]

Poor recruitment figures for Slovenes are mentioned in Chapter 3. The issues involved were different ones concerning the 'liberal' quest of an affluent, would-be Western society, but the effect was the same. More than half of all young Slovenes showed no interest at all in a military career, according to one survey.[156] In 1987, not one Slovene enrolled at the Military Academy in Belgrade; there were, in all, 25 per cent fewer Slovenes accepted than in the previous year.[157]

The YPA bent its rules to try to maintain ethnic proportionality. This had to happen to ensure that future leading cadres were not exclusively Serb and Montenegrin. Because the upper reaches, above all, were dependent on the national key (see Chapter 2) it was necessary to recruit from all nationalities to form a pool from which to draw. However, there seemed to be little chance of improvement. The effects of YPA units conducting 'counter-insurgent' action against Albanians in Kosovo would not attract many from that nationality. The fallout from the Jansa trial seemed certain further to deflate Slovene interest in military occupations. Matters such as this and the language issue fostered the impression of YPA disregard for Slovenes. In addition, the fact that almost half of all Slovenes supported the civilian option for military service undermined the YPA's position. Perhaps even more discouraging for the Generals was the level of faith in YPA capability; as many as 15.9 per cent thought it would not perform successfully in the event of an attack.[158] The confidence of only half the population (53.3 per cent) on a matter such as this did not suggest a large swell of support (although 58.7 per cent would resist an enemy attack).

Much of this did not bode well for the army. The psycho-social distance of Albanians and Slovenes from the YPA had dysfunctional consequences. According to Westbrook, 'there is a negative correlation between sociopolitical alienation and military efficiency'. Alienation is found to 'limit seriously the Army's ability to produce efficient soldiers';[159] a high level of alienation equates with low morale. This conclusion on the US Army was even more applicable to the YPA: 'If a substantial portion of the most capable and well-integrated members of society continue to refuse to serve in the Army, the alienation drain on military efficiency will probably exist to some degree regardless of the internal efforts of the army to combat it.'[160] Given the importance of 'recognition' in counteracting alienation, prospects were not good.[161] There seems little chance of Slovenes and Albanians according 'status' to the military profession and so conferring the 'recognition' that might encourage enlistment; more likely in the longer term, perhaps, was erosion of the 'recognition' that had backed individuals from other nationalities in becoming officers.

Ultimately, an even greater problem than attitudinal matters for the YPA in maintaining its national proportionality and morale was Yugoslavia's demographic development. The severe decline in the Slovene birth-rate would diminish even further the small pool from which it had to recruit officers.[162] Conversely, the factorial expansion of the Albanian population was going to bring even greater problems of language, alienation, low morale and weak unit cohesion; the number of Albanians in Yugoslavia (despite the exodus of 250,000 to other parts of Europe) appears to grow by half every ten years.[163] Unless Yugoslavia took enormous affirmative action not seen previously, the number of malcontents was destined to become vast.

Although the YPA might have tried to create units in which Albanians could be trained in their own language, which would operate on the cohesive principle of identity, it was unlikely to do so. The level of discontent was such that an 'Albanian' republican army could become a potentially troublesome nationalist instrument. Oppressed Albanians might use military might to gain politically, which gain might well imply civil war.

The YPA could not tolerate proposals, such as Jansa's, for ethnically complete regiments, in spite of theoretical advantages that might occur. By vehemently countering such initiatives the YPA did not help its predicament. Increasingly, its intonations of 'brotherhood and unity' had the opposite effect of that desired; as the YPA increased centralization (among other things to escape the ramifications of nationalist politics) and emphasized 'unity', it lost touch with 'brotherhood'.

Nationalism seriously impinged on the YPA's functional imperative. To avoid the possibility of being dragged towards republican regiments, as much as for reasons of strategy and command and control, the YPA drew into its centre. In doing so, it invited further stretching on the nationalist rack.

The social matrix of defence: GPD

The question of support for GPD has not been widely studied (at least openly – no doubt the Federal Secretariat has considered it). One valuable light has been cast on the issue by John Allcock.[164] He has analysed the social supports that underpinned the Partisans' victory. For him that success was linked to particular features of Yugoslav society. He divides these supports under the labels 'recruitment' and 'supply'. Social conditions that sustained the Partisan effort, Allcock demonstrates, were not available in the 1980s.

The Yugoslav revolution was essentially a peasant revolution, Allcock argues (in a good tradition).[165] This provided specific patterns of 'recruitment' and 'supply'. At the time, almost two-thirds of the population lived 'directly from agriculture'. Every Yugoslav economically active in agriculture 'supported' roughly two other citizens with food. By 1981, the number of people directly living from the land had fallen to 11 per cent; an agriculturally economically active individual in the 1980s supported nine other citizens. The countryside had been depopulated; the towns had swelled. Yugoslav society had become industrial and urban. There is no longer a rural population, poor and discontent, to furnish 'another generation of Partisans'.[166]

Not only were people no longer inhabiting villages, but those who did in the 1980s were increasingly aged. The younger, more active population had left for the towns. Contingent upon this are cultural changes. The Communists manipulated the hostility felt by poor, often unemployed peasants towards the bourgeois who lived in the towns. This could no longer be the case.

Allcock's point that the constituency from which the NLA derived membership and support was no longer available is indisputable. However, as a former Yugoslav defence minister reminded his readers, should it come to a war, the Yugoslavs would be fighting one of a different character.[167] This is true not only of the technologies involved, but for the very nature of the war. For all the talk in Yugoslav defence literature about drawing on Partisan experience, GPD was necessarily different: in a future war, Yugoslav armed forces would not be mobilizing to conduct a revolution, but to protect the status quo; the fight would not be against the system, but for it. More than this, the purpose of GPD was deterrence.[168]

For GPD to be an effective deterrent, it had also to work. Could Yugoslavia defend itself? Was GPD efficient enough to act as a 'detonator' with 'unpredictable reverberations'?[169] The question on the social foundations of Yugoslav defence was this: could the mechanisms of GPD successfully mobilize general support? Which is to say, would GPD work?

The social dimensions of Yugoslav defence placed a shadow of doubt on the chances of GPD mobilizing successfully. One problem stemmed from the country's under-development. The number of

Yugoslavs working abroad created major mobilization problems. In the early 1970s, 90 per cent of Yugoslavs working abroad were eligible for military service. In the event of war or a threat of war, there would be the logistical problem of how to transport all those people due to return. Another problem would concern the willingness of those abroad to return to Yugoslavia. Alternatively, there could be political difficulties with the West European host countries in which the 6–7 million *gastarbeiter* are active. This could be because of the involvement of the states in question, or the economic effect of losing a sizeable section of the workforce, or merely because of the chaos moving so many individuals *en masse* would involve. However, if these potential impediments to mobilization stemmed from Yugoslavia's economic weakness, even greater ones resulted from the degree of economic development and industrialization that had taken place in the Communist era.[170]

The urbanization of Yugoslav society spawned problems in this area. First, Yugoslavia was now well urbanized; its economic growth depended on industrial towns; what it had to protect, essentially, were towns and cities. GPD's focus was the mountains where Partisan success was cradled.[171] This created a question addressed by Rusinow: would the urban centres be conceded?[172]

If the towns and cities were to be seriously defended, 'supply' would become significant. Whereas 'recruitment' is of limited value in exploring the social facets of GPD, Allcock's second social support of the Partisan victory is compelling. Resistance within cities requires supplies. This support may come from 'other local inhabitants – by theft, bribery, or the restriction of their own consumption, or by supplies smuggled in from outside'.[173] To evade the occupier's detecting them, such supplies would be small. From this it follows that those engaged in active resistance would be few. Their acts of resistance would be of a correspondingly low intensity.

If the industrial conurbations were to be abandoned as GPD implied, the question of supplies remained. Loss of towns means loss of industrial capacity, most importantly, of arms' production. Beyond this, an evident corollary of a large urban population's taking to the hills to become fighters is survival. The relatively inhospitable mountains to which the fighters would go had become 'less able than they ever were to yield a food surplus'.[174] This would be so with skilled rural dwellers; 'townies' would face considerable unhappiness as they found themselves unable to 'live off the land'.

Another result of urbanization that would register in mountain-based resistance is transport. Helicopters might provide some service into and among the mountains, but these would be limited by number, opportunity and vulnerability. There would be little alternative to pack animals, as with the Partisans. But the number of horses in Yugoslavia had fallen enormously from 1,242,000 in 1955 to 409,000 30 years later.[175] This dearth, compounded by urban ignorance of how to handle horses, would constrain Partisan-type operations.

Finally, there could be problems mobilizing an urban population in the event of attack. The threat of imminent attack might induce chaos in towns and cities, as was reported in one major study.[176] Certainly the complexities of mobilization for GPD would appear to enhance this possibility. Experience demonstrated that in mobilization, preparations were not coordinated – the appropriate bodies had not achieved the 'expected results' in their work.[177] As a result many people did not know what their GPD role was. Fifty-one per cent of Slovenes say they knew what their role was in GPD;[178] nearly half the population did not know what to do. In this situation, the complexities of mobilization could create 'panic'.[179] It appears that the mechanisms of GPD would generate support which was both inadequate and confused. Inter-ethnic frictions, as when 500 reservists in Koper, Slovenia, left their positions on exercise to protest against their Serbian officer, would exaggerate this.[180]

A report in *Mladina* on the reservists' strike during exercises attributed to an officer commanding the group statements in which JBTZ were called 'spies' and Jansa was subject to coarse abuse; the new Slovene Alliances were anarchists hiding behind democratic slogans; moreover, the Slovene reservists were told they understood nothing of the Serbs. Although it is common for soldiers the world over to be subjected to any kind of abuse by their superiors, it seems unwise to use this approach with reservists, given the atmosphere in Yugoslavia at the time. Certainly the fact that the reservists protested and, later, left their positions, did nothing to recommend the approach; nor did it augur well for the likely cohesiveness of such units in time of war – and, therefore, for the performance of the territorial defence system as a whole.

It seemed possible that Yugoslav society could not provide the supports to sustain GPD. If this were so, GPD in its current form was inappropriate for modern Yugoslavia. The implications for YPA legitimacy of having to lead a misplaced defence system were not good. As Yugoslavia entered the 1990s GPD seemed to be faced with specific social impediments to its operation. Moreover, these were relatively straightforward, to some extent, inevitable features of industrializing society. The big question-mark against a successful defence of Yugoslavia was the effect of social crisis. In this sense, any comparison with social conditions in 1941 should focus less on how Partisan victory was nurtured, but more on how the old Yugoslavia fell apart, swiftly overrun and abjectly unable to defend itself.

Defending Yugoslavia in 1941 and the 1990s: the social matrix of defence

It cannot have escaped defence planners' consideration that in 1941 an economically decadent and nationally divided Yugoslavia fell apart when attacked. The possibility that history might be repeated placed a question-mark against the surety of Yugoslavia's defence. Inability to guarantee the country's defence was detrimental to the YPA's functional legitimacy: the YPA legitimated itself by ensuring – through its own immediate activity and the TDF system – defence against external threat; it could only achieve this, should it be necessary, if Yugoslavia itself were strong and united.

Similar weaknesses in Yugoslavia's political, social and economic infrastructure could be observed in the 1980s to those that characterized the country in 1941. Aleksa Djilas argued that there was also similarity between the Royal Army's situation in 1941 and the YPA's today.[181] Like the YPA, he argues, the Royal Army was large and highly regarded internationally. In the creation of the *cetnik odredi* after 1939, it had even prepared for guerrilla war.[182] Yet the Army's defence lasted only 12 days and the Chetnik operations were unsuccessful. Djilas believed contemporary Yugoslavia's defence was equally vulnerable.

However, observable differences exist between the two periods. These differences permit some confidence in the prospects for defending Yugoslavia. First, the military at the end of the 1980s still had greater social legitimacy than its inter-war predecessor. The inter-war governments lasted in total 268 months. During that period, the defence minister was always a Serb general. Indeed, in 1938, of 165 Generals, 161 were Serbs – leaving two Croats and two Slovenes.[183] The YPA's generals are better proportioned in the High Command. With a spread of 38 per cent Croats, 33 per cent Serbs and 8.3 per cent Slovenes, the higher reaches of the YPA are clearly less Serb dominated than those of the Royal Army. In addition, the top soldier in 1990, Kadijevic, was half-Croat and, although an ethnic-Serb, his predecessor as Defence Secretary, Branko Mamula, was from Croatia and a naval man – which gave him a Croatian profile.[184]

Another difference is inter-nationality morale. The predominating Serb Generals in the Royal Army perceived their colleagues from the 'national minorities' as unreliable, subversive German agents. Discipline and morale were undermined by these Serbs suspicious of their fellow officers.[185] As noted above, the YPA, in contrast, carries the banner of 'brotherhood and unity' from the Partisan days and is today a repository of 'Yugoslavism'. Against the suspicions debasing the prewar army, we may juxtapose a 'Yugoslav' trust among YPA officers. Greater trust meant greater cohesiveness and higher morale; these made it more likely that YPA officers would lead a fight and, indeed, fight more effectively.

This conclusion, finally, is reinforced by a consideration of the 'guerrilla' similarity between the two periods. The Chetnik idea, although a traditional notion, did not feature in military planning until 1940. A late arrival, it had little support among the highest ranks whose thought had been forged in the 1914–18 war and earlier. The weakness of conviction in the policy is evident in the position the Mihailovic-led Chetniks took when war came: wait for the Allies and then fight.[186] In contradistinction, the YPA was fully committed to its role in leading Yugoslavia's system of GPD. This commitment to a 'guerrilla' defence on a scale far more vast than the Chetnik strategy, and with immensely greater organization and preparation, indicated that, for the time being, albeit sagging, the Yugoslav defence posture remained just about firm enough.

However, although YPA leadership, command and control was likely to be strong, Yugoslavia's defence position was dependent on the army's receiving full support. If, in the event of war, there was a dissipation of support for territorial defence along national lines, as intimated above, GPD would not work. As well as YPA commitment and effectiveness, GPD rested on the engagement of all its citizens, of all nations and nationalities. It was the dread that such engagement would not happen as Yugoslavia dissolved in the welter of invasion which prompted YPA Generals in their political activity. They wished to secure Yugoslavia in a way in which it had not been in 1941. Although the position was clearly healthier *vis-a-vis* the army and its role – the 1980s Yugoslav defence posture was a fairly strong one – the political, economic and social infrastructure betrayed similar ills. These frailties began to affect the YPA's functional legitimacy as the technically expert, highly trained, unified, cohesive, leading element in the Yugoslav defence forces. This began to weaken YPA capability. That capability could not be maintained without adequate political, economic and social support. More importantly, in the unlikely arrival of war on the Yugoslav doorstep, the weaknesses in the Yugoslav infrastructure raised questions a propos the system of GPD. It does not seem unreasonable to share the Generals' implicit view that Yugoslavia could not be guaranteed to remain intact in the face of attack. Although militarily better prepared for invasion than in 1941, Yugoslavia was not necessarily politically, socially or economically any fitter.

Yugoslav civil-military relations, as has been argued, may be understood in terms of regime and military legitimacy. Yugoslavia in the 1980s was faced with a multi-faceted legitimacy crisis. The military's role in that crisis was both prompted and constrained by weaknesses in its legitimacy that emerged during those years. Frailties in regime and military legitimacy suggested that Yugoslavia might fall apart, as it had in 1941, should it be attacked. Weaknesses in military legitimacy placed question-marks over its probable performance in war. Although the difficulties were growing and generated worries for the future, strengths continued to outweigh weaknesses. However, the intensification of nationalist statements increased societal instability and did nothing to reassure anyone that Yugoslavia would hang together if attacked. Prospects, in this regard, resembled 1941, *de plus en plus*.

To compound this, the YPA's 'immune' system increasingly appeared to be deficient. 'Facts of social affairs have a most direct influence on the army' it was reported. The situation was clearly fraught: 'Negative features influence the consciousness of YPA members, their mood, motivation and conduct,'[187] it was reported. The Generals' admission that it 'would be very dangerous to underestimate its negative effect on YPA members' of nationalist influences was a clear sign that all was no longer well.[188] The army was becoming increasingly alienated. Exactly what this implied for the YPA's likely performance could not be gauged. Certainly neither this nor the general societal degeneration augured well for the prospect of defending Yugoslavia.

The YPA's legitimacy was weak. Functionally, we have identified various impediments to its effective leadership of a defence system that was open to question. Sociopolitically, the impossibility of immuring itself from the effects of societal crisis and preserving GPD from the consequences of that crisis undermined the army's position. As Yugoslav Generals had always been very much aware, a country's security results from the social matrix of defence. The YPA faced a crisis of military legitimacy, which, in part, depended on the crisis in regime legitimacy.

Unless the regime's legitimacy could be restored, Yugoslavia's security would be dependent on and better guaranteed by the international situation in which an attack, even on a severely weakened country, seemed ever more improbable. The outcome of a defence relying on Yugoslavia's capability might have been 'too close to call'.

5 The Disintegrative Country and Relegitimation: the End of Tito's Yugoslavia

The 1980s saw both regime and military in Yugoslavia delegitimated. As a consequence, both entered the last decade of the century needing to renew legitimacy. 1990 and 1991, therefore, must be considered as pivotal years (indeed, 50 years after the Axis turned on the first Yugoslavia and destroyed it, 1991 may be the axis Yugoslavia turns on between self-preservation and self-destruction). Renovation of military legitimacy is largely dependent on regime relegitimation. However, regime relegitimation is impossible without new military legitimacy. How could they achieve this?

The many-sided crisis of the 1980s gave rise to a quest for a new constitution, which would need to restore political legitimacy in the country. The bases of legitimacy that had emerged in the past no longer had currency. The key elements in the system's liturgy were apparent in the earlier discussions of legitimacy: the Partisan struggle during the war to create a better Yugoslavia based on the AVNOJ principles of brotherhood and unity and the equality of nations and nationalities; the independent Yugoslav road of socialist self-management and non-alignment after the split with Stalin; a devolved and decentralized political system with power resting in the republics and autonomous provinces; a relatively prosperous and progressive economy in which things would get better, fostered by the political structures and values just mentioned. These decreasingly generated support. Yugoslav politicians presented with the task of drafting a new constitution were, by the end of the 1980s, being tested to devise a completely new set of arrangements for the conduct of political and economic activity in Yugoslavia – which set of arrangements would necessarily have to accommodate the radically divergent positions adopted by various constituencies in the Yugoslav entity.

In the second half of the 1980s, the terminal condition of the old bases of legitimacy created a need for alternatives. Nationalism, managed initially by the LC authorities in the republics, but later also the focus for opposition parties, became the cornerstone of political support. This meant that the federal authorities were increasingly devoid of legitimacy, which was devolved almost completely to republican equivalents. The passing of legitimacy from the federation to the republics meant that any third Yugoslavia would be the product of negotiations between representatives of relatively strong republics, not a central creation offered to the country. The framers of a new constitution had much to do. Legitimation was required at all levels in the political system – authorities, regime and, most distressingly of all, community.[1] A legitimacy deficit with regard to those making and enacting policy (the authorities) is more easily made up than one concerning the way in which policy is framed and achieved (the regime); both these, however, will have much greater chances of restoring legitimacy than a state in which the very community itself is in question – which was clearly becoming the case vis-a-vis Yugoslavia at the end of the 1980s. The new constitution would have to find a way in which to reconcile the various elements of the Yugoslav federation to living with one another.

Relegitimation (1): from party to state

The problems confronting those charged with constitutional renovation became clear in the way Titoist and Communist Yugoslavia came to its end in the first two months of 1990. Predictions of Yugoslav disintegration were sparked by events at either end of the country. The Slovene declaration of the right to secede had given rise to such speculation in the latter stages of 1989. Concomitant with a particularly violent outbreak of the recurring troubles in Kosovo, the Slovene party left the federal party, accentuating speculation about a split with the federation itself. The circumstances of the federal party's break-up demonstrated the extremes any new ordering of Yugoslav politics would have to reconcile.

The LCY was dealt a fatal blow in January when the Slovene delegation walked out of the emergency 14th LCY Congress, called to revitalize and reorient Yugoslavia. At that congress, the LCY began to dissolve and the paths towards a third Yugoslavia began to be opened. The Slovene exit came after their reform proposals had been defeated in the congress. The proposals centred on the idea of a further federalization – or confederalization – of the LCY into a 'League of Leagues'; they also included amendments calling for the abolition of provisions for political crimes in the penal code, the release of existing political prisoners, a ban on torture and backing for Yugoslavia's seeking full membership of the European Community.

Although the LCY had already voted for an end to 'verbal crime' by deciding to abolish Article 133 of the Criminal Code and had also conceded its monopoly on power, paving the way for multiple-party elections, this was not enough for the Slovenes. To them, failure to adopt the other amendments constituted a lack of serious commitment to reform: democracy would remain distant while political crimes were still possible. Most of all, the refusal to decentralize the party further indicated that other Yugoslavs were still inclined to make the mistakes of the JBTZ trial and remained reluctant to accept the principle of republican sovereignty – which principle was now cardinal for the Slovenes.

Despite having voted to revoke its power monopoly, the LCY did not formally do so because the declaration of which it and other proposals above were part was not adopted. The declaration, the party and the country were put in limbo when the session was suspended and an emergency congress of the LCS called for Friday, 2 February. The meeting was put back two days as Ciril Ribicic (who had taken over from Kucan before the LCY Conference, freeing the latter to become a candidate in the presidential elections in the spring) received an eleventh-hour visit from the leader of the LCY-YPA, Vice-Admiral Petar Simic.[2] The content of their meeting went unreported. Almost certainly, there was a plea from Simic for a reconsideration. Discussion must have focused on the implications of a decision by the Slovene Communists to disengage from the federal party, particularly with regard to GPD.

At that conference, which took place on Sunday, 4 February, the LCS abolished itself.[3] With this act, *de facto*, the LCY ceased to exist and Yugoslavia became a multi-party system. For the Slovenes, the decision meant that they no longer had a voice in the federal party, which at that stage remained, technically, the only legal party and the 'leading force' in Yugoslav politics. However, the Slovene decision effectively neutered the LCY's leading role and gave a further push towards liberal democracy. The federal party could no longer function as the most important institution in Yugosalvia.

From the ashes of the LCS rose a phoenix-like (LCS) Party of Democratic Renewal. The new party retained the initials of the old party, presumably to indicate some continuation as well as to keep the advantage of name recognition (particularly with older supporters) in the Slovene elections due in March and April; at the same time, the change of name proclaimed the party's West German-style social-democratic freshness. The Slovene leadership wanted to give Yugoslavia a chance to become 'West European' – an ambition that was reflected in their election slogan 'Europe Now!'

The new name also left open an avenue for the establishment of a new federal party. Both Slovenia and Yugoslavia were now multi-party systems. In the federal parliament sat Communists and Renewal Democrats. In the absence of a 'Slovene' appendage to the new party's name, there remained the possibility of there being Renewal Democrats throughout Yugoslavia some time in the future.

Slovene actions in this period were undoubtedly influenced by the collapse of Communism elsewhere in Eastern Europe. For so long, Yugoslavia – in particular Slovenia – had been in the forefront of reforming the Communist state. Suddenly, Yugoslavia was lagging behind. Under Kucan's leadership, the Slovenes had made great advances in the process of liberalization. (See Chapter 3.) Yugoslavia's geostrategic position and Slovenia's situation within Yugoslavia meant that the old formulas and habits were due lip service and constrained the advancement of new ideas. Communism's crumbling and utter discrediting in Czechoslovakia, East Germany and Romania made it possible for the reformist Slovene leadership openly to declare its hand. In declaring multi-party elections and emphasizing Slovenia's right to self-determination, Kucan and his cohort, unlike the majority of Communists elsewhere in Eastern Europe and Yugoslavia, were continuing a policy that had been adopted long before.

However, their behaviour now had another dimension. The Slovene leadership's decision was taken with a view to surviving the spring elections. Given the outcome of the emergency 14th Conference, not to have distanced themselves from the Federation would have invited disaster at the polls in face of an ardently nationalist opposition. None the less, the new name and Ribicic's statements suggested that the erstwhile Communists would be more inclined than their antagonists to follow a wait-and-see-if-Yugoslavia-can-be-healed policy.

The demise of the Slovene party enhanced the role of the state – particularly of the Prime Minister. The party was no longer central because it was no longer the forum in which representatives from all parts of Yugoslavia could talk to each other. Political dialogue with Slovenes on executive matters would have to take place in some other primary institutional structure. At the federal level, it was Prime Minister Ante Markovic who now attempted to reconcile Slovene-Serb differences. All such disputes now had to be dealt with by state institutions, not the party, which was no longer all-Yugoslav. The last LCS, first (LCS)-PDR congress, completed the shift from party to state governance. Legitimacy would no longer embrace party rule. The question it left unanswered concerned which state would receive the governmental role: republic or federation?

In the first half of 1990, the basic lines of potential relegitimation were drawn. Three models for the continuation of Yugoslavia emerged in discussions; in addition, a fourth option, the spectre of disintegration loomed – notably with regard to talk about Slovenia's seceding; such a notion was an obvious corollary of the transfer of legitimacy to republican level. A propos establishing a third Yugoslavia, the models were associated with particular names: Kucan and Tudjman; Markovic; and Milosevic and Jovic.

Relegitimation (2): unionists and confederates

Throughout 20 years, there occurred a process in which authority passed from the centre to the republics in Yugoslavia. The crisis of legitimacy as the country approached the last decade of the twentieth century reflected this. Legitimacy, in a vein of nationalism, had been transfused from federation to republic. Federal government had difficulty in demonstrating that it was in possession of that quality by which it could justify its holding power and its making demands on and acting on behalf of the Yugoslav people. Indeed, the demands made were increasingly not acceded to, as republican governments and representatives withheld both contributions to the federal budget and agreement to legislation. At the same time, they began to question the actions made on their behalf by federal institutions and the rights of those institutions to do so.

In 1990, the transposition of legitimacy from federation to republic was *de facto* formalized in the holding, at republican level, of the first multi-party elections in Yugoslavia since before the war. These produced cohabitation in Slovenia between a former Communist as president in Slovenia (Kucan) and a coalition of former opposition parties (the fragile DEMOS) with a relatively weak parliamentary majority. In Croatia, centre-right parties decisively ousted the Communists. The leader of the right-wing Croat Democratic Community, Franjo Tudjman, (a former Partisan and General) was elected President and proved to be far more pragmatic than his highly nationalistic campaign rhetoric; the Croats were also responsible for appointing the first non-Communist, Stjipe Mesic, to the Federal Presidency. Macedonia produced a mixed result, with the 120-seat parliament containing four sizeable blocs. An alliance of nationalist parties held 37 seats, reform Communists 30, a coalition of two pro-Albanian parties 25, and a grouping of Young Democrats and Socialists 18. However, the most prominent Macedonian politician remained its representative on the Federal Presidency, Vasil Tupurkovski.

In Bosnia, results were predominantly along nationalist lines. The Muslim Party for Democratic Action gained 41 seats in the Chamber of Citizens, followed by 34 for the Serbian Democratic Party and 20 for the Croatian Democratic Community (the Bosnian cousins of nationalist parties in Serbia and Croatia); lastly, the reform Communists won 13 seats. The distribution of seats was proportional to the ethnic composition of the republic. The Bosnian elections were notable for securing the return to political life of Fikret Abdic, notorious in some parts of Yugoslavia for his part in the Agrokomerc financial scandal of the mid-1980s, but a hero in his own community. Abdic obtained the highest vote in polling for the collective Republican Presidency. In doing so, he finished ahead of his PDA colleague, Alija Izetbegovic, who none the less subsequently became President. (Izetbegovic was just one of a crop of seemingly highly able politicians in Bosnia.) Finally, the delicate balance of political forces in the republic (and perhaps their maturity) could be measured in the outcome in the Mostar municipal vote: the CDC gained a majority, but a Serb was chosen as Municipal President.

In the remaining republics, Serbia and Montenegro, there were overwhelming votes for the pre-democratic forces. Milosevic's not-so-reformist ex-Communists won an easy victory against an Albanian electoral boycott and a Serbian opposition led by Vuk Draskovic; and the Serbian Socialist Party leader was himself voted in on the first ballot as President of the Republic. His counterpart in Montenegro, Momir Bulatovic, on the other hand, only secured 40 per cent of the first-round votes and had to wait for a second ballot for the Republican Presidency. Meanwhile, his unchanged League of Communists of Montenegro took 85 of the 125 places available in parliament at the first vote.[4]

The process of legitimacy transfer was not complete, however, with Ante Markovic's federal government generally retaining support throughout Yugoslavia (Serbia appeared, to some extent, to be an exception in this regard). That support reflected economic policy successes. But inter-republican squabbles undermined his achievements and hampered their progress. At the centre of Yugoslavia's surviving its critical condition was the competition between federal and republican institutions and between different republican authorities.

During the 1980s, legitimacy had been denuded at all levels. It therefore had to be restored at all levels – authorities, regime and community. Indeed, the most salient of the Yugoslav crises was the crisis of community. Questions of relegitimation concerned not only how Yugoslavia would organize its future but whether or not Yugoslavs would have a future together. The Slovene disconnection from the LCY, following declarations of its sovereign right to secede the previous autumn, began speculation that lasted throughout the year, on the break-up of Yugoslavia. Apocalyptic prognostications abounded as Yugoslavia's valiant attempt to make six plus two equal one came closer than ever to disaster.

In the course of 1990, four ideas could be identified a propos the future for Yugoslavs. One of these was proposed by the President of the Federal Presidency, Borisav Jovic, a Milosevic ally. His proposal for a new federation appeared to have support from Serbia and the YPA. The basic points of his outline contained many features of the present federation. However, clauses on the role of federal institutions vis-a-vis republican ones indicated the intention to strengthen the former in relation to the latter. In particular, items such as the need for all republics to consent to changes in the borders of Yugoslavia and the 'obligatory' nature of federal documents and laws throughout the federation while government on Republican territories was to be nobody else's affair seemed to be designed to maximize central control.[5] This proposal was wholly unacceptable to Slovenes and Croatians who characterized it as 'unitarian' and 'bolshevik'.[6] Indeed, to the Slovenes, who were not prepared to remain part of a Yugoslavia built on the 1974 Constitution, promoting even greater central control appeared to be a move designed to precipitate the country's disintegration. Instead, they and the Croatians said that they would only stay as part of a confederal Yugoslavia – and if that could not be achieved, then they would become independent.

In other parts of Yugoslavia, response was split. Montenegrins favoured the Jovic proposal. Bosnians preferred it, but would also accept a confederation of all the existing republics (one suggestion of a Yugoslavia made up of federal and confederal elements was strongly dismissed in Bosnia).[7] Macedonia, in the guise of its old Communist leadership, began by supporting the federal option, but by the time of the elections in that republic, in November, virtually all parties' programmes favoured confederation. The Albanians in Kosovo were more in tune with the confederalists, but their position was complicated by the desire for a confederation that would include republican status for Kosovo. A confederal arrangement, otherwise, would leave them even more at the mercy of Serbian repression. When Serbia closed the provincial parliament, its Albanian members stood on its steps and declared Kosovan sovereignty. This action was a symbolic gesture; Kosovo remained under firm Serbian dominion.

The Jovic proposal was disliked in most parts of Yugoslavia. Above all, there was no possibility of its being accepted by the Slovenes (aside from its message, the messenger's association with Milosevic and 'Serbian unitarism' left little possibility of the proposal's being well received). They would not remain part of such a Yugoslavia. They promulgated the idea of a confederal Yugoslavia of sovereign states. Kucan and Tudjman jointly presented a confederal model. Kucan's republic would only continue to be a part of Yugoslavia on the basis of the principles inherent in that model. For the Croatians and, in particular, for the Slovenes, the question of 'how to be?' became less of a question than 'to be or not to be?'

The Kucan-Tudjman axis produced a discussion document, based largely on European Community (EC) arrangements, which presented options for degrees of confederation.[8] The independence of sovereign states would be the only fixed point; everything else would be a question of voluntarily (the voluntary nature of confederation was stressed) giving up areas of sovereignty and transfer of certain responsibilities to confederal bodies.

According to the proposal, confederal Yugoslavia would be based on international principles, values and laws recognizing human and property rights, market economies, parliamentary democracy and the right to secede from the confederation and the possibility of being expelled from it if confederal courts consistently found a member breaching its obligations. Its essential characteristics would be monetary union (as distinct from a single currency), a single market and harmonized infrastructure elements, such as communications' networks, separate but coordinated armed forces, with the possibility of permanent joint forces (particularly air forces) and separate subjects of international law – and, therefore, foreign relations, although for certain matters common or joint diplomatic action would be possible. Its chief institutional features were envisaged to be a Council of Ministers, and Executive Commission, a consultative Parliament and a Confederal Court (all along EC lines); in addition, other bodies, for example, a Development Bank – or even a Central Bank – might be created.

Among politicians and in the press, the proposal met with the mixed response that might have been expected: Slovenia and Croatia were for it, the Federal President, the Generals, Serbia and Montenegro were against it, Bosnia-Hercegovina and Macedonia were somewhere in between, with the former leaning towards federation and the latter more interested in confederation. According to a poll published in *Borba*, confederation was supported in each republic by the following percentages: Bosnia-Hercegovina 12; Croatia 43; Macedonia 9; Montenegro 4; Serbia 9; Slovenia 49.[9] However, these figures were achieved with a sample of only 70 people in each republic, making their reliability low. Indeed, a radically different result of opinion-polling in Slovenia showed around 80 per cent of its population supporting confederation or independence.[10]

In truth, the confederalists were offering something likely to be transient. The transitional nature of confederations was recognized on both sides of the debate. The question was: transitional to what? For the anti-confederal pessimists at *Vecernje Novosti* (Belgrade), the evidence that, in the past, confederations had not lasted meant that promoters of confederalism were 'continuing to bury Yugoslavia with their proposal'. This view of transition was supported by *Dnevnik* in Novi Sad which thought the confederal model to be 'most probably simply a way of breaking up Yugoslavia'.[11]

The view of confederation as merely a way of breaking up Yugoslavia in a gentler, slower, more orderly manner was counter to the hopeful statements of one of its authors. Speaking of RTVLj, Kucan maintained, like *Vecernje Novosti*, that throughout history, confederal models had only provided transitional solutions. However, for him the proposed model offered opportunity for coexistence and further integration. At the same time, though, he also declared pessimistically that the Serbian authorities were trying to compel Slovenia to secede as soon as possible. He defended the 'Crovene' confederal concept, saying that it was not tabled under the supposition that it would be unanimously acceptable, but was based on the idea that it 'ought to be acceptable for us and our interests', which interests were 'no longer ideological'. Kucan emphasized his optimism by detecting signs of a mood in favour of confederation emerging in all republics.[12]

Whereas the confederalists identified federation with the old system of Serb-dominated centralism, federalists understood it as the only sense in which Yugoslavia could continue to exist. Conversely, for the federalists, confederation was a code for breaking up Yugoslavia, to the confederalists it could be seen as a way of enabling the Yugoslavs to remain together. In other words, the authors of the confederalist proposal (as shown in the 37 alternatives suggested in the document) were looking for an arrangement that would recognize their interests and at the same time avoid the dissolution of Yugoslavia; the accommodation of those interests within a confederated Yugoslavia was preferable to their protection outside it.

The confederal model had the virtue of attempting to render the *de facto* situation one which was *de jure*. Slovenia was going to become an independent sovereign state. The only question to be asked was if this new status would be established within or without a Yugoslav commonwealth. For all their preference for a continuation of Yugoslavia, Slovenes would not remain part of a non-confederal Yugoslavia: federation was unacceptable.

Relegitimation (3): the viability of independent states – or breaking up is hard to do

A question remained over Slovenia's ability to become independent. However, two things were to its advantage: the degree of ethnic homogeneity in the population and the relatively autonomous nature of its economy. This was geared towards international markets and obtained only around one per cent of raw materials from the pan-Yugoslav market; otherwise these were found locally in the Republic, or purchased on international markets. One study distinguished the approximate autarky of the Slovene economy from the more or less dependent one in Vojvodina, although both were prosperous by Yugoslav standards.[13] The study of official federal statistics on internal trade showed that throughout the 30 years it covered, the Slovene economy had, to a large extent, operated apart from the rest of Yugoslavia.

The large share of Yugoslav export earnings emerging from Slovenia was not even, as was commonly supposed, dependent on the Yugoslav market for cheap raw materials with which to manufacture the goods it sold abroad. Only 1.6 per cent of Slovenia's raw materials were imported from other parts of Yugoslavia.[14] Indeed, the (non-Slovene) Yugoslav market accounted for only 14.8 per cent of total purchases and 21.2 per cent of sales.[15] Of the Slovene economy 80–85 per cent was apparently independent of the all-Yugoslav market.

None the less, it was clear that secession would add further economic hardships to those produced by economic reform, such as closure and unemployment. The Serb trade boycott of Slovene goods, for example, was reported to have adversely affected one per cent of Slovene GDP; Serbia proper was the destination of less than 6 per cent of Slovene manufactured goods and its province of Vojvodina accounted for another 2 per cent.[16] However, it was not unreasonable to suppose that, in considerable measure, Slovenia's trade with other parts of Yugoslavia would remain largely intact – everybody would continue to do business through necessity and convenience. A more difficult economic problem to be considered in the event of a break-up was Yugoslavia's debt: who was responsible for what share of the US $16 billion owed?

If complete independence was viable, albeit at a price, for Slovenia, then it was impracticable for the Croats and others who could only become independent with the peaceful agreement concomitant with confederation. Most parts of the country were too poor seriously to consider moves to independence. Moreover, even Croatia, easily second to Slovenia in the republican wealth stakes, was too tied to the other parts of Yugoslavia for its economic well-being. Yet even if the necessity and convenience that could be hoped to soften the dents in an independent Slovenia's economy were to overcome reliance on raw materials from Bosnia (for example), Croatia's ethnic divisions would cause headaches.

Signals of what could be expected were in full evidence in the autumn of 1990 when parts of Croatia occupied by ethnic Serbs became no-go areas for the Croatian security forces, as armed mobs barricaded roads and held an unofficial referendum on autonomy.[17] It appeared to be inconceivable that Croatia could split from the federation without precipitating a war between Croats and the Serbs living on the republic's territory – and, most probably, those living in Serbia proper. These fears were aggravated by Serbian political leadership declarations that it would pursue political autonomy for the Serbs in Croatia if a confederation came into being and that it would seek to 'unify' Serbia if the Croats attempted to become independent.[18]

The ethnic interpenetration of Yugoslavia's nationalities meant that blurred boundaries and large minorities could be found everywhere. Apart from Slovenia, the only political division of the federation with over 90 per cent of its population of one ethnic group was Kosovo – which remained an Autonomous Province only in word: all its authority was finally removed by amendments to the Serbian Constitution re-integrating both autonomous provinces and 'making Serbia whole again'. The federal authorities more or less washed their hands of the affair, acquiescing in the constitutional changes and backing repressive measures against protest by deploying YPA units in Kosovo.[19]

Political leaders in the more liberal Republics complained and withdrew their national contingents from the federal security forces in the province; these moves were followed by the withdrawal of all federal forces.[20] This and a federal decision to drop 18 month-old proceedings against the erstwhile leader of the LC Kosovo, Azem Vllasi, who was being tried on wholly spurious charges, indicated a federal policy shift vis-a-vis Kosovo.[21] That development probably owed much to the democratic changes afoot in some parts of the country and the prospering of more liberal leaderships, on the one hand, and to international pressures on the other. Both the federal government and the remaining Republics wanted to demonstrate to the international bodies that had been so critical of the situation in Kosovo, that it was all the responsibility of the Serbs. While this was largely true, the complicity of other Yugoslavs up to that point could not be denied. In addition, one effect of this policy was to leave the

Kosovan Albanians entirely to the mercy of Serbia's interior forces.

Ethnic Albanians in neighbouring Macedonia got little better treatment. Similar policies to those found in Kosovo were followed by the Macedonian authorities – political trials, dismissals, 'differentiation', restrictions on Albanian activities and the types of business they could go into and forceful suppression of pro-Albanian demonstrations. As the elections in the republic approached towards the end of 1990, the leader of one pro-Albanian party, the People's Democratic Party, noted that they were, at least, better off than their counterparts in Serbia: they had been permitted to compete freely in the elections and there had been no killings or arrests.[22]

Matters were at once more complicated yet easier in Bosnia. The complication arose from the diverse nature of the population there – 40 per cent Muslim, 32 per cent Serb and 18 per cent Croat. Life was a little less threatening, however, because the inhabitants of this Yugoslav-crossroads community seemed better able to get along with each other, despite the shadow cast from other republics. This was shown in the wake of the elections held in November 1990, when nationalist parties were successful in almost exact proportion to the size of the ethnic community for which they stood. Immediately the elections were over, the three party leaderships began to form a united-front coalition.[23] Bosnian political behaviour seemed to imply, in spite of ethnic divisions, a curious, contingent, non-concrete, nebulous, unlabelled Bosnian identity. That identity, rather than being stated, emerged in characteristics such as communication and cooperation.

Yet the claims of those other republics with regard to Bosnia caused some unease. The Communist leadership had earlier begun to abandon its support for Milosevic in the LCY when it was found that Serbia's interior forces were, contrary to the constitution, active in the Bosnian Republic.[24] The notions of independence and confederation presented dangers to the Bosnians: the republic might become subject to irredentist claims from other republics. The prospect of a Serbo-Croat conflict elsewhere spilling over into Bosnia could not be ignored.

The Bosnian attitude to the federalist-confederalist debate reflected its delicate position between Serbs and Croats. In declaring itself for either option provided all constituents remained part of Yugoslavia the Bosnian leadership avoided offending either side, while advancing its own prime interest in preserving some sort of Yugoslavia. In so far as it had a preference for federation over confederation, this was an expression of its desire to encounter the least trouble – and the spectre of irredentism if confederation were to be chosen would make trouble more likely than an arrangement in which all the Yugoslav parts remained a whole, thereby obviating discussion of who and what belonged in which state.

During 1990, the biggest factor impending confederal prospects was Serbia. The Serbian Republic pursued a *contre tout azimuts* (against all points) policy, antagonizing virtually all other sections of Yugoslavia. The conflicts with Albanians, Croats and Slovenes have received attention above, so too have irredentist claims on Bosnia and interference in that republic's internal affairs. In addition, Macedonia was thought of as Southern Serbia, creating unease there. Indeed, only Montenegro failed to be at odds with Serbia. Having antagonized so many people outside Serbia, the idea gained currency in that republic that 'everyone' was against the Serbs – an idea that was extended to the world community as criticisms of the Serbian regime and its repressive policy and human rights abuses in Kosovo emerged from international bodies and foreign governments.[25] For the Serbs, confederation appeared not only to be something that undermined Belgrade's influence, but a manifestation of the way in which they were being victimized by the rest of Yugoslavia and the world. Perhaps as much as Slovenes would not accept anything labelled 'federation' because of associations with Serbian hegemony, 'confederal' labels were interpreted as 'anti-Serb' in Serbia (an interpretation that was without doubt partially true some of the time).

One further factor obstructing the formation of independent states – whether or not in a confederation – was defence. Restructuring armed forces would present problems – all the more so in the face of YPA opposition to such moves. Although the confederalist document addressed the formation of armies in each republic and the utility of some joint forces, there remained other defence-system ties: notably the Yugoslavia-wide arms and technology industries covered by the Ministry of Defence, which were responsible for $2 billion export trade.[26] The redistribution of YPA resources would provoke major headaches.

The desire to establish common elements of defence was, in effect, recognition of the vulnerability of small states. Not even an independent Slovenia could sustain a full and effective defence force and continue its relatively prosperous life, unless security could be guaranteed. Other republics would have even smaller resources to devote to defence. Moreover, the definition of common security requirements would ease the most dangerous threats faced by any of the Yugoslav republics – actions by their neighbours: it is often better to have a potential enemy on your own side and to know what that enemy is doing.

Perhaps the following Yugoslav paradox was emerging as central to the country's future: independence was only likely to be prosperous and successful if the harmonious relations necessary to the construction of a confederation were possible, yet the existence of such harmony would to a large extent obviate the perceived need for independence. Whether the relationship between the republics of Tito's Yugoslavia was to be characterized by federation, confederation or complete separation, the base line was that tolerance and respect not only of other republics, but national minorities within republics, was the only beneficial way forward.

The old Titoist bases of legitimacy had ceded ideological dominion to a variety of nationalisms. These became the foundation of relegitimation, first for the republican Communist parties, and, later, for the majority of parties contesting the democratic elections of 1990. Those elections confirmed the dissipatory tendencies of the previous 30 years in Yugoslavia.

The difficulty, however, with nationalism is its nature. Consciousness of a common identity – usually a blend of ethnic, linguistic and territorial features – is the essence of nationalism. The trouble is that whereas ethnicity provides strategic bonding, it offers little at local level. (At its most extreme, 'strategic', from the Greek *strategos*, meaning *general*, is the most correct expression of this kind of bonding as it involves defining one's own community *vis-a-vis* others which are potential enemies against whom wars might be fought; this, of course, is not to say that all nations must go to war with each other.) It is one thing to be motivated to distinguish one's political community from another, something else to deal effectively with good management of political life.

Nationalism, rather like confederation, has limited durability as a mobilizing force. Its strength lies in motivating a people during a period of change. The partial nature of legitimation provided by consciousness of ethnic identity as a policy platform was reflected in the fact that all the parties in the various elections during 1990 espoused concepts such as democracy, independence, civil society and human rights. There was more to politics than nationalism.

Inherent in the political and philosophical tradition of the concepts promoted from most points of the political spectrum in Yugoslavia was the tolerance necessary to democratic politics. Something akin to the system of accommodation of human fallibility and fractiousness described by Madison in the *Federalist Papers*,[27] was now being sought by most Yugoslavs (at least in principle). Not always evident in that Yugoslav search was the promulgation of policies and undertaking of practical measures to deal with the status of national minorities in ways consistent with the idea proclaimed.

The gulf between Serbia and the Western Republics concerned the idea of 'civil society'. Whereas Milosevic and his cronies could be brought to realize that multi-party elections were inevitable, notions of civil society did not appear to have been taken to heart. The transfer of power from party to state had to be accompanied by the values of the civil society if the *rechtstaat* were to replace rule by arbitrary central authority. Moreover, even where the values of civil society seemed earnestly to be espoused, there was room for concern. One example of this was the crass initial handling by the newly elected nationalist authorities in Croatia of the Republic's large ethnic-Serb minority.[28]

The essence of civil society, whether in its old sense as non-authoritarian society, or in the sense developed in places such as Czechoslovakia, Hungary and Slovenia in the 1980s of non-political society (wherein political referred to anything to do with Communist rule), is found in the concepts of citizenship and communication.[29] The big problem with nationalism, in the long term, is that political identity is equated with ethnic identity; another problem is that language functions more as an aspect of identity than as an instrument of understanding.

It was evident that language and education policies would have to be better calibrated to the needs of national minorities than was sometimes previously the case.[30] The crux of this was the need to distinguish between national or ethnic identity and citizenship status. For example, it had to be possible to be both a citizen of the Republic of Slovenia and a Muslim, or a Serb, or an Albanian; likewise, an ethnic Hungarian or Albanian would have to have rights as a citizen of the Republic of Serbia – and so on for all the nationalities in all the republics. Therefore, while within a republic, there might be an official language of the majority group, but linguistic proficiency could not be allowed to become a prerequisite for citizenship (as was suggested by some Slovenes and Macedonians).

In short, the same conditions existed for the Yugoslav republics to be successful either together, apart, or somewhere in between. The establishment of democratic practices and the pursuit of the humanitarian values contained in the documents referred to in the Kucan-Tudjman proposal for confederation (such as the 1950 European Convention on Human Rights) were those essential to renewal and health in any future arrangement of the Yugoslavs. Adherence to those principles, particularly demonstrations of tolerance and the granting of rights to minorities in sovereign republics inhabited by citizens, was the best way to neutralize the impact of those, such as Milosevic, who were taking the nation, wheresoever it was to be found, as sovereign.

By regarding the nation, rather than political-territorial communities, as sovereign, Milosevic claimed the right to speak for Serbs in other republics, to make appeals to them and to make Serbian communities part of Serbia should the federation cease. By removing any grounds for grievance, authorities in other republics, particularly Croatia, could defuse the potency of Milosevic's calls. Similarly, it could be argued, Serbia itself could only have truly improved prospects once new policies addressing the real need for reform were adopted. In the meantime, the opportunity for a break with the past – which would have offered the prospect of policies of economic reorientation and the chance for improved relations with other republics, even with ardent nationalists opposing the Serbian President and his party – was missed when Milosevic was elected on a policy of Serbianism. While nationalism provided a partial, transitional basis for relegitimation, other features were required – and this would be increasingly so. Future well-being and durable relegitimation lay in the establishment of a new political regime, the core of which was Western-style democracy.

Curiously, most parties in most republics had broadly similar election programmes, except with regard to nationalist issues. All these shared support for democratic and humanitarian values and practices, for membership of the European Community and the economic reform policy of federal Prime Minister, Ante Markovic. In Slovenia in April this was the case, as it was later in Croatia, Macedonia and Bosnia-Hercegovina.[31] Only in Serbia and Montenegro was this pattern not consistent; yet even in Serbia, the opposition parties were broadly in line with this trend and Milosevic paid lip service to much of it.

Relegitimation (4): the Markovic option

It was a paradoxical feature of Yugoslav politics that throughout a year of declarations of sovereignty and consolidation of republican rule, most parties in all parts of the country supported the economic programme of the President of the FEC, Ante Markovic. Equally surprising was the extent of the Prime Minister's popularity. Markovic's popularity was high, despite his administering harsh economic medicine.

In the first half of 1990, support for Markovic as Prime Minister was extremely high, giving a degree of relegitimation at the level of the authorities. Support for Markovic assisted the shift from party to state governance, a prerequisite for regime legitimation; the process was further aided by the Prime Minister's policy successes in the economic sphere. Markovic and his government gained credibility and a measure of social and political capital by meeting their self-set demands.

At the end of 1989, Markovic revealed a radical reform plan to tackle inflation which was running at 2,600 per cent per annum.[32] The central feature of the reform was monetary control. A dinar devaluation gave one new for ten thousand old and made that new one convertible by tying it to the deutschemark. In addition, black-market pressure was taken away by allowing Yugoslavs freely to exchange dinars for hard currency. Finally, perhaps most importantly, wages would be held for six months; at the same time, price restrictions were removed from 85 per cent of commodities, leaving only certain raw materials and essential utilities under control. Alongside the basic monetary policy went the continuing promotion of market criteria, independence of enterprises, equal status of all forms of ownership (essentially, this meant privatization) and a profit consciousness.

Markovic's accomplishment in merely getting the reforms passed was considerable. Only after the Federal Presidency had acceded to the Prime Minister's request for a declaration of support were six of the new laws adopted as temporary measures. Moreover, particulars of the plan received criticism during debate in republican assemblies;

those criticisms were then transposed to the debate in the Federal Assembly.[33] The programme's most ardent opponents were found in Serbia where it was argued that its adverse effects would be greatest, further devastating Yugoslavia's poorest regions. Serbian opposition was, however, thought to stem most of all from Milosevic's desire to ruin Markovic. The poorest parts of the country – Montenegro, Macedonia and the then still autonomous Kosovo – all voted in favour of the reform because it, at least, held the prospect of a way out of economic crisis.

Performance of the Markovic programme in its first six months was dramatically impressive.[34] The month-on-month inflation rate fell: 65 per cent in December; 46 per cent mid-January; 17 per cent in late-January; 8.4 per cent at the end of February; in June, it dropped below 0 per cent. At the same time hard-currency reserves rose to US $7.1 billion at the end of February – twice its May 1989 level. Moreover, the country's debt fell to US $16 billion. Where the policies were most thoroughly implemented, in Slovenia, a spate of liquidations began; in one week, 230 firms in the republic had their bank accounts closed and were heading for the 60-day limit on illiquidity at which point bankruptcy would become automatic if payments still failed to be made. Elsewhere, the reforms were practised with various lesser degrees of commitment. In Serbia, there were flagrant breaches of the wage freeze which led to Serbian average income equalling that in Slovenia, despite no increase in productivity. Markovic's FEC ordered all excessive payments to be returned over a three-month period from March.

The trend towards a looser federation increased with the Slovene split from the LCS and the democratic elections held during the spring, while, paradoxically, opening up a greater role for the federal government of Ante Markovic. By completing the shift from party to state governance, the Slovenes apparently enhanced Markovic's chances of bringing Yugoslavia back from the brink. Indeed, in the first months of 1990, Markovic's federal government appeared to become the most important element in the Yuogslav political system.

The enactment of a well-designed reform package for the economy, the government's acting as the authority (rather than the party or the presidency) for making executive decisions a propos matters such as the troubles in Kosovo and Markovic's attempts to act as peacemaker between Slovenia and Serbia in February,[35] pointed to a shift towards democratic government and recognition of the LCY's terminal condition. Markovic's standing also owed something to his not being part of the inter nationality squabbling all around the country. It was this squabbling, however, which most undermined his prospects for outright success.

The second half of 1990 favoured Markovic much less than the first. Further reforms and constitutional amendments were blocked by republican non-cooperation. Serbia again seemed to be the major culprit; but both Slovenia and Croatia refused to agree to essential measures and withheld federal contributions, ostensibly in protest at Serbia's suppression of Kosovan autonomy – although this may be regarded as a pretext.[36] Reform of the banking system proved difficult to effectuate in many areas.[37] Once the wage freeze ended on 30 June, the pressures that had been building up during the previous two months were released. Further, inflation quickly began to climb again. Unemployment was also on the rise.[38] All economic difficulties were exaggerated by international action against Iraq, which had broad ramifications for Yugoslavia. Up to 10,000 Yugoslavs were employed in Iraq and a further 50,000 in Yugoslavia itself, working on contracts with Iraq. The overall cost to Yugoslavia ran into several billions of dollars.[39]

Markovic's popularity across the country remained extremely high, reaching up to 79 per cent in pan-Yugoslav opinion-polling.[40] However, he was unable to convert this personal support into political capital, in spite of spearheading a political movement, the Alliance of Reform Forces of Yugoslavia (ARFY). Launched on July 29 in Bosnia where, because of the ethnic mix, Markovic was sure of a good reception, the idea behind the ARFY was to provide an umbrella to shelter individuals and parties from all parts of the country interested in economic reform and a future in which Yugoslavs would live together, not tear themselves apart. It was not formally a party.

However, Markovic's popularity notwithstanding, the ARFY fared poorly in the later Republican elections where it fielded candidates (it was formed after the April elections in Slovenia and Croatia – but there is no reason to suppose that it would have been more successful there, given the votes in both cases along national lines). In Macedonia and Bosnia, the ARFY gained some promising results, but it was left far behind the nationalist parties. In Montenegro and Serbia, it made next to no headway.[41]

Markovic was therefore in a curious position: clearly successful and, it seemed popular, he was unable to confirm this electorally. As federal elections were not held before the end of the year as they should have been, Markovic did not have to subject his government to electoral vetting, the result of which could not confidently have been predicted to be favourable, in the light of the way the electoral cookie crumbled along nationalist lines in the republics. So there was some benefit for him in the delay. Markovic remained in a position to continue his policy battle against the odds, although, particularly when the odds against included apparent acts of economic guerrilla warfare by Serbia, that position was always (and became increasingly) vulnerable.

Without doubt, Markovic represented the best, if not the only, real chance of federal relegitimation when legitimacy lay to such an extent with Republican regimes. In the confederal-federal debate, Markovic was fairly agnostic: for him it did not matter so much whether Yugoslavia was to be labelled federal or confederal, so long as it remained one entity with a single market and currency and followed the reform programme. In effect, this had to mean something closer to the federal option than its challenger. Markovic expressed this. However, what it meant most of all was his opposition to dismemberment.

The absence of federal elections allowed Markovic to persist with his government. This state of limbo – or grace – would continue until arrangements for such elections were made. There seemed little prospect of an early conclusion as the electoral laws would have to be agreed by the various republican leaderships as acceptable to everyone. It was not easy to envisage this as rapidly achievable because of the deep inter-republican schisms. Markovic could not be said to be facing an easy prospect, but he was in a position to guide Yugoslavia, which would probably have been denied to him had federal voting taken place.

Markovic was not being offered a clear run. Without support from the republics, his limbo-leadership would be inoperable. Although some considered the absence of a democratic mandate to be a factor that would gradually undermine his leadership after parliamentary elections had been held in all the republics, this did not necessarily have to be the case. As long as his own popularity remained buoyant and republican behaviour did not completely torpedo his policies, his government could continue. It would do on the basis of limited (somewhat negative) legitimation through non-destruction and some degree of support and compliance from the republics that had the power to ruin his economic programme.

It is notable that amid the fog of relegitimation there was apparent economic consensus. Despite the passing of so much authority to the republics creating a *de facto* confederation in which the basis of authority was representation of perceived national interests, in most cases, economic policies of the new nationalist parties coming to power were pro-Markovic. That is either similar policies were advocated, or the policy itself was 'support for the reforms'.[42] Even Milosevic's newly named Serbian Socialist Party professed economic reform as its policy, although practice often belied this. Moreover, the various nationalist parties also shared Markovic's adherence to the institution of democratic procedures and the aim of gaining membership of the European Community.

Shared policy orientation did not mean complete harmonization. Each republican government and each party would have points at which its particular interest would mean non-conformity. Each instance of this phenomenon would weaken Markovic's chances of success. But in the absence of wholesale disruption, the government and its policies could muddle along, continuing to achieve limited progress. The longer the period in which federal elections were not held, the greater Markovic's room for manoeuvre would grow, and the more probably would Yugoslavia hold together.

It is possible to see the behaviour of a large family growing up in all this. While the various adolescents attempt to establish their emerging personalities, some by screaming, shouting and declaring that they are going to leave home, others by demonstrating their insecurities and wanting to hold on to the apron strings, the parents, tried and tested at every point, get on with life, trying to keep the family together, diligently getting on with the serious business of paying the bills and securing the family's income for the future. With the Republican authorities 'acting out' as immature teenagers, it is easy to discern in Markovic the diligent parent figure doing the hard work.

The lack of any serious alternative economic policy and the shared orientation on democracy and EC membership meant that, in reality, there was a limited federal consensus underpinning Markovic's government, albeit one that could only be perceived through a glass darkly. Like atomic structure, the fact that it was not readily observable did not mean it did not exist. Perhaps central in this consensus was the common desire for entry into Europe.

'Europe now!' had been the rallying cry in Slovenia in the period before the elections. The confederal model, proposed jointly by Croatia and Slovenia, took the EC as its frame of reference. Everyone in Yugoslavia was persuaded of the virtue of the European option (Serbia included, although the authorities there did not appear committed enough to end the much criticized human rights practices in Kosovo, above all the suppression of its parliament). Moreover, the basic conditions for EC membership seemed to correspond with those on which a viable Yugoslavia would have to be based. 'We sincerely hope that Yugoslavia will solve all of its political problems by 1992 and that it will be able to enter the Europe of 1992,' said the managing director of one large Belgrade firm, addressing this question.[43]

The European Community and the idea of a 'new' Europe had a large role to play. (This applies to other democratizing, former Communist, regimes.) A summary comparison of the transition from authoritarian rule to democracy in Latin America and Southern Europe suggests that an external carrot is instrumental in assuring stability and the survival of the newly sprung democracy, enabling it to take root. Whereas attempts to establish democracy in Latin America tended to revert to authoritarianism, the experience of Portugal, Spain and Greece was more positive. A major difference between the two cases is the presence of the outside carrot: all three Southern European countries were encouraged to develop in democratic directions by the promise of accession to the European Community, with the attendant benefits of its vast market once their shifts to democracy had been confirmed.

The European Community was clearly in a position to play such a role with regard to Yugoslavia. The country was most likely to survive and prosper – and, therefore, re-establish a legitimate political system – if it met the requirements of EC membership: continuation of the single state, a market economy, multiple-party electoral systems and legally codified human-rights guarantees. Given the desire of virtually all strands of Yugoslav society to join the EC, the promise of EC membership was a decisive factor likely to keep Yugoslavia together and develop these concomitant features. Developments such as the Pentagonale initiative, involving Yugoslavia with Italy, Austria, Hungary and Czechoslovakia enhanced this: here was a forum through which accession to the EC could be facilitated for the four non-members. (On the other hand, the Italian and Austrian foreign ministers were the first to acknowledge the possibility of recognizing independent Yugoslav states.)

There were many reasons inhibiting a parting of Yugoslav ways. In a curious manner, while the Republics became increasingly autonomous, the real limitations on full independence became clearer. Confederation to a large extent could be seen as confirming what, in fact, existed. None the less, it was by no means inconceivable that separation would happen. Slovenia, at least, was capable of achieving this and ever more likely to do so, it appeared. At the end of 1990, following the comfortable return of Milosevic in the Serbian elections, a plebiscite on independence in Slovenia found more than 90 per cent support for full independence in the absence of agreement on confederation.

The major impediment to Slovenia's independence – or, indeed, to the successful negotiation of independence within a confederation – was the EC's insistence on maintaining a single-state Yugoslavia. Without international recognition, Slovenia would find itself in a difficult position. This was particularly the case because of the way the EC position shaped the Yugoslav debate. By not admitting the possibility of transition to a loose association of sovereign states, the EC inadvertently facilitated deadlock in Yugoslavia's constitutional talks. Serbia and the army wanted what Europe wanted – a unitary state. Therefore there was no incentive for these two actors to alter their absolutist stances in favour of compromise. Instead, they would be legitimised in using violence and the threat of violence against Slovenia and Croatia as they sought to redefine Yugoslavia.

At the end of 1990, the chances of a stable, joint future for Yugoslavs appeared evenly balanced. The Economist Intelligence Unit wished to avoid gloom, but found that 'the present balance of political forces in Serbia' made it hard to put the chances for Yugoslavia at more than '50:50'.[44] The Markovic government's continued success and its policy orientation towards 'Europeanization, not Balkanization' added to the structural impediments to dissolution and were foundations upon which to rebuild Yugoslavia. However, these foundations were reliant on the good will of the republics. Should any republic sabotage the Markovic option, particularly by rejecting the European direction, Yugoslavia would almost certainly succumb to its divisions.

In some ways it was possible to discern two phenomena: a Yugoslavia that continued to operate under the federal leadership of Markovic; and a set of independent republics ('states', as they were increasingly dubbed), functioning on a different plane, as though Markovic and the federation did not exist most of the time. We can conceive of federal and republican governments as parallel universes. This seemingly unreal situation could continue as long as necessary, so long as there was no decisive intervention either from federal or republican actors. One actor, in particular, had an important role in this situation: the YPA. Once again its actions would be telling for a fissiparous Yugoslavia.

6 The Delegitimating Army and Relegitimation: Conclusion

It is notable that in the autumn of 1990, *Narodna Armija* was carrying articles on themes such as integration in Europe as a priority of foreign policy, the integrity of the country as a necessary condition for European acceptance and a factor in European stability, and humanitarian practice in the armed forces.[1] Even if there was a hint of an old vocabulary merely being replaced with a new one, of new formulations being adopted that corresponded closest to the old ideas of a unified, federal Yugoslavia, the reality was that those new 'values' were the ones that could provide the secure foundation of a third Yugoslavia.

However, despite signs of support for the European idea, the Generals were not otherwise doing much to help Markovic, even though he was clearly providing the most serious prospect of a unified Yugoslavia – something cardinal for them. Despite the persistent bickering between Slovenia and Serbia, and between the latter and most of the other republics, Markovic's federal government was, with regard to the economy at least, the strongest since the days when Tito still held the reins of power. In the middle of fissive chaos, federal government was pursuing its business to reasonably good effect, given the fragile circumstances. The case for a federal option would have been even stronger if Markovic's efforts had had the benefit of YPA approval. Instead, the military seemed to be doing the opposite.

Relegitimation and the military

Relations between defence minister Kadijevic and Markovic were cool. Kadijevic was reported to be a rare attender at FEC sessions. Moreover, it was suggested that the Prime Minister and his Defence Minister disagreed on a number of issues – or would have done so had they discussed them in cabinet. These included freezing certain military programmes, notably the supersonic fighter project; Kadijevic's insistence on enforcing the call-up in Slovenia; the YPA's removal of territorial defence armaments from Slovenia and Croatia; army tanks being painted in the blue of the Serbian interior forces and being used in Kosovo; the intervention of Mig 23s and military helicopters in Croatia; the army's provision of a guard of honour to Milosevic; and, the central issue with regard to a democratic future for Yugoslavia, the depoliticization of the military.[2]

There was speculation that the Generals were planning a *coup*.[3] Military behaviour provided some basis for such rumours, although it could not be denied that the Croatian and Slovenian authorities were the chief beneficiaries of them: the positing of such a threat was a sure way to rally support. In reality, there remained little chance of the YPA seizing power. Its political legitimacy was weaker now than ever *vis-a-vis* the republics that troubled it most in the North-West. It could threaten intervention and rattle sabres; but these only harmed its case. To take action would have been to obviate any chance for a united Yugoslavia, the Generals' primary objective. This was rammed home by the (legally questionable) import of arms from Austria and Hungary by the new republican defence secretaries in Slovenia and Croatia: armed intervention would mean wars of independence.[4]

The import of arms began, following two events in Slovenia. One was the transfer of some heavy arms to new locations. This was interpreted as removing equipment from control by republican territorial defence authorities. However, this was a misinterpretation as the armaments in question belonged to the YPA.[5] The other event was the occupation by military police of the Slovene Defence Ministry building. However, they met no resistance and were said to have occupied an empty building: Jansa and his team had been warned and had moved out; they opened for business again a few days later in a new home.[6] The Slovenes responded to these events by ensuring that if it came to pass, they would have the means to fight for their independence.[7]

Military conduct in the North-Western republics undermined the efforts of Markovic and others to preserve a federation, despite the army's frequent declarations in favour of preserving Yugoslav unity. Putative support for Markovic was further weakened in November by the formation of a revamped Communist party, the League of Communists–Movement for Yugoslavia (LC-MY).[8]

The new party was formed with the support of Kadijevic and Brovet, plus retired Generals such as Mamula, Buncic, Mirkovic and Gracanin, who was Federal Interior Minister; in addition, old stalwarts of the LCY were involved, such as Stipe Suvar, Raif Dizdarevic, Lazar Mojsov and Milan Pancevski. The new party's purpose was to prevent the disintegration of the Socialist Federal Republic of Yugoslavia and stem the anti-Communist revolution. Although not theoretically inimical to Markovic's ARFY because of that body's character as an umbrella for everyone wanting to preserve Yugoslavia through reform, neither was it a boost to the Markovic project. Indeed, because it highlighted the military's political profile, it ran contrary to his attemps to institute a *rechtstaat*, as a key element in the institutionalization of the legal state would be the depoliticization (or 'decommunization') of the military.

The major issue confronting both the YPA and its civilian counter-parts was depoliticization. The YPA's professed aim of encouraging a unified future for Yugoslavs would have been best served by depoliti-cization and withdrawal from political prominence. The implementa-tion of such a policy was clearly the best way to lend support to Markovic in his attempts to preserve Yugoslavia and generate regime relegitimation. In effect, this meant that regime relegitimation was, in part, a function of military relegitimation; of course, this was reciprocal. So the military role in politics was crucial to the future development of Yugoslavia.

Depoliticization of the military was an enormous challenge facing both civilians and soldiers. If Yugoslavia were to develop as a multi-party system, then the Generals would have to learn to live without a governmental role. Previously, their political role has been founded in their association, both traditional and formal, with the LCY. These were Communist Generals, operating as party members in a party-army organization. Their position would necessarily have to change as the political topography shifted. The traditional association with the Communist party could not realistically sustain a continuing political life: as Communism dwindled, there would be little role for either Communists or soldiers in government (and room would be even harder to find for Communist soldiers).

An obvious corollary of this was for a civilian to become Minister of Defence. Unless another Communist regime emerged (Republican election returns suggested this to be highly unlikely), a new demo-cratic government would end the appointment of serving officers as Secretary for Defence. As in liberal-democratic states elsewhere, the military would have to become completely subservient to political will. Where political authority changes periodically between the representatives of one set of values and those of another, the military serving political masters cannot be overtly partial (although it would have its own preferences as is always the case): military profes-sionalism dictates the equal serving of political overlords.[9]

From this point of view, the formation of a new Communist party around a core of Generals was not likely to be beneficial either to the military or to the Yugoslav cause. Indeed, even in the short term, it was difficult to see what benefit this move could bring; in the long term, it was unlikely to have any whatsoever. It was perhaps a fairly desperate act of Generals with problems coming to terms with change and clinging to the past. The army, as was shown in Chapter 2, shared roots with the party. A creation of the Communist movement, it was experiencing difficulty in adjusting to the post-Communist world.

The YPA's political role in the past had been founded on its rela-tionship with the Communist party. This had been central in its legitimacy as a political actor. That legitimacy was limited to acting in concord with another legitimate force within the political system – in reality, this meant within the party. In alliance with Tito, the army had been able to intervene decisively in Croatia in the early 1970s. In the absence of such an ally and with persistent erosion of its bases of legitimacy, the military in the 1980s was unable to perform the same role. In the absence of a ruling party within which the military's political involvement was legitimized, its political participation was now restricted to the Defence Minister's *ex officio* presence in the collective Federal Presidency. So the existence of a new Communist party was of little relevance in the YPA's attempt to maintain its political prominence.

A telling military intervention relied on military legitimacy becoming allied to another part of the political constellation. Any military intervention would have to have a sociopolitical base. It emerged during 1990 that sympathies within the military were towards Serbian causes. Even if, as in previous years, Kadijevic was not an unreserved Milosevic supporter, he was surrounded by some who were. Moreover, there appeared to be a legitimacy *crisis* forming at the middle and junior rank level where the officer corps was overwhelmingly dominated by Serbs. Sixty per cent of officers were Serb; a further 5.4 per cent were 'Yugoslavs' and likely to be Serbs; and 6.2 per cent were Montenegrins. These all shared a perspective of Yugoslavia that coincided in many ways with that of the neo-Communist Serbian leadership. The political attitudes of the remaining officers were generally to be expected to have a Communist orientation, but they were probably less likely to find Milosevic attractive. The ethnic distribution of the rest of the 60,000 officer corps in early 1991 was put at: Croats, 12.6 per cent; Macedonians, 6.3 per cent; Muslims, 2.4 per cent; Slovenes, 2.8 per cent; Albanians, 0.6 per cent; Hungarians 0.7 per cent; others, 1.6 per cent.[10] This structure, even more so the conscript element in the army, could not be unaffected by political events.

This was demonstrated in two features of the events in the Knin region of Croatia where the local Serb population created a no-go area, conducting terrorist attacks on railway lines. The first of these was the intrusion of two military aircraft which intercepted and turned away helicopters of the Croatian militia heading for the area. Investigations produced the conclusion that this operation had been ordered at a relatively low level by the air base commander. It was an indication of pro-Serbian sentiment among officers in the middle and junior ranks of the officer corps. A similar case was the stealing of YPA armaments by Serbs in Croatia. This seemed only to have been possible with the collusion of local military personnel.[11]

This kind of activity at lower echelons was reinforced by higher level interventions and non-interventions. Non-intervention applied to the military reaction to the suppression of the Kosovan parliament by the Serbian authorities, despite the military leaders' liberal proclamations in favour of preserving Yugoslavia's constitutional integrity and the blatant unconstitutionality of that act. Intervention came towards the year's end with an interview given by Kadijevic and the formation of the new party.

In his interview with *Danas*, Kadijevic made statements that clearly positioned the military closer to Serbian opinion than any other. In particular, his statement of intent to deal with 'abuses' of the GPD system and the creation of armed militias, acting as paramilitary forces, by the republican governments in Croatia and Slovenia showed this. Yugoslavia would not, according to the Defence Minister, become 'another Lebanon'. However, he overlooked military complicity in the Knin events and the extent to which those events were central to discussions of the country becoming 'another Lebanon' and the formation of paramilitary forces. Thus Kadijevic appeared to be condemning and threatening the actions of elected and constitutional authorities, while continuing to ignore the wholly unconstitutional armed groups in the Serb-populated regions of Croatia.[12]

Kadijevic's hardening line clearly owed something to the formation of the LC-MY. There he was surrounded by a group of ex-generals identified as part of a Milosevic clique: Mamula, Mirkovic, Ljubicic and Gracanin.[13] It was telling that, in addition to the party-army old guard, the new party counted among its luminaries Milosevic's wife, Mirjana Markovic. Perhaps the most significant thing to emerge from the new party was the intervention of Stevan Mirkovic immediately after the party's formation, telling the press in Belgrade that Milosevic's Socialist Party was the only party worth voting for in the forthcoming Serbian elections.[14]

Elements from the military elite had clearly begun to align them-selves with Milosevic. However, in a political system in which republican and federal political authority was invested in state bodies, not party ones, this was futile. Whereas in the past, party disciplinary mechanisms could be invoked and political charges concocted, this was no longer so. Measures against recalcitrant individuals and groups would have to be taken through the institutions of an independent legal system – in the North-Western republics, at least. Any kind of alliance with a particular republican leadership could only serve further to undermine the YPA's all Yugoslav character and increase alienation in other republics.

Kadijevic's own position was hard to define clearly. While turning an occasional blind eye to affairs in Serbia, he had also shown signs of reluctance to see Milosevic prosper (see Chapter 3). Moreover, in his interview with *Danas*, he gave the first signs of military depoliticization of the YPA. He did so by recognizing that although the Communist party had played a major role in forming the army's pan-Yugoslav character, especially through the LC-YPA, with the demise of Communism, political organization within the party was no longer tenable. Members of the armed forces, he said, would be allowed to be members of any legally and constitutionally recognized political party, but no party would be allowed to organize within the YPA; 'concrete measures' in connection with this would, he continued, be announced, 'soon'. These statements were formally confirmed at the 12 December FEC session, where it was also signalled that depoliticization of the armed forces would be discussed at a future joint session of the FEC with Republican presidents.[15]

With regard to this, an early sign of depoliticization came as early as the autumn of 1989, when Mirkovic was replaced as Chief of the General Staff by General Blagoje Adzic. Adzic was the first appointee to the job to be an army career man; all his predecessors had party-army organization track records. Moreover, unlike previous appointments, the press gave no biographical details about the new man.[16] However, this kind of depoliticization perhaps carried risks with it: Generals (and lower ranking officers where appropriate) without the political skills and experience of someone like Kadijevic, a man tailored to his task, might seek to use the army's physical capacity for intervention in politics. The emergence of less politically astute military men was a possibility.

There were, therefore, contradictory signs. On the one hand, Generals prominent in the formation of an essentially reactionary political party; on the other, moves towards a necessary depoliticization of the YPA. That depoliticization was unavoidable if the disintegration of the country was to be avoided and democracy established. Moreover, it was the first step to the renewal of military legitimacy. If a third Yugoslavia were to be constituted, political legitimacy for the YPA would have to mean its becoming apolitical.

However, depoliticization would not in itself be enough. Political legitimacy would also require structural changes to satisfy republican and nationalist demands. A corollary of this would be measures to encourage functional relegitimation. The changes needed had military and political virtues. In addition, attempts to persevere with the old structural arrangements were likely to result in no Yugoslavia, ergo no YPA. If Yugoslavia was to remain together, either as a looser federation or as a confederation, it seemed that restructuring would be necessary. That restructuring would have to involve the creation of more regionally based units.

Such was the situation at the end of 1990. At the beginning of 1991, all issues of regime and military relegitimation were in flux. But, as was the case with regime legitimacy, the lines along which military restructuring and, therefore, relegitimation could be achieved were not obscure. A model for restructuring that could be adapted was provided by Yugoslavia's war-time experience.

As was shown in Chapter 2, the Partisan army was formed on an essentially territorial, regimental basis. There seems to be a good case for supposing that such a structure for a peacetime standing army would be workable. Political and socializing functions would be vastly diminished, enhancing the military purpose. Units would be composed of more or less coherent regiments on an ethnic-regional foundation; they would not, however, be ethnically pure – like the war-time units, they would be formed around a national core, but would almost certainly, because of the nature of Yugoslav demography, contain members from different nationalities. There would also need to be elite units, modern equivalents of (or successors to) the Proletarian Brigades. These would be formed on a multinational basis by volunteers. Such units would comprise national regiments designated to the multinational force. To some extent this could be seen as a parallel with the structure of NATO as a multinational force. However, unlike NATO practice heretofore (which practice may be in the course of changing) it would require co-stationing: that is, perhaps in the vein of British military tradition, units from various regiments would combine to form a larger entity. In this scenario, at divisional level or below, contributions could be expected from Serbian, Croatian, Slovenian, Bosnian (and so forth) regiments.

The nationally based units could be treated as regiments of one army, or as republican armies in themselves which made contributions to a collective defence force; that is, either the British model or the NATO model – although in practice, a hybrid would probably emerge. Either model would offer the chance to satisfy demands, such as those from Slovenia, that military service should be carried out on home territory, in units where their native tongue was used. (Canada provides something of a model here.) This arrangement would also cater for sentiments of national identity – everybody would be able to identify their own military, although that military would form part of a pan-republican whole.

The central command and the elite central units would provide overall strategic command. Central command would certainly have charge of units delegated to the multinational force. The degree and circumstances of republican control would correspond with whatever arrangement could be achieved for the establishment of a third Yugoslavia. Command and control arrangements would be a product of whatever negotiations resulted in a new Yugoslavia.

However, with regard to military legitimacy, broad political and social changes did not just affect the YPA. The pan-Yugoslav character of the defence economy was another major factor in restructuring Yugoslavia's military institutions. The domestically developed M-84 tank had parts made in factories from one end of the country to the other, involving all parts of the country – from Jesenice near the Slovenian-Austrian border to the Macedonian capital, Skopje, and Prizren in Kosovo in the South.[17] Anything other than a federal future for Yugoslavia would automatically concern the army from the military-industry viewpoint. Defence projects involving more than one republic would have to become cooperative ventures in a confederal Yugoslavia. Should any of the republics realize independence, the nature of the cooperative arrangement would be more difficult.

No matter which configuration of republics emerges, basic economic and political reforms impact on the defence sector. The shift to multi-party parliamentary politics and a market economy with all kinds of ownership and property rights, not just social ones, requires changes to be made a propos the defence industrial base. New laws and regulations on commercial activity require alterations in the balance of rights and responsibilities with regard to war-time functioning. In particular, this means that GPD obligations could no longer be on the basis of self-management accords, but would become contracts in law between particular business and state actors.[18] In addition, YPA financing and the whole GPD planning system would be difficult issues with which to deal. Indeed, the scope and complexity of GPD planning indicate the need for a complete overhaul leading to simplification. The goods and services budget would have to lose a significant number of its 1990 total of 3,600 items.

One part of the Yugoslav defence system would be likely to continue, whatever political shape Yugoslavia gains. Apart from the removal of the leading role of the Communist party, which must necessarily wither, it seems likely that even independent republics would retain the relatively cost-effective territorial defence arrangement. The emphasis on this aspect of life could, however, be expected to decline; for example, it is unlikely that GPD will remain a core item on many school timetables. The only topic in need of elaboration would be the source of political authority in the event of war. It could be possible that restructuring along the lines indicated above might extend the territorial dimension of defence and, thereby, strengthen military legitimacy. This would be achieved through the more organic links between regular and non-regular units.

Both the sociopolitical and the functional imperatives of military legitimacy require redefinition. There seems little prospect of the 'Yugoslav idea' providing an adequate component of the legitimation crasis, although it could undoubtedly retain some relevance. Whatever the extent of that relevance, there can be no doubt that the defence of Yugoslavia, rather as in 1941, could not be judged sustainable as Yugoslavia enters the 1990s. The likelihood of concerted common action against an aggressor of the magnitude of Hitler's Germany can be considered far less than a collapse similar to that after the Nazi invasion. An attack by one of Yugoslavia's neighbours would almost certainly result in the particular republic involved and the army resisting while the other Yugoslavs tried to ignore the matter and go their own way.

Military legitimacy could be given limited fortification in the short term by alliance with one part of the Yugoslav community – as appears to have been the case with Serbia towards the end of 1990 and during the first part of 1991. However, such alliances could only be poison for soldiers trying to hold Yugoslavia together. For such an alliance gave them a political and a national profile that could only antagonize other Yugoslavs. Relegitimation for the YPA had to mean dangling carrots, not brandishing big sticks. This meant willing depoliticization and restructuring. By embracing these notions, the YPA could enhance both regime and military relegitimation. Failure to do so would destroy any prospect of either surviving. At the beginning of 1991, much depended on whether Kadijevic's tendency to reform or the views of more conservative generals would prevail in the YPA. Chances of survival reduced every time the Generals made attempts to assert authority which could only be counterproductive. The more the Generals tried to take the initiative, the worse they made the situation. The sum of Milosevic's dominion of Serbia and the shadow it cast across the whole country, added to sabre-rattling senior soldiers, edged the country closer to a break. Attempts to intimidate Slovenia and Croatia, towards the end of 1990 and as 1991 began, only served to catalyse dissolution. If the Generals were to end up without a country to defend, it would have been largely their own doing.

Legitimacy and civil military relations

Civil-military relations in Yugoslavia can be understood as a function of the interaction of regime and military legitimacies. Post-war Yugoslavia was forged on the strength of political and military legitimacy resting with Tito's Communist-led Partisans. This legitimacy was attested in the conflict with Stalin of 1948 and the redesigning of Yugoslavia's legitimating principles in terms of socialist self-management. Over a number of years, the notion of decentralized power inherent in the post-1948 revisions became a reality. As a consequence the authority of the federal regime was undermined. This led to the crisis of 1971 in which regime legitimacy was defective. Defects were restored by the lending of military legitimacy based on its role in the regime's creation, its adherence to the war-time principles of brotherhood and unity, and its formal position in the political system to strengthen President Tito's federal arm. Regime legitimacy and military legitimacy were functions of each other.

However, as Yugoslavia slipped deeper into crisis in the 1980s, and without Tito's charismatic presence, the army was unable to repeat its role of the early 1970s. Military legitimacy too had been eroded. Intra-Yugoslav disputes and divisions had begun to undermine the YPA as the bastion of brotherhood and unity; the war was no longer a strong motivational theme; and in the clamour of competing nationalisms, yet without an ally of Tito's calibre, the Generals were impotent in the political vacuum. Social and political developments had debased the army's legitimacy as a political force.

The YPA's functional legitimacy was challenged by the national and economic crises in Yugoslav society. The economic crisis forced it to reduce its size, slow down its modernization plans and personally affected individual soldiers. This meant its leading role in the defence system was weakened by technical inadequacies and diminished morale. Its leading role was damaged by its failure to be, or to be seen to be, nationally and proportionally representative, while a clamour of particularist national voices attacked it as a Serb preserve. Unable to satisfy all these conditions, it was not fully suited to performing its function. The YPA's functional legitimacy was impaired.

The various threats to its legitimacy explain the military's growing voice in Yugoslav domestic politics in the 1980s. This is why the seeming extension of its role from defence to non-defence issues was only an apparent change. For Yugoslav soldiers, everything was a matter of defence. The Generals' concern for the welfare of society rested, above all else, on an understanding of the effect the crisis of legitimacy in Yugoslavia had upon the YPA as the leading component in the defence system and upon Yugoslavia's wider defence capability.

As the 'backbone' of the defence system, and aware of the importance of morale as a vital factor of military power, the YPA was anxious about a decadent Yugoslavia's defensive strength. On one side was the question of economic difficulties reflecting on the modernization of the YPA, its standards and the mood of its members, particularly officers. On another, the issue was one of the importance of the army's links with the people whose support was a prerequisite for the efficient functioning of the system of all-people's defence; the implication of social divisions was that the unified support required for effective defence would not be forthcoming.

The Generals' concern was that the disintegrative processes which developed with the crisis should not be allowed to affect the army. Although some undesirable influences infiltrated the YPA, and in spite of broad societal difficulties, until very late in the decade, the general state of the army was said to be politically secure. There was certainly awareness that unacceptable influences should be withstood. In this regard, it was necessary that the army should be above inter-republican or Provincial discords, and a guard against nationalism and other sociopolitically unacceptable forms of influence. In short, the prospect of defending Yugoslavia was not favourable if the various constituencies in the country were antagonistic to each other and unable to work together effectively.

The premise of the YPA's political activity was the desire to assure the internal cohesion, stability and effectiveness of Yugoslavia, because the state of internal security was the first condition for a successful struggle and resistance against invasion. Socioeconomic (and political) stability was understood as the key to strong defence. Conversely, countries were most vulnerable to attack when internal stability was disturbed. In the Marxist terminology dear to the Generals, the YPA's role was determined by an awareness that its internal and external functions were 'in dialectical unity'. If internal tensions within a society increase beyond a certain point, the capability of resisting dangers from outside diminishes. Although, realistically, the threat of international war was unlikely (and considered to be so), there remained a consciousness in Yugoslavia that internal divisions might be exploited by foreign powers and a belief that this, in fact, was the case – that subversive 'special wars' were being waged within and against Yugoslavia, especially in Kosovo. However, the YPA's concern must be seen as tacit expression of a greater fear than subversion. That fear concerned what would happen if Yugoslavia were attacked.

In the final analysis, the YPA appears to have been fighting a losing battle. Its commitment to defending and preserving Tito's united Yugoslavia has blinkered the military. If Yugoslavia breaks up, particularly if that break up involves Slovene secession, the role of the YPA leadership will have been paramount. Without its panicky blunders in dealing first with *Mladina*, then with the Slovene political establishment, it is possible that events would have taken a different course. Had it taken firmer and more obvious stands against Milosevic's constitutional machinations, things might have been different. It is even conceivable that military pressure could have limited the damage done to the federation from that quarter. As it is, an accumulation of actions and inactions led to dissolved legitimacy.

As the 1990s got under way, both regime and military in Yugoslavia had been delegitimated. On the regime side, a notable degree of legitimacy could be found at the republican level, while to some extent the quality was still to be traced, albeit weakly, at the federal level. Whatever Markovic's success, his efforts were continually diminished by republican recalcitrance. The actions of any one republic could terminally sabotage the Prime Minister's fragile programme. It cannot be doubted that decisive authority rested with the republics: the federal government was dependent on their support. Legitimacy at the federal level, such as it was, derived from republican endorsement of its performance and republican agreement that a federal government should exist at all.

Change was ineluctable. Slovene political authority had been established on the basis that the republic would never again be part of a country ruled directly from Belgrade. The same was applicable to Croatia, Macedonia and, to a lesser extent, Bosnia. The only options were these: a very loose association in which republican sovereignty was paramount and central authority could not be exerted, or full independence. Thus the old Yugoslavia would never be again.

Whatever succeeds, it is unlikely, however, to be decided by Ljubljana. The fate of Yugoslavia will be decided by the Zagreb-Sarajevo-Belgrade axis. Indeed, to a considerable extent, it will be decided in Belgrade. Responses in the Croatian and Bosnian capitals to Belgrade politics, whether from the Serbian or federal authorities there, will be a large determinant of what occurs. Both republics' conduct will be shaped by the presence of large ethnic Serb populations. In this sense, it is within the power of the Serbian political leadership to make life easier or harder for its neighbours.

The increasing focus of military attention on Croatia, rather than Slovenia, towards the end of 1990 may have been recognition of the centrality of the triangle just delineated and the possibility that intimidation, added to the economic and inter-ethnic bonds, could be enough to limit Croatia's claims to independence. With Slovenia undoubtedly prepared to leave its confederalist ally behind, the concentration on Croatia may have been a sign that Slovenia was written off, but Croatia was thought to be redeemable.

If this was so, then it boded ill. The army's predominantly Serb and still old-style Communist composition was pushing it to act in the interest of the Serbian and still essentially Communist political leadership – albeit, in many cases, probably with grave reluctance. Acting in effect as a Serbian army, this was a recipe for war with the Croat and Slovene republican armed forces, created with militia and territorial reservists.

Unless a suitable commonwealth of sovereign states could be accommodated, at least as a temporary measure, Yugoslavia would certainly cease to have the same components. It would, perhaps, cease to exist at all. Even if a unified Yugoslav rump according to Serbian designs survived Slovene secession with Croatia still in its embrace, then it would be an unhappy place, bedevilled by the problems that have beset Yugoslavia since its inception as a Serbian realm. If a Serbo-Croat war were averted, a violent backlash from Kosovo would be ever more threatening as the Albanians, stripped of the support for its human-rights demands found in Slovenia, became ever more impatient of their treatment.

Alternatively, if the realities of power distribution in 1990s Yugoslavia are recognized by those in Belgrade and an accord reached that formalizes the *de facto* confederation in existence for some years. whatever title it is actually given, then it possible that Yugoslavia can be reincarnated. That reincarnation would, ironically, need to be along the lines of the Illyrian and Yugoslav movements, whose conceptions of the South Slav state were discussed in the Introduction: these ideas found less favour than Serbian arguments in the talks to establish the first Yugoslav state. In this case, Yugoslavs would be giving themselves breathing space and time to allow the introduction of new blood. In many ways, whatever happens, the present actors on the Yugoslav stage – the Milosevices, the Kucans, the Kadijevices, the Tudjmans and the Markovices – are history.

Whatever the political outcome – centreless association as a community or confederation, or independent states – relegitimation for the military will mean readjustment and restructuring. If military legitimacy is not dispersed to the corners of Yugoslavia and reformed in the armed forces of two or more independent states, then it will need to be renewed in a way appropriate to a new Yugoslav context. In that context, both sociopolitical and functional imperatives will demand attention. Relegitimation thus must involve depoliticization and restructuring.

Restructuring should include development towards a more regionally based regimental system and greater professionalization. Relegitimation will also involve consolidation of changes in the defence sector of the economy and de-Communization of the defence system as a whole. This will all require much work. The sooner that work is begun, the better.

Conclusion

Throughout this study, I have argued for the use of two concepts in civil-military analysis: regime legitimacy and military legitimacy. Based on an understanding of legitimacy as a *crasis* – that is, a necessary combination of elements, none of which is sufficient – these are logically and lexically consistent complements. They have been used to sustain the thesis that the Yugoslav civil-military relationship is a function of the interaction of regime legitimacy and military legitimacy.

The thesis has met with a considerable degree of success at the theoretical level. It has defined and developed two new and specific basic concepts. These can be used to guide and structure investigation and analysis. (Although only applied here to the Yugoslav case, they are concepts transferable to any civil-military relationship.) The operation of the two concepts in combination has enabled an explanation of Yugoslav civil-military relations at different stages and the conditions of change using the same terms. We have followed the relationship through the assessment of military and regime legitimacies in three distinct phases. The second Yugoslavia was built on the strength of political and military legitimacy derived from the Partisan struggle. In 1971, military legitimacy was called upon to compensate for weak regime legitimacy. As Yugoslavia plummeted further into multiple crisis in the 1980s, the army, its legitimacy increasingly in question, was unable to replay its earlier role.

In the Yugoslav case, neither regime nor military legitimacy were strong at the federal level; there was regime legitimacy at the republican level. Frailties at the federal level were connected to each other and to the growth of republican legitimacy: diminishing federal plus accruing republican regime legitimacy undermined military legitimacy; YPA attempts to restore its own position by reinforcing the federal regime's only served further to undo both legitimacy *crases*. This meant that legitimacy renewal for both was reciprocal: the legitimacy of each was a function of the other's.

As both regime and military sought to adapt to changing circumstances and to establish new bases of legitimacy, the functional nature of their relationship was quite clear. Military legitimacy was dependent on regime revitalization. Whatever its details, that revitalization required profound transformations of the armed forces. Without redefinition of the bases of military legitimacy, any regime relegitimation would be virtually impossible. Any chance of a third Yugoslavia embracing its present members receded, the longer it took for the military to withdraw from politics. Unless change was thorough-going and began to be implemented quickly, it would be too little, too late.

At the beginning of 1991, the military that gave birth to the second Yugoslavia and preserved it once through legitimate intervention in political affairs perhaps still held the power – but only just – to preserve the country again. It could have been the midwife to the birth of a third Yugoslavia by non-intervention.

Notes

1: Introduction

1. I have analysed events in Yugoslavia in the first half of 1991, leading up to the declarations, in James Gow, *Yugoslav Endgames: Civil Strife and Interstate Conflict*, London Defence Studies, No. 5, Centre for Defence Studies and Brasseys, London, 1991. The events surrounding the actual declarations are dealt with in my article, 'Deconstructing Yugoslavia', *Survival*, Vol. XXXIII, No. 4, July–August 1991.
2. See Gow, *Yugoslav Endgames*, p. 39 ff.
3. Robert W. Dean, 'Civil–Military Relations in Yugoslavia, 1971–5' in *Armed Forces and Society*, Vol. 3, No. 1, 1976, p. 17.
4. For example, Slobodan Stankovic's *Radio Free Europe Research* papers for the post-Tito years reflect this increase. See especially, 'Yugoslav Defence Minister calls the Army the "backbone" of the system', 28 April 1983 and 'Yugoslav military leaders warn against disunity', 25 November 1983. See also Milovan Djilas' article in *The Wall Street Journal (Europe)*, 22 August 1985.
5. Dean, loc. cit., p. 47.
6. *Ibid.*, pp. 48–50.
7. A. Ross Johnson, 'The Role of the Military in Communist Yugoslavia: An Historical Sketch', *RAND P 6070*, Santa Monica, 1978, p. 21.
8. For example, Defence Minister and Admiral of the Fleet Branko Mamula's speech at the 9th session of the LCY Central Committee, Belgrade, 25 July 1983, reported in *Narodna Armija*, 28 July 1983, translated in *FBIS-EEU*. 5 August 1983.
9. Quentin Crisp, *The Naked Civil Servant*, Thames Films, 1975.
10. Stevan K. Pavlowitch, *Yugoslavia*. Ernest Benn, London, 1971, p. 20.
11. Pavlowitch, op. cit., pp. 17–21, offers examples of this. John Allcock of Bradford University conducted a personal survey of the British press for a year, in which time every piece on Yugoslavia contained at least one error.
12. See Bogdan D. Denitch, *The Legitimation of a Revolution: The Yugoslav Case*. Yale U.P., New Haven and London, 1976, p. 17.
13. See Fred Singleton, *Twentieth Century Yugoslavia*, Macmillan, London, 1976, pp. 8–16, for a geographer's summary.
14. Constraints on space mean that the medieval Serbian and Croatian empires cannot be discussed. However, their importance in national memory should be emphasized. This is particularly the case with the Serbs whose nationally specific Orthodox Church was founded at this time. On the Slavs in medieval times, see Stephen Clissold, (ed.): *A Short History of Yugoslavia*, Cambridge U.P., Cambridge, 1966; Singleton, op.

cit., and *A Short History of the Yugoslav Peoples*, Cambridge U.P., Cambridge, 1985; Pavlowitch, op. cit.

15. See Francesco Altimari et al., *Albanci*, Cankarjeva Zalozba, Ljubljana, 1984, pp. 12–22.
16. Ivo Banac, *The National Question in Yugoslavia: Origins, History, Politics*. Cornell U.P., London, 1984, p. 78.
17. 'Illyrian' was a misnomer: the Illyrian language had no connection with any of the Slav tongues; as noted, only the Albanians in the modern world have any connection with the autochthonous Balkan population.
18. Banac, op. cit., p. 79.
19. Teodor Pavlovic, cited ibid, pp. 79–80.
20. This linguistic typology placed the kajkavians with the Slovenes to leave only the cakavians of Istria, parts of the Adriatic coast and of most of the islands strung along the littoral as Croats. In their eagerness to encourage integration, Gaj and the Illyrianists abandoned kajkavian; they were pushed into this by the belief that only a national programme could counter intense 'Magyarisation' by their imperial masters.
21. Singleton, *Twentieth Century Yugoslavia*, p. 53.
22. On the formation of Yugoslavia, see Ivo J. Lederer, *Yugoslavia at the Paris Peace Conference*, Yale U.P., New Haven, 1963; Alex N. Dragnich, *Serbia, Nikola Pasic and Yugoslavia*, Rutgers U.P., New Brunswick, New Jersey, 1974; and D. Djordjevic, (ed.): *The Creation of Yugoslavia 1914–18*, Clio Books, Santa Barbara, 1980.
23. Banac, op. cit., p. 12.
24. On inter-war Yugoslavia, see the relevant parts of Joseph Rothschild, *Eastern Europe Between the World Wars*, University of Washington Press, Seattle, 1974.
25. J. R. Hoptner, *Yugoslavia 1938–41*, Columbia U.P., New York, 1963, gives a strong analysis of the events leading to the coup and the axis invasion.
26. On the structures of Yugoslav politics, see Jim Seroka and Radoslav Smilijkovic, *Political Organs in Socialist Yugoslavia*, Duke U.P., Durham, 1986; see also April Carter, *Democratic Reform in Yugoslavia: The Changing Role of the Party*, Frances Pinter, London, 1982.
27. My use of 'military' is, for the most part consistent with others – many though they are. Where it differs is the understanding that a military exists for political reasons. A mob may operate using various levels of force to coerce, but it does not do so in a knowingly restrained way to achieve political ends. The political dimension is *necessary* to a definition of 'military'.
28. The role as an instrument of conquest is rarely found these days.
29. As Foot writes, 'the world today exposes those without forces to the will of those with them: no manned weapons, no security,'. M. R. D. Foot, *Men in Uniform*, Weidenfeld & Nicolson, 1961, p. 21. Of course, this was just as true of the world of yesterday – as Machiavelli is witness: 'I conclude, therefore, that without having one's own soldiers, no principality is safe; on the contrary, it is completely subject to Fortune, not having the power and the loyalty to defend it in times of adversity.' Machiavelli, *The Prince*, Chapter XIII in *The Portable Machiavelli*,

P. Bondanella and M. Mufa, (eds), Penguin, Harmondsworth, 1979, p. 123.

30. Of course, this is not strictly true. But, as Edmonds suggests, 'the exceptions scarcely warrant close inspection.' M. Edmonds, (ed.): *Central Organisations of Defence*, Westview Press Inc. and Frances Pinter Ltd, London, 1985, p. 1.

31. In his expansion of *The Military in the Political Development of New Nations*, University of Chicago Press, 1964, Janowitz includes a long, useful section on the rise of paramilitary internal security forces which are used to increase regime stability. M. Janowitz, *Military Institutions and Coercion in the Developing World*, University of Chicago Press, Chicago, 1977, pp. 3–73.

32. Which part in particular is usually stipulated or evident from the context. See, for example, A. Perlmutter, *The Military and Politics in Modern Times*, Yale U.P., 1977, p. 17 or Finer, *The Man on Horseback: The Role of the Military in Politics*, Penguin, Harmondsworth, 1978, pp. 141–8 and 174–8.

33. Examples include S. E. Finer, *The Man on Horseback: The Role of the Military in Politics*, (2nd edn) (enlarged) Penguin, Harmondsworth, 1976, on the civil side and Morris Janowitz, *The Military in the Political Development of New Nations*, University of Chicago Press, Chicago, 1964, on the military. Neither is exclusive.

34. See for example, A. R. Luckham, 'A Comparative Typology of Civil–Military Relations' *Government and Opposition*, Vol. 6, No. 2, Spring 1971.

35. Finer himself recognized this, op. cit., p. 240; see also, for example, George Sanford, *Military Rule in Poland: The Rebuilding of Communist Power 1981–1983*. Croom Helm, London, 1986, p. 24.

36. Finer, op. cit., p. 17.

37. *Ibid.*, p. 78.

38. Finer expressed reservations about such characterizations, but, none the less, accepts them (ibid, pp. 241–2).

39. *Ibid.*

40. *Ibid.*, p. 241.

41. *Ibid.*, p. 238 ff.

42. Samuel P. Huntington, *Political Order in Changing Societies*. Yale U.P., New Haven, 1968, p. 1.

43. *Ibid.*, p. 12.

44. *Ibid.*, p. 1.

45. *Ibid.*, p. 78 ff.

46. *Ibid.*, p. 196.

47. *Ibid.*, p. 195.

48. *Ibid.*, p. 196.

49. Samuel P. Huntington, 'Political Development and Political Decay', *World Politics*, Vol. XVII, 1964–5.

50. Huntington, 'Political Order', p. 201.

51. *Ibid.*, p. 221.

52. Finer, op. cit., p. 233.

53. Samuel P. Huntington, *The Soldier and the State: The Theory and Politics of Civil–Military Relations*. Belknap Press of Harvard U.P., Cambridge, Mass., 1957.

54. M. Needler, *Anatomy of a Coup d'Etat: Ecuador, 1963*. Institute for the Study of Comparative Political Systems, Washington, 1964, p. 45.
55. A. R. Luckham, *The Nigerian Military*. Cambridge U.P., Cambridge 1971, p. 279.
56. Finer, op. cit., p. 234.
57. *Ibid*.
58. Janowitz, op. cit., and *Military Institutions and Coercion in the Developing World*, University of Chicago Press, Chicago, 1977.
59. Luckham, loc. cit.
60. C. E. Welch and A. R. Smith, *Military Role and Rule*. Duxbury Press, North Scituate, 1974.
61. *Ibid.*, p. 29.
62. Martin Edmonds, *The Armed Services and Society*. Leicester U.P., Leicester, 1988, p. 91.
63. H. Lasswell, *Politics: Who Gets What, When, How*, Whittlesey House, New York, 1936. The present definition of politics also synthesizes with Lasswell's classic attempt the following: David Easton in *A Systems Analysis of Political Life*, John Wiley, New York, 1965, p. 350; and S. E. Finer in *Comparative Government*, Penguin Books, Harmondsworth, 1974, pp. 6–10.
64. See Roderick Martin, *The Sociology of Power*, Routledge & Kegan Paul, London, Chapter 4; esp., pp. 55–6.
65. *Cf.* William H. McNeill, *The Pursuit of Power*. Basil Blackwell, Oxford, 1983, pp. 2–4.
66. We should be careful in our use of the term 'right'. In one sense it could be taken to mean the perception of 'rightfulness'. Alternatively, it could refer to the accuracy or correctness of an analysis or diagnosis.
67. It is important to recognize that, *in extremis*, the principle which legitimates a division of power may be simply 'might is right'; if one is strong enough to get one's own way, this in itself is sufficient justification. 'Might is right' is one type of morality. More usually, however, might needs to prove itself right. Pascal summarized this process: 'Being unable to make what is just strong, we have made what is strong just.' ('Et ainsi ne pouvant faire que ce qui est juste fut fort, on a fait que ce qui est fort fut juste.') Pascal, *Pensees*, Michel Autrand, (ed.), Bordas, Paris, 1976, p. 111.
68. Here I shall bear in mind the difficulties inherent in social scientific theory discussed in Morris R. Cohen and Ernest Nagel, *An Introduction to Logic and Scientific Method*, Routledge & Kegan Paul, London, 1934, and 1966; Vernon van Dyke, *Political Science: A Philosophical Analysis*, Stanford U.P., Stanford, 1960; David Potter, (ed.): *Society and the Social Sciences*, Routledge & Kegan Paul, London, 1981; Karl R. Popper, *The Logic of Scientific Discovery*, Hutchinson, 1980.
69. See Max Weber, 'Science as a Vocation' in Weber, *From Max Weber: Essays in Sociology*, H. H. Gerth and C. Wright Mills, (eds) Routledge & Kegan Paul, London, 1948, esp., p. 145 ff; see also Anthony Giddens, *Studies in Social and Political Theory*, Hutchinson, London, 1979, p. 85 ff.
70. Dolf Sternberger, 'Legitimacy' in *International Encyclopedia of the Social*

Sciences, Macmillan, New York, 1968, p. 247.

71. Max Weber, *Economy and Society*, p. 215. The following understanding of Weber's work is, in particular, informed by Rigby, loc. cit., and J. G. Merquior, *Rousseau and Weber*, Routledge & Kegan Paul, London, 1980.

72. For example, see Sternberger, loc. cit., p. 247; Merquior, op. cit., *passim*; Martin, op. cit., p. 76; Anthony Giddens, *Politics and Sociology in the Thought of Max Weber*, Macmillan, London, 1982, and op. cit., p. 90 ff.

73. See Merquior, op. cit., Chapter 7.

74. *Ibid.*, p. 6.

75. Weber, *Economy*, p. 212.

76. See Sternberger, loc. cit., p. 247; Merquior, op. cit., Chapter 6.

77. Giddens, *Studies*, p. 92.

78. Rigby, loc. cit., notes that Weber's view of legitimacy is deeply imbued with the values of his bureaucratic culture (p. 7).

79. Seymour Martin Lipsett, *Political Man*, Heinemann, London, 1969, p. 77.

80. Easton op. cit., p. 278.

81. *Ibid.*

82. One of the major problems in social scientific theory is to establish the truth or falsity of beliefs, feelings and attitudes – either as professed or observed. *Cf.* Stephen White, *Political Culture and Soviet Politics*, Macmillan, London, 1979, pp. 14–19.

83. *Cf.* Harry Eckstein and Ted Robert Gurr, *Patterns of Authority: A Structural Basis for Political Enquiry*, John Wiley, New York, 1975, pp. 208–11.

84. *Cf.* Archie Brown, 'Introduction', p. 20 in Brown and Jack Gray, (eds): *Political Culture and Political Change in Communist States*, Macmillan, London, 1977.

85. Merquior, op. cit., p. 5.

86. Arthur L. Stinchcombe, *Constructing Social Theories*, Harcourt, Brace and World Inc., New York. 1968.

87. *Ibid.*, p. 168.

88. *Ibid.*, pp. 159–60.

89. Merquior, op. cit., p. 8.

90. *Ibid.*

91. *Cf.* McNeill, op. cit., p. 4.

92. This interpretation is perhaps a little simplistic in view of the complexity of modern politics; since the American revolution brought the 'no taxation without representation' notion into widespread practice, there has been an understanding that the ruled control the rulers in democratic societies. To whatever extent this is the case, in essence the situation remains the same: if we want to be a member of a community and have a quiet life, unpestered by freelance thugs or the agents of the state on behalf of those who hold power (even if this is 'everybody'), we must pay what is due.

93. Merquior, op. cit., p. 9. *Cf.* Martin, op. cit., p. 56.

94. Gugliemo Ferrero, *The Principles of Power: The Great Political Crises of History*, Puttnams, New York, 1943, p. 134, writes: 'Legitimacy can only be established by a clear, fixed standard of comparison, bearing the same meaning for everyone and uncontrovertible in its application.' This may

be true for evaluation in terms of our own moral preferences; however, for scientific observation, the standard must be to identify the mechanical elements which explain a distribution of power – this means no 'fixed' standard of what constitutes legitimacy. (See below.)

95. Cf. Sternberger, loc. cit., p. 247; Ferrero, op. cit., p. 144. The variety of legitimacies should be self evident from the different interpretations discussed here and found in the literature.

96. James M. Buchannan, *Freedom in Constitutional Contract: Perspectives of a Political Economist*, Texas A & M U.P., College Station and London, 1977, p. 124.

97. *Idem.*, *The Calculus of Consent: Logical Foundation of Constitutional Democracy*, University of Michigan Press, Michigan, 1962, and *The Limits of Liberty: Between Anarchy and Leviathan*, University of Chicago Press, London, 1975.

98. *Ibid.*, p. 7.

99. *Ibid.*, p. 125.

100. *Ibid.*, p. 124.

101. *Ibid.*, p. 16.

102. *Idem.*, *Freedom*, p. 127.

103. Merquior, op. cit., p. 3.

104. Alfred G. Meyer, 'Legitimacy of Power in East Central Europe' in S. Sinnanian et al., (eds): *Eastern Europe in the 1970s*, Praeger, New York, 1972, p. 66.

105. Paul. G. Lewis, 'Legitimation and Crises: East European Developments in the Post-Stalin Period' in Lewis, (ed.): *Eastern Europe: Political Crisis and Legitimation*, Croom Helm, London, 1984, suggests that this approach is particularly useful a propos of Eastern Europe. He also, however, supports this by noting that 'under the entry for "legitimation" in the 1933 *Encyclopedia of the Social Sciences* the social researcher is succinctly enjoined to "see Illegitimacy"; anyone who does follow the reference will find that it only bears upon inheritance law'.

106. Jurgen Habermas, *Legitimation Crisis*, Heinemann Educational Books, London, 1970, pp. 1–2.

107. *Ibid.*, p. 69.

108. *Ibid.*

109. Alternative terms to the 'bases of legitimacy' include 'legitimating ideologies' (Easton, op. cit., pp. 289–97), legitimating 'doctrines' (Bruner, loc. cit., p. 28 ff) and 'political religion' – an adaptation of Machiavelli's concept (Carl A. Linden, 'Marxism–Leninism: Systemic Legitimacy and Political Culture') in T. Rakowska-Harmstone, (ed.): *Perspectives for Change in Communist Societies*, Westview, Boulder, 1979.

110. This corresponds with the criterion of 'adaptability' which is essential in Huntington's concept of 'institutionalization'. See Samuel P. Huntington, *Political Order in Changing Societies*, Yale U.P., New Haven, 1969, p. 13.

111. Merquior uses the adjective *cratic* in his discussion of Stinchcombe's 'power reserve' legitimacy. To avoid confusion, that term has been expressly eschewed in the present consideration. Merquior's *cratic*

concerns *power*; *crasis* refers to a necessary *combination of elements*. The former stems from the Greek *kratos* (power); the latter from the Greek *krasis* (mixture). Whereas 'bureaucracy' is from *kratos*, 'idiosyncrasy' is from *krasis*. However, both words form the same adjectival ending: bureaucratic, idiosyncratic. To avoid any confusion with notions of power and Merquior's use of '*cratic* legitimacy', I shall deploy the adjectival form *crastic*.

112. Ferrero, op. cit., p. 135, says that a government is legitimate if power operates in agreement with principles and rules 'accepted without discussion by those who must obey'.

113. 'Ideology' is used here in the sense of Weberian 'legitimating ideologies'; however, as the present argument contends, we must see these only as one part of legitimacy.

114. Cf. Joseph Rothschild, 'Political Legitimacy in Contemporary Europe' in Bogdan Denitch, (ed.): *The Legitimation of Regimes*, Sage, London, 1979, Chapter 3; and Lucien W. Pye, 'The Legitimacy Crisis' in L. S. Binder et al., *Crises and Sequences in Political Development*, Princeton U.P., Princeton, 1971, p. 136.

115. See A. Ross Johnson, *The Transformation of Communist Ideology*, MIT Press, Cambridge, Mass., 1972.

116. See Dennison Rusinow, *The Yugoslav Experiment 1948–1974*, Charles Hurst and Co., London, 1977.

117. Robin A. Remington, 'Armed Forces and Society in Yugoslavia' in C. M. Kelleher, (ed.): *Political Military Systems*, Sage, London, 1974. p. 184.

118. *Ibid.*, p. 178.

119. A. Ross Johnson, 'The Role of the Military in Communist Yugoslavia', *RAND*, P 6070, p. 14.

2: The Legitimating Army

1. For example, Jonathan R. Adelman, loc. cit., p. 6; William Turley, 'The Vietnamese Army' in Adelman, (ed.), op. cit., p. 77; Amos Perlmutter and William Leo Grande, 'The Party in Uniform: Towards a Theory of Civil–Military Elations in Communist Political Systems', *American Political Science Review*, Vol. 76, 1982, p. 788.

2. For example, Claude Welch and Arthur Smith set the 'extent and nature' of political participation and the strength of civil institutions against 'military strength'; they then add the 'nature' of the civil-military boundary. The first of these notions complicates the analysis; it (and the last) are a hindrance in that they do not 'fit' the other two concepts used. They do not facilitate clear understanding. See Welch and Smith, *Military Role and Rule*, Duxbury Press, North Scituate, 1974, Chapter 3.

3. A. R. Luckham, 'A Comparative Typology of Civil–Military Relations; *Government and Opposition*, Vol. 6, No. 2, Spring 1971.

4. Samuel P. Huntington, *The Soldier and the State: The Theory and Politics of Civil–Military Relations*, Harvard U.P., Cambridge, Mass., 1957, pp. 11–18; Morris Janowitz, *The Military in the Development of New*

Nations: An Essay in Comparative Analysis, University of Chicago Press, Chicago, 1964, esp., p. 31 ff.

5. See Huntington, *Political Order in Changing Societies,* Yale U.P., New Haven, 1968.

6. On the need for economy and simplicity in the construction of theory, see S. E. Finer, op. cit., p. 243.

7. Jacques van Doorn, 'The Military and the Crisis of Legitimacy' in G. Harries-Jenkins and Jacques van Doorn, (eds): *The Military and the Problem of Legitimacy,* Sage, London, 1976, p. 21.

8. See Maury D. Feld, *The Structure of Violence,* Sage, London, 1977, p. 123.

9. John Erickson and T. N. Wolfe, 'Introduction' in Erickson and Wolfe, (eds): *The Armed Services and Society: Alienation, Management and Integration,* Edinburgh U.P., Edinburgh, 1970, p. 1.

10. *Cf.* Martin Edmonds, 'The Function of the Armed Forces: A Framework for Analysis of the Armed Forces of France, West Germany and Britain', USSG Paper, p. 1. Edmonds discusses this point, arguing that 'security' is a 'cathectic' notion.

11. Karl von Clausewitz, *On War,* A. Rapoport, (ed), Penguin, Harmondsworth, 1968.

12. See Huntington, *Soldier,* pp. 11–18 and 60–86.

13. See *ibid.,* p. 71. However, this notion of 'neutrality' is spurious. Any army is always political. *Cf.* Martin Edmonds, 'Armed Forces and Legitimacy in Britain: Emerging Stresses and Dichotomies', paper presented at the Colloque sur les systems militaires britannique et francais, Toulouse, 1976, p. 5.

14. For example, Soviet military doctrine is a qualitative concept from that understood in Western countries. Whereas in a Western context, the idea relates specifically to guiding notions in military science, for a Soviet officer it is understood as a part of the whole social and political system. Mensur Ibrahimpsic, 'Vojna subordinacija kao determinanta strukture: Princip Organizacije Armije', *Zbornik Radova 1,* Belgrade, 1969, writes of the military's technical and social roles (pp. 66–7). See also Christopher N. Donnelly, *Heirs of Clausewitz: Change and Continuity in the Soviet War Machine,* Institute for European Defence and Strategic Studies Occasional Paper, No. 16, London, 1985, Part III, esp., pp. 20–1.

15. In a liberal democracy, the state is a go-between that separates those who make policy – the government – from those it affects. For example, in the United Kingdom, the Ministry of Defence mediates between the Secretary of State for Defence and the Armed Forces; the Department of Health and Social Security lies between the Secretary of State for that Department and the Health Authorities and Hospitals, and so on. The Secretary of State and those on the receiving end of the policies have no immediate contact.

This is the formal position in a Communist system. However, the reality is somewhat modified. Whereas liberal democracies rely on the notion of a permanent, independent, professional and neutral bureaucracy, in a Communist system the bureaucrats are controlled by the party's *nomenklatura* system. Indeed, the 'politicized bureaucracy' of the state intercedes between those with power, the party elite, and the objects of their policies, the soldiers, enterprise managers and so forth, who will also be party-vetted. See S. E. Finer, *Comparative Government*, Penguin, Harmondsworth, 1974, pp. 69–71; Neil Elder, 'The Function of the Modern State' in J. E. S. Hayward and R. N. Berki, (eds): *State and Society in Contemporary Europe*, Martin Robertson, Oxford, 1979, pp. 62–3; H. Gordon Skilling, *The Governments of Communist East Europe*, Thomas Y. Crowell, New York, 1966, Chapter 12, esp., pp. 147–9; Ota Sik, *The Communist Power System*, Praeger, New York, 1981, pp. 54–86; Gary K. Bertsch, *Power and Policy in Communist Systems*, John Wiley, New York, 1978, pp. 115–16, 124–8 and 140–3; Radoslav Selucky, *Economic Reforms in Eastern Europe: Political Background and Economic Significance*, Praeger, New York, 1972, p. 10 ff.

16. Perlmutter and Leo Grande, loc. cit.
17. See Jim Seroka and Rados Smilijkovic, *Political Organs in Socialist Yugoslavia*, Duke U.P., Durham, 1986, pp. 55–6 and 60.
18. See George Sanford, op. cit., Chapter 2, esp., p. 81.
19. Edmonds, 'Armed Forces', p. 2.
20. See Colton, loc. cit., pp. 132–3.
21. See Martin Edmonds, *The Armed Services and Society*, Leicester U.P., Leicester, 1988, pp. 96–8. In a Communist context, the GDR's NVA may be interpreted as particularly performing this function in a delicate situation. *Cf.* Martin McCauley's 'Legitimation in the German Democratic Republic' in Paul G. Lewis (ed.), *Eastern Europe: Political Crisis and Legitimation*, Croom Helm, London, 1984, p. 60.
22. David B. Bobrow, 'Soldiers and the Nation State', *Annals of the American Academy*, No. 358, 1965, p. 68.
23. *Ibid.*
24. Janowitz, op. cit., p. 32; see also Janowitz, *Military Institutions and Coercion in Developing Nations*, University of Chicago Press, Chicago, 1977, p. 115.
25. Colton, loc. cit., p. 122.
26. *Ibid.*, pp. 122–3.
27. *Ibid.*, see also William H. Odom, 'The Soviet Military–Educational Complex' in Dale R. Herspring and Ivan Volges, (eds): *Civil–Military Relations in Communist Systems*, Westview, Boulder, 1978.
28. Colton, loc. cit., pp. 124–5.
29. This is particularly the case where major nationality issues are found, such as in the USSR or Yugoslavia. In another sense, it is peculiarly important to the GDR. See Teresa Rakowska-Harmstone, 'The Soviet Army as the Instrument of National Integration' in John Erickson and E. J. Feuchtwanger, (eds): *Soviet Military Power and Performance*, Macmillan, London, 1979; Ellen Jones, *Red Army and Society: A Sociology of the Soviet Military*, Allen & Unwin, London, 1985.
30. Van Doorn, loc. cit., p. 30.
31. Edmonds, 'Armed Forces', p. 8.
32. Erickson and Wolfe, loc. cit., p. 1.
33. Edmonds, 'Armed Forces', p. 4.

34. In analysing military legitimacy in WTO East European cases, our understandings would have to incorporate the fact that, in terms of environmental support, there was a dual aspect. Even more so than for the regimes of Eastern Europe, the armed forces' legitimacy included a substantial Soviet dimension. Both civil and military leaders had a compact not only with their own society, but with the USSR. The national armies of Eastern Europe had to have support not only of their own community, but also of the Soviet Union.

35. Edmonds, 'Armed Forces' passim.

36. See Lawrence J. Korb, The Fall and Rise of the Pentagon: American Defense Policies in the 1970s, Greenwood Press, London, 1979; R. Giradet, (ed.): La Crise Militaire Francaise 1945–1962: Aspects sociologiques et ideologiques, Cahiers de la Fondation Nationale des Sciences Politiques – Libraire Armand Colin, Paris, 1964; J. S. Ambler, The French Army in Politics 1945–1962, Ohio State U.P., Ohio, 1966.

37. International Pravda. October 1987.

38. Vojna Enciklopedija (hereafter VE), Vol. 4, p. 136; resistance preparations were begun earlier in Slovenia. The Communist-led Liberation Front took the decision to organize on 22 June, whereas the CPY only made that move on 4 July.

39. See Tito's 'Letter from the Central Committee of the CPY to the Regional Committee of the CPY for Montenegro, Boka and the Sandzak', Tito, Military Thought and Works: Selected Writings (1936–1979), Belgrade, 1982, p. 92 ff.

40. Milovan Djilas, Wartime, Secker & Warburg, London, 1980, p. 24.

41. Ibid., p. 54.

42. On the use of the term 'Partisan' see ibid., p. 57.

43. Ibid., p. 100.

44. Tito, 'Consultation of HQ Representatives and Commanders of the National Liberation Partisan Detachments of Yugoslavia', op. cit., pp. 81–2.

45. The OF (Osvobodilna Fronta) was a Communist Party of Slovenia (CPS) led coalition, formed from the Anti-Imperial Front organized on 27 April 1941 against the axis invasion. The CPS had been criticized by Tito for creating the Anti-Imperial Front as this was an action counter to Moscow's will – and therefore Tito's. It changed its name after the 22 June invasion of the Soviet Union. The OF was a broad-based organization that involved a majority of the population. See Metod Mikuz, Pregled Zgodovine NOV v Sloveniji (Vol. 1) p. 96 ff. However, in spite of the degree of popular participation, proportionally few became engaged in Partisan activities – to Tito's irritation. Indeed, the situation in Slovenia was distinct from that in other parts of Yugoslavia – until the latter stages of the war (as in much else later) events in Slovenia were separate from those in the rest of Yugoslavia; Slovenia was not present at the first AVNOJ session in 1943, and then only an observer at the second a year later. See Djilas, op. cit., pp. 338–9 and Zdravko Klanscek, Oris Narodnoosvobodilne Vojne na Slovenskem 1941–1945, Partizanska Kniga, Ljubljana, 1982, pp. 74 and 80–1.

46. Djilas, op. cit., p. 338.
47. See Ljubo Sirc, *Between Hitler and Stalin*, Andre Deutsch, London, 1989, pp. 26-7.
48. *VE*, Vol. 4, p. 136.
49. Tito, 'Consultation', op. cit., p. 82.
50. Djilas, op. cit., p. 17.
51. *VE*, Vol. 2, p. 254.
52. Tito, 'Order on partisan insignia, saluting and national flags', op. cit., p. 84.
53. Tito, 'Instructions of the Supreme Headquarters to National Liberation Partisan Detachments of Yugoslavia', op. cit., p. 85 ff.
54. Tito, 'Order establishing the Quartermaster General and Commissariat', op. cit., p. 100.
55. Tito, 'Statute of the National Liberation Proletarian Shock Brigades', op. cit., p. 103.
56. Djilas, op. cit., p. 31.
57. Nikola Anic, 'Stvaranje Oruzanih Snaga 1941-1945', *Oruzane Snage Jugoslavije 1941-1945*, VIZ, Belgrade, 1982, p. 34.
58. Blazo S. Jovanovic, *Cetvrta Proletarska Crnogorska Brigade*, VIZ, Belgrade, 1975.
59. Anic, loc. cit., p. 26.
60. *Ibid.*, p. 35.
61. 'Statut Proletershih Brigada', *Zbornik Dokumentata i Podatka Narod-noslobodilacke Borbe Jugoslavije*, VIZ. Belgrade, Vol. II, pp. 134 and 175.
62. Anic, loc. cit., p. 35.
63. Djilas, op. cit., p. 32.
64. *VE*, Vol. 4, p. 137.
65. Tito, 'Formation of the National Liberation Army of Yugoslavia', op. cit., p. 138.
66. Tito, 'To the Regional Committee of the CPY for Serbia', op. cit., p. 135.
67. On the basis of 6 independent batallions, each with around 3,000 fighters (thus, 18,000) plus 17 Partisan detachments; see Anic, loc. cit., pp. 25 and 28.
68. *Ibid.*, pp. 26 and 28.
69. Klanscek, op. cit., p. 33.
70. Sirc, op. cit., p. 40; *cf.* Branko Latas, 'Cetnici Draze Mihailocica u Sloveniji - Plava Garda 1941-1943 Godine', *Vojnoistoriski Glasnik*, Vol. XXXIV, 1983, p. 186; Klanscek, op. cit., gives 5,145 for 28 February (p. 60).
71. *Ibid.*, p. 64, reports 4,000 fighters organized in two divisions and 5,500 Partisans in the whole of Slovenia; this is consistent with Stanko Petelin, *Enaintrideseta Divizija*, Zalozba Borec, Ljubljana, 1985, pp. 264-83 *passim*.
72. *VE*, Vol. 4, p. 137.
73. *Ibid.*
74. Tito, 'Formation', op. cit., p. 138.
75. *VE*, Vol. 2, p. 478.
76. Tito, 'Formation', op. cit., p. 139.
77. *VE*, Vol. 4. p. 478.

164 NOTES

78. Petelin, op. cit., p. 266.
79. Anic, loc. cit., p. 48.
80. *Ibid.*, p. 65.
81. *VE*, Vol. 4, p. 478.
82. Anic, loc. cit., p. 48.
83. For example, Petelin, op. cit.
84. Anic, loc. cit., p. 48.
85. Petelin, op. cit., pp. 268–72.
86. *Ibid.*, pp. 272–82.
87. *Ibid.*, Petelin, op. cit., p. 266.
88. Anic, loc. cit., pp. 48–9; see the subsequent pages for the development of corps in various parts of the country.
89. *Ibid.*, p. 72.
90. *Ibid.*, p. 72–3.
91. Rade Roksandic, 'Organizacijsko-Formacijsko Razvoj Oruzanih Snaga', *Oruzane Snage Jugoslavije 1941–1981*, VIZ, Belgrade, 1982, p. 153.
92. Milojica Pantelic, 'The Role of the Armed Forces in the System of National Defence', *Yugoslav Survey*, No. 4, 1969, p. 30.
93. Roksandic, loc. cit., pp. 152–3.
94. Sveto Kovacevic, 'Koncipiranje Uloge Komunista u Posleratnom Razvitku Jugoslovenske Narodne Armije', *Zbornik Radova 1*, Politicka Skola JNA, Belgrade, 1968, p. 9.
95. Drago Nikolic, *Razvoj Politickih Organa u Jugoslovenskoj Narodnoj Armiji*, VIZ, Belgrade, 1985, p. 35.
96. Milija Stansic, *KPJ u Izgradnji Oruzanih Snage Revolucije 1941–1945*, VIZ, Belgrade, 1973, pp. 302–3.
97. On political cultural work see Nikolic, op. cit., pp. 31–41.
98. Mensur Ibrahimpsic, *Armija Kao Drustvena Institutacija*, Magister Thesis, Political Science Faculty, Belgrade University, 1973, p. 151.
99. See Stansic, op. cit., pp. 438–44.
100. Nikolic, op. cit., p. 37.
101. *Ibid.*, p. 427.
102. 'The People's Liberation War and the Socialist Revolution in Yugoslavia 1941–1945', *Yugoslav Survey*, No. 5, 1961, p. 610.
103. *Ibid.*, p. 613.
104. See Tito, 'Address at the First Session of the National Anti-fascist Council for the Liberation of Yugoslavia', op. cit., p. 141; for a full study of the Partisan economy in one part of Yugoslavia, see Metod Mikuz, *Slovensko Partizansko Gospodarstvo*, Zavod Borec, Ljubljana, 1969.
105. Djilas, op. cit., p. 103.
106. Klanscek, op. cit., pp. 96–7.
107. Petelin, op. cit., p. 396.
108. Anic, loc. cit., p. 73.
109. Pantelic, loc. cit.
110. *VE*, Vol. 4, p. 139; Bosko Todorovic, 'Neke Bitne Karakteristike Razvoja Oruzanih Snaga u Posleratnom Periodu', *Oruzane Snage Jugoslavije 1941–1981*, VIZ, Belgrade, 1982, p. 101.
111. Roksandic, loc. cit., p. 161; see also Kovacevic, loc. cit., *passim*.

112. Rade Susa, 'Naoruzani narod – Crvena Nit u Posleratnoj Izgradnji Nasih Oruzanih Snage', *Vojno Delo*, No. 6, 1983, p. 51.
113. Svetozar Vukmanovic-Tempo, *'Revolucija Koja Tece: Memoari*, Komunist, Belgrade, 1971, Vol. 1, p. 24.
114. *VE*, Vol. 4, p. 140.
115. Blazo Nikolovski, 'Drustveni Razvoj i Izgradnja Nasih Oruzanih Snaga', *Oruzane Snage*, VIZ, Belgrade, 1982, p. 131.
116. Todorovic, loc. cit., p. 103.
117. Reneo Lukic, 'La Dissuasion Populaire Yougoslave', *Cahiers d'Etudes Strategiques No. 5*, CIRPES, Paris, 1985, p. 26.
118. *VE*, Vol. 4, p. 140.
119. The Allies' concerns in Greece were pursued in line with the Churchill–Stalin accords at Yalta.
120. Adam Roberts, *Nations in Arms: The Theory and Practice of Territorial Defence*, Chatto & Windus, London, 1976, p. 143.
121. Ibrahimpsic, op. cit., p. 166.
122. Todorovic, loc. cit., pp. 103–4.
123. Ibrahimpsic, op. cit., pp. 163–4.
124. *Ibid.*, p. 164.
125. Lukic, op. cit., p. 26.
126. Between 1945 and 1951, 9,600 YA personnel obtained qualifications from Soviet military schools and academies – see Milos Prelevic, *Drustvena Sustina Vojne Sile*, VIZ, Belgrade, 1972, p. 158; on Yugoslav military education, see Djordje Stanic, 'Military Schools of the Yugoslav People's Army', *Yugoslav Survey*, No. 2, 1975.
127. Ibrahimpsic, loc. cit., p. 168.
128. *Ibid.*, p. 165.
129. Vukmanovic-Tempo, op. cit., p. 31.
130. Roberts, op. cit., p. 144.
131. *Ibid.*, p. 149.
132. Todorovic, loc. cit., p. 104.
133. *VE*, Vol. 4, p. 141.
134. *Ibid.*, p. 143; Nikolovski, loc. cit., p. 135 ff.
135. Lukic, op. cit., p. 20.
136. Nikolic, op. cit., pp. 102–13.
137. Kovacevic, loc. cit., p. 12.
138. Todorovic, loc. cit., p. 104.
139. *VE*, Vol. 4, p. 141.
140. Roberts, op. cit., pp. 152–3.
141. Todorovic, loc. cit., p. 105.
142. Prelevic, op. cit., p. 160.
143. Todorovic, loc. cit., p. 105.
144. Roberts, op. cit., p. 147.
145. Roberts, op. cit., p. 150, cites the report of an American general making a visit to assess the YA in 1951.
146. *Ibid.*, p. 149.
147. *VE*, p. 142.
148. Pantelic, loc. cit., p. 31.

149. *Ibid.*
150. Todorovic, loc. cit., pp. 105–6.
151. Roberts, loc. cit., pp. 172–3; Lukic, op. cit., p. 20.
152. Cited by Pantelic, loc. cit., p. 31.
153. Nikolovski, loc. cit., p. 139.
154. *VE*, Vol. 4, p. 142; Pantelic, loc. cit., p. 32.
155. See Lukic, loc. cit., pp. 24–5.
156. A. Ross Johnson, 'Total National Defence in Yugoslavia', *RAND*, P 4746, Santa Monica, 1971.
157. *Borba*, 6 June 1970.
158. Pantelic, loc. cit., pp. 36–7.
159. General Viktor Bubanj, *Narodna Armija*, 15 May 1970.
160. See for example, 'Tito's Ljubljana Speech Analysed', *RFE*, 12 December 1969.
161. Savo Drljevic, 'The Sources of Our Concept of National Defence', *Socialism* (Belgrade), No. 4, 1969; or Roberts, op. cit., p. 174.
162. *Borba*, 28 June 1970.
163. Lukic, op. cit., p. 25.
164. Dusan Dozet, 'Social Factors of the Nationwide Defence System', *Narodna Armija*, 19 June 1970.
165. Pantelic, loc. cit., p. 31.
166. *Narodna Armija*, 24 July 1970.
167. Anton Bebler, *Marksizem in Vojastvo*, Komunist, Ljubljana, 1975, p. 101.
168. Todorovic, loc. cit., p. 106.
169. Zdenko Antic, 'Yugoslavia Prepared to Wage All-out People's War in Case of Attack', *RFE*, 26 November 1968.
170. *Ibid.*
171. Roberts, op. cit., pp. 157–8.
172. *Ibid.*
173. *Narodna Armija*, 1 December 1967.
174. General Rade Hamovic, *Ibid.*, 6 January 1967.
175. Pantelic, loc. cit., p. 31.
176. *Ibid.*
177. Communications between the Supreme Staff and the Main Staffs presented little difficulty. The real problems lay in communications between the Main Staffs and the corps, divisional and brigade commands. Anic, loc. cit., p. 61.
178. Todorovic, loc. cit., pp. 106–7 and 109–12; Pantelic, loc. cit., pp. 36–8.
179. Dennison Rusinow, 'The Yugoslav Concept of "All-National Defence"', *AUFS Field Report: South-East Europe*, Vol. XIX, No. 1, November 1971, p. 2.
180. Roberts, op. cit., p. 161.
181. *Sluzbeni List*, 19 February 1969.
182. 'Croatian National Assembly to Adopt Own Defence Law', *RFE*, 21 January 1971.
183. 'Yugoslavia Prepared to Wage All-out People's War', *RFE*, 26 November 1968.
184. Rusinow, loc. cit., p. 2.

185. Roberts, op. cit., p. 168.
186. Article 12, 1974 National Defence Law, cited, *Ibid.*, p. 179.
187. Roberts, op. cit., pp. 169–70.
188. See Ibrahimpsic, op. cit., pp. 133–4.
189. Janowitz, op. cit., argues that in many countries the army is the best educated, most technically advanced and, therefore, best equipped part of the community to provide these.
190. Dusan Pejanovic, *The Yugoslav People's Army in the Reconstruction and Development of the Country*, VIZ, Belgrade, p. 84.
191. *Ibid.*, pp. 87–8.
192. Roberts, op. cit., p. 195.
193. Pejanovic, op. cit., p. 88.
194. Anic, loc. cit., p. 31.
195. Stevo Gajic, 'Inzinjera', *Oruzane Snage*, p. 330.
196. Aleksandar Sekulic, 'Veza', *Ibid.*, pp. 351–3.
197. Hajro Kulenovic, 'Sanitetska Sluzba', *Ibid.*, pp. 506–7.
198. *Ibid.*, p. 508.
199. Svjatopolk Urbancic, 'Gradjevinska Sluzba', *Oruzane Snage*, p. 535.
200. Milan Perunovic, 'Intendantska Sluzba', *Ibid.*, p. 479.
201. *Ibid.*, p. 479.
202. Pejanovic, pp. 31–4.
203. Kovacevic, loc. cit., p. 70–1.
204. Pejanovic, op. cit., p. 47.
205. Predrag Pejcic, 'Ratno Vazduhplovststvo i Protivazdusna Odbrana', *Oruzane Snage.*, p. 365.
206. Nikolovski, loc. cit., p. 132.
207. *Ibid.*, p. 133.
208. Pejanovic, op. cit., p. 138.
209. Dusan Pekic, 'Neki Aspekti Daljeg Razvoja Oruzanih Snaga', *Oruzane Snage*, p. 457; see also Pejanovic, pp. 94–107.
210. Nikolic, op. cit., p. 143.
211. See John Erickson and T. N. Wolfe, 'Introduction' in Erickson and Wolfe, (eds): *The Armed Services and Society: Alienation, Management and Integration*, Edinburgh U.P., Edinburgh, 1970.
212. See Ibrahimpsic, op. cit., pp. 192–219, *passim.*
213. See Jozo Tomasevitch, 'Yugoslavia During the Second World War' in Wayne S. Vucinich, (eds): *Contemporary Yugoslavia: Twenty Years of Socialist Experiment*, California U.P., California, 1969.
214. *Mladost*, 11 October 1973.
215. Nikolic, op. cit., pp. 141–4.
216. PIC/276, *National Liberation Movement of Yugoslavia*, Public Records Office, Political Intelligence Command Middle East, June 1944, p. 29.
217. Prelevic, op. cit., p. 148 and 'Neki podaci o oruzanim godina formacija NOR-a', *Zbornik Radova*, No. 3, Politicna Skola JNA, Belgrade, 1970, p. 123.
218. PIC/276, p. 29.
219. For example, Jankovic, op. cit., pp. 68–9.
220. Ibrahimpsic, op. cit., pp. 147 and 198–222.

221. Prelevic, op. cit., p. 169 ff.
222. *Ibid.*, p. 144.
223. This point was made by Major General Joze Ozbolt in an interview with *Tribuna*, 19 December 1973.
224. The Croat figure includes Muslims in Bosnia and Hercegovina.
225. PIC/276, p. 24.
226. Nikolic, op. cit., p. 143; these figures appear to be for 1972.
227. Zdenko Antic, 'National Structure of the Yugoslav Army Leadership', *RFE*, 12 April 1972.
228. *Ibid.*
229. Bogdan Denitch, *The Legitimation of a Revolution: The Yugoslav Case*, Yale U.P., New Haven and London, pp. 113–20.
230. A. Ross Johnson, 'The Role of the Military in Yugoslavia: An Historical Sketch' in R. Kolkowicz and A. Korbonski, (eds): *Soldiers, Peasants and Bureaucrats: Civil–Military Relations in Communist and Modernizing Systems*, Allen & Unwin, London, 1982, p. 198.
231. *Mladina*, 31 July 1973.
232. See the interview with Major General Joze Ozbolt, loc. cit., that with Colonel Alojz Hren, *Mladina*, 31 July 1973, *Delo*, 24 November 1973 and the articles in *Mladina*, by Boris Lenic (11 December 1983) and Dusan Gacnik (18 December 1973) on the difficulties faced in recruiting Slovenes.
233. *Illustrovana Politika*, 6 April 1982.
234. Pejanovic, op. cit., p. 54.
235. On Rankovic, see Dennison Rusinow, *The Yugoslav Experiment 1948–1974*, Hurst, London, 1977, pp. 184–91.
236. A. Ross Johnson, *The Transformation of Communist Ideology*, MIT Press, Cambridge, Mass., 1972, pp. 33–4.
237. A. Ross Johnson, 'The Role of the Military in Communist Yugoslavia: An Historical Sketch', *RAND*, P 6070, 1978, p. 5.
238. In the Huntingdonian sense of expertise, responsibility and corporateness. S. P. Huntingdon, *The Soldier and the State*, Cambridge, Mass., 1957, pp. 11–18.
239. A. Ross Johnson, *RAND*, P 6070, p. 6.
240. R. W. Dean, 'Civil–Military Relations in Yugoslavia, 1971–75', *Armed Forces and Society*, Vol. 3, No. 1, November 1979, p. 24.
241. A. Ross Johnson, *RAND*, P 6070, p. 10.
242. The Officer Corps was traditionally Serb dominated. Only in the High Command was there proportionality. See Denitch, op. cit., p. 114.
243. In 1971, 54 per cent of officers thought 'nationalism and chauvinism' the greatest single present danger to Yugoslavia. See Johnson, *RAND*, P 6070, p. 11 ff.
244. A. Ross Johnson, *Yugoslavia in the Twilight of Tito*, Washington Paper No. 16, Sage, Beverly Hills and London, discusses 'opening to society', pp. 13–14.
245. On All-People's Defence, see Dennison I. Rusinow, 'The Yugoslav Concept of "All-National Defence"', *American Universities Fieldstaffs Reports, South Eastern Europe Series*, Vol. XIX, No. 1, 1971; A. Ross

Johnson, 'Total National Defence in Yugoslavia' *RAND*, P 4746, Santa Monica, 1971; Adam Roberts, op. cit., Chapters 5 and 6.

246. Ross Johnson, 'Twilight', p. 19.

247. Paul Lendvai, *Eagles in Cobwebs: Nationalism and Communism in the Balkans*, Macdonald, London, 1970, pp. 131–3 and 166.

248. Robin Alison Remington, 'Armed Forces and Society in Yugoslavia' in Catherine McArdle Kelleher, (ed.): *Political-Military Systems: A Comparative Perspective*, Sage, Beverly Hills and London, 1974, p. 176.

249. *Ibid.*, p. 177.

250. *Ibid.*, p. 176.

251. Rusinow, 'Crisis in Croatia: Part IV', American Universities Field-staffs Reports, *South Eastern Europe Series*, Vol. XIX, Nos. 4–7, 1971, p. 1.

252. Stoyan Pribichevich, 'Tito at 80: An Uncomplicated Marxist', *New York Times*, 25 May 1972. Rusinow refers to this piece in 'Crisis in Croatia: Part IV', p. 11.

253. Remington, loc. cit., p. 184.

254. Johnson, 'The Role of the Military', p. 14.

255. Remington, loc. cit., pp. 45–6. On the YPA's constitutional position, see Jim Seroka and Radoslav Smilijkovic, *Political Organs in Socialist Yugoslavia*, Duke U.P., Durham, 1986, pp. 55–6 and 60.

256. See A. Ross Johnson, 'The Role of the Military', 1982, pp. 183–6.

257. Dean, loc. cit., p. 48.

258. Tito, cited by Johnson, 'The Role of the Military', 1982, p. 189.

259. Johnson, 'The Role of the Military', 1978, p. 46.

260. *Ibid.*

261. The YPA was not, I believe, coopted in preparation for the succession to Tito as has been suggested – although this was a contingency. See S. K. Pavlowitch, 'The Grey Area on NATO's Balkan flank', *Survey*, Vol. 25, No. 3, 1978, p. 74.

262. Dean, loc. cit., p. 29.

263. The military in fact kept a low profile on non-defence issues.

264. Dean, loc. cit., p. 30.

265. *Ibid.*, p. 50.

3: The Multiple Crises of the 1980s

1. See Dennison Rusinow, 'Nationalities Policy and the "National Question"' in Pedro Ramet, (ed.): *Yugoslavia in the 1980s*, Boulder, 1985.

2. Rusinow, 'Yugoslavia' in Martin McCauley and Stephen Carter, (eds): *Leadership and Succession in the Soviet Union, Eastern Europe and China*, Macmillan, London, 1986.

3. Paul Shoup, 'Crisis and Reform in Yugoslavia', *Telos*, No. 79, Spring 1989, p. 132.

4. Chris Martin and Laura D'Andrea Tyson, 'Can Titoism Survive Tito?

Economic Problems and Policy Choices Confronting Tito's Successors' in Ramet, (ed.), op. cit., p. 189.

5. *Ibid.*

6. EIU, *Yugoslavia*, No. 1, 1989, p. 4.

7. *Ibid.*, pp. 9–10 and No. 4, 1988, pp. 9–10.

8. Shoup, loc. cit., p. 133.

9. Martin and D'Andrea Tyson, loc. cit., p. 192.

10. *Ibid.*, p. 191.

11. EIU, *Yugoslavia*, No. 1, 1987, pp. 3–5.

12. Shoup, loc. cit., p. 133.

13. Stevan K. Pavlowitch, *The Improbable Survivor: Yugoslavia and its Problems 1918–1988*, Hurst, London, 1988, p. 143.

14. Shoup, loc. cit., p. 133.

15. EIU, *Yugoslavia*, No. 4, 1988, pp. 9–10.

16. Pavlowitch, op. cit., p. 145.

17. *Delo*, 31 December 1988.

18. *Danas*, 24 January 1989.

19. Shoup, loc. cit., p. 134.

20. Sharon Zukin, 'Self-management and Socialisation', Ramet, (ed.), op. cit., p. 94.

21. George Schopflin, 'Political Decay in One-Party Systems in Eastern Europe: Yugoslav Patterns', ibid., p. 317.

22. *NIN*, 10 and 17 April 1983.

23. Slobodan Stankovic, 'Poll Claims Yugoslavs Are Losing Confidence in Communism', *RFE*, 30 June 1986.

24. Slobodan Stankovic, 'The Kosovo Unrest – The Causes and the Consequences', *RFE*, 7 April 1981. For a chronological record of events, see Patrick Moore, 'The Kosovo Events in Perspective', *RFE*, 28 April 1981.

25. Elez Biberaj, 'The Conflict in Kosovo', *Survey*, Vol. 28, No. 3, 1984, p. 50, cites various death totals.

26. Zdenko Antic, 'Long Prison Terms for Albanian Nationalists in Kosovo', *RFE*, 14 August 1981.

27. Biberaj, loc. cit., p. 54.

28. Cited *Ibid.*, p. 51.

29. Pedro Ramet, *Nationalism and Federalism in Yugoslavia 1963–1983*, Indiana U.P., Bloomington, 1984, pp. 162–3.

30. *Ibid.*, p. 157.

31. Biberaj, loc. cit., pp. 43–5.

32. Moore, loc. cit., cites Bernhard Tonnes, *Sonderfall Albanien*, Oldenbourg, Munich, 1980, pp. 47–52, on this.

33. Francesco Altimari et al., *Albanci*, Cankarjeva Zalozba, Ljubljana, 1984, which is a fairly balanced collection. See also Alex N. Dragnich and Slavko Todorovic, (eds): *The Saga of Kosovo: Focus on Serbian Albanian Relations*, East European Monographs, Boulder, 1984; Ranko Petkovic, *Kosovo: Proslost i Sadasnjost*, Medunarodna Politika, 1989; Vuksan Cerovic, *Kosovo: Kontrarevolucija Koja Tece*, Nova Kniga, Belgrade, 1989, for increasingly pro-Serb (and therefore propagandist) versions; Arshi Pipa and Sami Rapitshti, (eds): *Studies on Kosova*, East European Monographs, Boulder,

1984, is a collection generally more sympathetic to the Kosovo Albanians.

34. Bojan Koriska, (ed.): *Srbija i Albanci: Pregled Politike Srbije Prema Albancima od. 1878 du 1914 Godine*, Book 1, Casopis za Kriticno Znanosti, Ljubljana, 1989.

35. Biberaj, loc. cit., p. 40.

36. Bojan Koriska, (ed.): *Srbija i Albanci: Pregled Politike Srbije Prema Albancima od. 1913 do 1945 Godine*, Casopis za Kriticno Znanosti, Ljubljana, 1989, p. 58.

37. *Ibid.*, pp. 35–65, *passim.*, Biberaj, loc. cit., p. 40.

38. *Ibid.*, p. 41.

39. Shklezen Maligi, 'Kosovo Kao Katalizator Jugoslovenske Krize' in Slavko Graber and Toncni Kuzmanic, (eds): *Kosovo – Srbija – Jugoslavija*, Knjiznica Revolucionarne Teorije, Ljubljana, 1989, p. 72, states that 60,000 Albanians were tortured by UDBa.

40. Biberaj, loc. cit., pp. 40–1.

41. *Ibid.*, p. 41.

42. *Ibid.*, p. 48.

43. Branko Horvat, *Kosovsko Pitanje*, Globus, Zagreb, 1988, p. 100.

44. Ramet, op. cit., pp. 161–2.

45. Zdenko Antic, 'Kosovo Riots Stir Sharp Polemics Over Information Policy', *RFE*, 23 April 1981.

46. Horvat, op. cit., p. 100.

47. Stankovic, 'The Kosovo Unrest'.

48. Branko Horvat, op. cit., p. 98.

49. Zdenko Antic, 'Kosovo's Socio-Economic Development', *RFE*, 23 April 1981.

50. *Ibid.*

51. Zdenko Antic, 'Exodus of Serbs from Kosovo', *RFE*, 18 May 1981.

52. Hivzi Islami, 'Demografiski Problemi Kosova i Njihovo Tumacenje' in Graber and Kuzmanic, (eds), op. cit., p. 52 and Horvat, op. cit., p. 98.

53. Horvat, op. cit., pp. 98–9.

54. *Gesellschaft fur bedrohte Volker*, Gottingen, cited by Islami, loc. cit., pp. 55–7.

55. Horvat, op. cit., p. 99.

56. Boris Koriska (ed.): *Srbija i Albanci: Pregled Politike Srbije Prema Albancima od 1944 do 1989 Godine*, Book 3, p. 76.

57. Biberaj, loc. cit., p. 46.

58. Horvat, op. cit., p. 99.

59. *Le Monde*, 6 April 1981

60. *Illustrovana Politika*, 6 April 1982.

61. *Ibid.*; Slobodan Stankovic, 'Yugoslav Central Committee Discusses Kosova, Party Problems', *RFE*, 24 November 1981.

62. *Vjesnik*, 19 September 1981.

63. See Ramet, op. cit., p. 166; Slobodan Stankovic, 'Kosovo Party Leader Replaced, *RFE*, 11 May 1981, and 'A Rising Kosovo Leader Tries to Combat Albanian Nationalism', *RFE*, 30 July 1981.

64. *NIN*, 6 August 1981.

65. See Rusinow, 'Nationalities Policy'.

66. Pavlowitch, op. cit., p. 145–6; see also *NIN*, 9 October 1988.
67. *NIN*, 9 November 1986.
68. See Shoup, loc. cit.
69. See Rusinow, 'Nationalities Policy', pp. 148–52.
70. See Steve Reiquam, 'Is Slovenian Nationalism on the Rise?', *RFE*, 9 August 1983.
71. Pavlowitch, op. cit., p. 146.
72. See Shoup, loc. cit., Milan Nikolic, 'Yugoslavia's Failed Perestroika', *Telos*, No. 79, Spring 1989, pp. 127–8; or almost any copy of *Mladina* in 1988 and 1989.
73. See Rusinow, 'Nationalities Policy', p. 141 ff.
74. Schopflin, 'Political Decay', p. 317.
75. *Ibid.*, p. 313.
76. This interpretation is borrowed from an international investment banker involved in handling Yugoslavia's debt.
77. See Shoup, loc. cit.
78. Taras Kermauner cited in Slobodan Stankovic, 'Yugoslav Military Leaders Warn against Disunity', *RFE*, 25 November 1983.
79. See Slobodan Stankovic, 'Controversy Surrounding the Yugoslav Army', *RFE*, April 1984.
80. Milovan Djilas, an article in *The Wall Street Journal (Europe)*, 22 August 1985.
81. Pero Car, *Delo*, 13 January 1984, translated in *FBIS-EEU*, 18 January 1984.
82. Mamula, *Politika*, 22 December 1983.
83. Cited by Remington, 'Armed Forces and Society in Yugoslavia' in Catherine McArdle Kelleher, (ed.): *Political-Military Systems: Comparative Perspectives*, Sage, Beverly Hills and London, 1974, p. 177.
84. Colonel-General Milan Daljevic, Assistant Secretary for Defence and Chair of the Co-ordinating Committee for All-People's Defence, *Narodna Armija*, 3 July 1986.
85. Cited in A. Ross Johnson, 'The Role of the Military in Yugoslavia' in R. Kolkowicz and A. Korbonski, (eds): *Soldiers, Peasants and Bureaucrats: Civil–Military Relations in Communist and Modernizing Systems*, Allen & Unwin, London, 1982, p. 189.
86. See K. Krishna Moorthy, *After Tito, What?*, Humanities Press, Atlantic Highlands N.J., 1980, pp. 53–4 and Robin Alison Remington, 'Political–Military Relations in Post-Tito Yugoslavia' in Ramet, (ed.), op. cit., pp. 67–8.
87. Tito is alleged to have denied such a role for the army in an interview with James Reston on 4 March 1978. See Gary K. Bertsch, 'Yugoslavia: The Eleventh Congress, The Constitution and the Succession', *Government and Opposition*, Vol. 14, No. 1, 1979, p. 107.
88. Daljevic, *Narodna Armija*, 28 April 1983, translated in *FBIS-EEU*, 11 May 1983. See also, Col.-Gen. Metodija Stefanovski's invocation of Tito's views, *Borba*, 18 December 1985.
89. Mamula, *Politika*, 22 December 1983.
90. Col.-Gen Georgije Jovicic, President of the Committee of the party-army organization, *NIN*, 27 April 1986.

NOTES 173

91. This feature was evident at an early stage. The Partisans' 'outlook on the nationalities question leads them to regard the movement as Yugoslav in character' was one war-time report. PIC/276 *National Liberation Movement of Yugoslavia*, PICME, June 1944, p. 25.

92. Mamula, *Narodna Armija*, 3 July 1986.

93. On the transition from a war-time to a post-war officer cadre, see the 'Koj je nas oficir?' pieces in *NIN*, 7 and 14 March 1976.

94. Mamula, *Politika*, 22 December 1983.

95. Col.-Gen. Dane Cuic, *Narodna Armija*, 22 December 1983, translated in *FBIS-EEU*, 4 January 1984.

96. Joze Smole's speech to Slovene SAWP Conference, Tanjug, 1735 GMT, 20 January 1987, *SWB*, 22 January 1987 was 'civil'; Jovicic, *Narodna Armija*, 19 June 1986 was military.

97. Mamula, *Narodna Armija*, 28 July 1983, translated in *FBIS-EEU*, 5 August 1983.

98. *Politika*, 29 June 1986.

99. Tanjug Domestic Service, 1421 GMT, 21 December 1983, translated in *FBIS-EEU*, 28 December 1983.

100. Daljevic, *Borba*, 22 April 1986.

101. *Politika*, 29 June 1986.

102. Daljevic, *Narodna Armija*, 28 April 1983, translated in *FBIS-EEU*, 11 May 1983.

103. The entry of former Secretary of Defence Nikola Ljubicic into first the Presidency of the Serb Republic and later the Federal State Presidency may be seen as an extension of the military's role into state bodies; its constitutional role was within the LCY. With no official representation in state organs, it is feasible that an army constituency was being built within them. If such a development occurred, it was probably not intended to be so initially. Ljubicic's swift move from the Ministry of Defence to the Serbian Presidency seemed to be one designed to ensure stability and reliability in the Serb leadership in the wake of Kosovo and the Serb 'nationalist' backlash.

104. Maj.-Gen. Svetozar Oro, *Narodna Armija*, 28 April 1983, translated in *FBIS-EEU*, 11 May 1983.

105. Stefanovski, *Kommunist*, 8 March 1985.

106. See, for example, Mamula's speech on the Economic Stabilization Programme at the 19th session of the LCY CC in *Narodna Armija*, 28 July 1983, translated in *FBIS-EEU*, 5 August 1983.

107. Mamula, *Narodna Armija*, 14 April 1983, translated in *FBIS-EEU*, 6 May 1983.

108. Cuic, *Narodna Armija*, 22 December 1983, translated in *FBIS-EEU*, 4 January 1984.

109. Slobodan Stankovic, 'Yugoslav Military: Leaders Warn Against Disunity', *RFE*, 25 November 1983.

110. Mamula, *Narodna Armija*, 28 July 1983, translated in *FBIS-EEU*, 5 August 1983. See also Daljevic, *Narodna Armija*, 31 March 1983, translated in *FBIS-EEU*, 11 April 1983.

111. Schopflin, loc. cit., p. 312.

112. See Mamula in *Narodna Armija*, 14 April 1983, translated in *FBIS-EEU*, 6 May 1983.
113. *Politika*, 19 December 1985.
114. Jovicic, *Narodna Armija*, 24 April 1986.
115. See Slobodan Stankovic, 'The Yugoslav Army adopts a wait-and-see attitude', *RFE*, 21 January 1986 on the importance of 'Yugoslavism' to the YPA. It is worth noting that 10 per cent of delegates to the 8th LCY-YPA organization conference were declared Yugoslavs, whereas only 5.4 per cent of the whole population were thus designated.
116. Bogdan D. Denitch, *The Legitimation of a Revolution: The Yugoslav Case*. Yale U.P., New Haven and London, 1976, p. 114.
117. *Cf.* Johnson, 'The Role of the Military' in R. Kolkowicz and A. Korbonski, (eds), op. cit., p. 198; Denitch, op. cit., p. 114; Drago Chas Sporer, 'Politics and Nationalism within the Yugoslav People's Army', *Journal of Croatian Studies*, Vol. XX, 1979, p. 127; and the figures for delegates to the LCY organization in the YPA conference (in percentages): 42.63 Serbs; 14.21 Croats; 10 Yugoslavs; 9.45 Montenegrins; 6.4 Slovenes; 6.31 Macedonians; 5.6 Muslims, 3.15 Albanians; 1.05 Hungarians; and 1.05 'others'; *Borba*, 22 April 1986. There was general agreement that 60–70 per cent of the officer corps were Serb or Montenegrin.
118. *Politika*, 23 April 1986.
119. *Narodna Armija*, 25 September 1986.
120. *Narodna Armija*, 14 April 1983, translated in *FBIS-EEU*, 6 May 1983.
121. Slobodan Stankovic, 'Controversy Surrounding Yugoslav Army', *RFE*, 26 April 1984.
122. Tanjug Domestic Service, 1741 GMT, 12 February 1987, translated in *SWB*, 17 February 1987.
123. *Ibid*.
124. Slobodan Stankovic, 'A Youth Paper Criticises the Army', *RFE*, 28 March 1985.
125. *Mladina*, 19 April 1984.
126. Slobodan Stankovic, 'Yugoslavia would resist any foreign aggressor', *RFE*, 16 May 1986. See also *Mladina*, 21 February, 7 and 14 March 1985.
127. Stankovic, 'Controversy Surrounds the Yugoslav Army', *RFE*, 26 April 1984.
128. Remington, loc. cit., note 44.
129. Col.-Gen. Dane Petkovski, cited by Slobodan Stankovic, '*The End of the Tito Era: Yugoslavia's Dilemmas*, Hoover Institute Press, Stanford, 1981, p. 47.
130. For example, Daljevic, *Narodna Armija*, 1 January 1987.
131. *Cf.* Tanjug 1643 GMT, 16 January 1987, translated by *SWB*, 19 January 1987 in which it is reported that there are 'no obstacles' to the posting of notices in Slovene.
132. *Narodna Armija*, 5 March 1987.
133. Capitulation is forbidden under Article 238 of the Socialist Federal Republic of Yugoslavia, *Constitution*, Belgrade, 1974. See also, Stankovic, op. cit., pp. 36–7.
134. Milan Kucan, *Danas*, 20 January 1987; Franc Setinj, Tanjug 1113 GMT,

13 February 1987, *SWB*, 18 February 1987.
135. *Narodna Armija*, 30 November 1986.
136. Daljevic, *Narodna Armija*, 1 January 1987.
137. *Ibid*.
138. *Narodna Armija*, 8 January 1987.
139. Daljevic, *Narodna Armija*, 1 January 1987; see also *Danas*, 13 January 1987 for the essentials of Daljevic's view.
140. Daljevic, *Narodna Armija*, 1 January 1987.
141. *Danas*, 20 January 1987.
142. Changes to the law on military service enabled conscripts who refused to carry arms on the grounds of religious belief to perform two years (rather than the usual 12 months) unarmed service instead. While this was short of complete excusing from conscription, it completely broke with the basic principles outlined by Daljevic. *Borba*, 24 March 1989.
143. *Mladina*, 20 and 27 May 1988.
144. See, for example, the editorial by the 'Counter-revolutionary Editorial Board', *Mladina*, 18 March 1988; also, the article that opened up the issues of a possible military occupation of Slovenia and the complicity of Slovene leaders in this at a secret LCY CC meeting – 'Night of the Long Knives: The Dangerous Games of the Secret State', *Mladina*, 20 May 1988.
    A review and source book for the Slovene-military discord is Igor Z. Zagar and Peter Tancig, (eds): *Kontekst ljubljanskega procesa, Kolovij pravnikov o procesu zoper cetverico, Racunaliska analiza 'napadov na JLA'*, Casopis za Kriticno Znanosti, Ljubljana, 1989.
145. *Politika*, 11 April 1988; *Narodna Armija*, 21 April 1988.
146. At a meeting in Belgrade, Robert Botteri is reported to have claimed that, in the previous year, of a total of 5,000 articles published in *Mladina*, only 36 dealt with the army. *SWB*, 9 June 1988.
147. For a review of its disputes on the YPA, see *Mladina*, 22 April 1988.
148. James Gow, 'Legitimacy and the Military: Yugoslav Civil–Military Relations and Some Implications for Defence', pp. 79–81, in M. Milivojevic et al., (eds): *Yugoslavia's Security Dilemmas: Armed Forces, National Defence and Foreign Policy*, Berg, Oxford, 1988.
149. *Mladina*, 19 February 1989.
150. *Mladina*, 4, 11, 18 and 25 March 1988.
151. *Narodna Armija*, 10 March 1988. This gave rise to a joke 'report' in *Mladina* when General Veljko Kadjevic succeeded Mamula in May. In it, Kadjevic is asked if he, too, will build a villa; he replies that there is no need – he has one already. *Mladina*, 20 May 1988.
152. Mamula continued with some activities – including writing a book published at the year's end. *Odbrana Malih Zemalja*, Vojnoizdavacki Centar, Belgrade, 1988. *Narodna Armija*, 24 November 1988.
153. *Teleks*, 18 February 1988.
154. *RFE*, 2 May 1988, reported that Tone Persek, a member of the Slovene Constitutional Commission, was alleged to have said this by Radio Belgrade.
155. *Politika*, 9 June 1988, referring to Jansa's candidacy, said that it should

not mean his being placed 'above the law'.
156. *SWB*, 30 June 1988.
157. It did so on 6 June 1988: *Mladina*, 21 October 1988.
158. *SWB*, 10 June 1988.
159. *SWB*, 30 June 1988.
160. For discussion of this article and the 'Jansa case', see *Nasi Razgledi*, 23 September 1988.
161. A statement by the Federation of Slovene Lawyers drew attention to this and other matters, *SWB*, 14 June 1988. See also the editorial in *Teleks*, 14 July 1988.
162. *The Guardian*, 28 July 1988.
163. *NIN*, 10 July 1988.
164. *Ibid*.
165. *Ibid*.
166. *Delo*, 8 June 1988. When the JBTZ sentences were given, the reason for Tasic's only having six months was because he had not done military service. Borstner was given four years because he was a serving soldier who should have recognized a secret; Jansa was given 18 months because he was an 'expert', and Zavrl because he had done military service and, therefore, should have had some knowledge. *SWB*, 29 July 1988.
167. *Mladina*, 21 October 1988; *Delo*, 20 July 1988.
168. *SWB*, 14 November 1988.
169. *Mladina*, 20 May 1988.
170. *Mladina*, 27 May 1988.
171. *Mladina*, 27 May 1988, published an open letter from various journalists and intellectuals, which included the demand for the official notes of the secret meeting of the CC LCY Presidency on 29 March. This was to establish whether the notes of a meeting held at this time, which had been passed to *Mladina*, were authentic.
172. This is clearly confirmed in a statement on the arrests by Tomaz Ertl, Republican Secretary for Internal Affairs, *SWB*, 22 June 1988. For the essential elements of the Kucan notes, see *Mladina*, 3 June 1988.
173. *SWB*, 1 July 1988.
174. *SWB*, 22 June 1988.
175. *SWB*, 22 June 1988; *Delo*, 20 July 1988.
176. *SWB*, 23 November 1988; *SWB*, 30 November 1988, reports a Radio Belgrade commentary on this.
177. The reports in *Il Giornale* and *La Repubblica* were referred to in *Mladina*, 13 and 20 October 1989.
178. *Delo*, 26 July 1988. For an extension of the constitutional points, see the open letters by Zavrl and Jansa in *Mladina*, 26 August 1988.
179. *Mladina*, 29 July and 5 August 1988.
180. *SWB*, 25 July 1988.
181. *SWB*, 27 July 1988.
182. *SWB*, 28 July 1988 – although in this instance the Article cited is not 21 but 3; the SFRY Presidency was asked to re-examine its conclusions, *Delo*, 26 July 1988.

183. *SWB*, 28 July 1988.
184. This view was expressed in a report of expert opinion by Mian Potrc, President of the Slovene Assembly, in the Assembly (ibid.).
185. See Article 240 of the SFRY Constitution.
186. *Delo*, 30, 31 March and 1 April 1989; *Mladina*, 7 and 21 April 1989.
187. *Delo*, 22 November 1988.
188. Kucan on RTV Ljubljana's 'Tednik', 28 July 1988; cited in *Mladina*, 21 October 1988. Sovereignty and the homogenization of Slovene politics were issues addressed at a second big rally in Ljubljana in November, *Teleks*, 24 November 1988. From a different viewpoint, the bringing together of the various elements in Slovene politics was recognized in a piece on the trial in *Narodna Armija*, 4 August 1988, in which the author complained that there was no difference between Borstner and the Slovene leadership.
189. *SWB*, 8 August 1988. Joze Smole made the linguistic-constitutional point by going against his usual practice and speaking in Slovene at a SAWPY session, *Delo*, 21 September 1988. Smole also complained about the holding of a SAWPY session on 22 July, the day of the Slovene uprising – therefore a Republican holiday – against the agreement on holding meetings on national days, *SWB*, 26 July 1988. It was later decided that the SAWP recommend that its delegates should use Slovene when appearing in federal bodies, *SWB*, 15 November 1988.
190. See, for example, *Nasa Obramba*, Nos. 3, 5 and 7, 1970, and Gow, loc. cit., p. 80.
191. It is commonly estimated that 60 or 70 per cent of junior officers are Serb and Montenegrin. For example, see A. Ross Johnson, 'The Role of the Military in Yugoslavia: An Historical Sketch' in R. Kolkowicz and A. Korbonski, (eds): *Soldiers, Peasants and Bureaucrats: Civil–Military Relations in Communist and Modernizing Systems*, Allen & Unwin, London, 1982, p. 198.
192. The *Daily Telegraph*, 29 July 1988, suggested that 'envy of Slovenia's superior economic performance' lay behind this.
193. On the development of Slovene nationalism as a 'new' phenomenon, see *RFE*, 9 August 1983.
194. Jansa wrote an article on the political reasons for his not going to prison, *Mladina*, 5 May 1989.
195. 'Socialism on a Human Scale' became Kucan's main theme, alongside the notion of the 'legal state'.
196. See *Mladina*, 13 January and 3 February 1989.
197. For comments by the then Prime Minister Mikulic, see *SWB*, 25 October 1988. For the amendment as finally agreed, see *Delo*, 2 November 1988.
198. *Delo*, 31 December 1988.
199. *FBIS*, 9 January 1989.
200. See Milan Andrejevich, 'General "Greatly Concerned" About Party Strife', *RFE*, 11 November 1988.
201. *Narodna Armija*, 17 November and 1 December 1988; see also Joze Smole's speech reported in *SWB*, 15 November 1988.
202. In saying this, we should note, however, the unsubstantiated and

unlikely claim that more interest had been shown in a military career among Slovenes during the previous year. *SWB*, 9 November 1988.

203. See Gow, loc. cit., pp. 82–94.
204. *Narodna Armija*, 5 February 1987.
205. Nikola Ljubicic, *Politika*, 31 December 1982, translated in *FBIS-EEU*, 14 January 1983.
206. See Stankovic, 'Yugoslavia would resist any foreign aggressor', *RFE*, 16 May 1986.
207. *Narodna Armija*, 5 April 1989.
208. *Narodna Armija*, 30 March 1989.
209. Ciril Ribicic and Zdravko Tomac, *Federalizam po Mjeri Buducnosti*, Globus, Zagreb, 1989.
210. This seems to me clearly to be the case, although it was never stated as such. It was certainly perceived to be the case in Serbia, where Slobodan Milosevic was able to manipulate Serbia's constitutional situation to mobilize mass support by arguing the need to make Serbia 'whole' again. See, for example, Milosevic, *Godine Raspleta*, BIGZ, Belgrade, 1989, pp. 187–278 *passim.*, esp., p. 264 ff.
211. On AVNOJ principles, see Janko Pleterski, 'Kaj je Avnojska Jugoslavia?', *Nasa Obramba*, October 1989.
212. See Biberaj, loc. cit.
213. See *The Times*, 3, 4, 6, 7, 28, 29, 30, 31 March and 1 April 1989 – the editorials on 3 and 30 March are especially worthy; Milan Andrejevich, 'Kosovo in Turmoil Again' and 'Yugoslavs React to the Situation in Kosovo as Arrests Begin', *RFE*, 8 March 1989; *idem.*, 'The Unrest in Kosovo Escalates', *RFE*, 15 April 1989; *Mladina*, 19 September 1989.
214. See Milan Andrejevich, 'The Army Stands Poised as Leaders Resign and Strikes Continue in Kosovo', *RFE*, 8 March 1989.
215. See David Goodlet, 'Serbian "Isolation" of Albanian Prisoners Criticized', *RFE*, 17 August 1989; and *Mladina*, 9 June 1989.
216. An article in *Mladina*, 1 September 1989, suggested that 'homogenization' had never really occurred.
217. *Teleks*, 6 July 1989; *Mladina*, 7 July 1989.
218. On the Belgrade press there is an interesting and curious piece in *Nova Hrvatska*, 14 March 1989. In it there was an apparently systematic substitution of the Slovene President's surname for that of the editor of the Croat nationalist emigre editor of that periodical – Kucan instead of Kusan was used, presumably with the intention of smearing the Slovene leader. See also the attack in *Politika*, 9 March 1989, on the generally respected Croat weekly *Danas*.
219. Michael Akehurst, *An Introduction to International Law*, Allen & Unwin, London, 1970.
220. Dimitrij Rupel, later to become President of the Social Democratic Alliance and President of the Slovene National Assembly after free elections in April 1990, in an interview; Milan Andrejevich, 'The Yugoslav Crisis and the National Question', *RFE*, 17 August 1989.
221. *Mladina*, 12 September 1989.
222. *Ibid.*; *Borba*, 28 September 1988.

223. Indeed, the situation recalls Ivan Cankar's *The Bailiff Yerney*, in which the greatest of Slovene writers created a metaphor for his country and his people under the Austro-Hungarian empire. This metaphor has relevance for 1989.

Bartholemew, the bailiff of the title, has faithfully served Old Sitar for 40 years, having built his master's house and worked every corner of his master's land. When Old Sitar dies, Young Sitar inherits and immediately stops Yerney from sitting by the corner of the fire in the house, as he always has. When Yerney laughs, thinking this and similar assertions by the brash new master cannot be serious, he is dismissed.

Bartholemew goes to Ljubljana in search of his rights, assuming that, having built the house and lived in it as his own for so long, he cannot be thrown out in this way. There, the courts treat him as a joke figure. He is sure that he has rights, having worked so long on the estate, and asks for justice. He is disappointed. So he goes to Vienna, convinced that there he will see the Emperor, who will dispense justice and affirm his rights. Instead, he is arrested as a vagrant, interrogated by men who do not speak to him in his own language (*plus ca change . . .* for German substitute Serbo-Croat), identified by his papers and sent back.

Broken and without his rights, Bartholemew returns to collect the pipe he left in the house. The book ends with Sitar's house, the one Yerney built, burning down. The former bailiff, standing with his fists on his hips, watching and laughing, is savaged by the villagers and thrown into the fire.

It is conceivable that the Slovenes' assertion of their rightful position in the Yugoslav house may be accommodated. If not, then like the partner in a marriage which has been on the rocks for years and subject to many efforts to save it, reluctantly the Slovenes may walk out. Like the bailiff in Cankar's novella in 1989 they did not want to leave the house, only to have their rights inside it recognized.

Should it come to a matter of secession, the outcome may be ominously prefigured in *The Bailiff Yerney*. After the secrets trial, Stanovnik described the Republic's disputing that matter as 'sticking one's hand in the fire'. To seek to secede may result in the Yugoslav house's burning down and the bailiff Kucan's Slovenia being thrown into the flames – along with the bailiff himself.

224. *Mladina*, 9 December 1988, carried a poll showing that 79 per cent believed a multi-party system necessary.

225. Shoup, loc. cit.

226. This view was expressed by a member of the Tito old guard, Franc Setinc, in an article in a Slovene military publication – a point, perhaps of some note. See *Nasa Obramba*, No. 10, October 1989.

227. *Delo*, 5 July 1989.

228. Brovet, cited in *Borba*, 4 and 5 February 1989.

229. For example, see *FBIS*, 8 December 1988.

230. According to Amendment XXXII, GDP would be organized throughout the whole Republic, that is, the Autonomous Provinces would be effectively left out; moreover, a key phrase declared that defence

would be organized 'in the interests of the Republic as a whole'. *Politika*, 7 January 1989.
231. The Ministry of Defence was responsible for a strongly worded document attacking the Slovene changes. The document, marked 'strictly confidential' was obtained and published by *Mladina*, 29 September 1989.
232. Slavoj Zizek, interviewed in *Delo*, 8 July 1989.
233. Kadijevic stated this in an otherwise reformist address to a session of the YPA-LCY Central Committee, *Komunist*, 14 July 1989.
234. Vice-Admiral Petar Simic, Head of the LC-YPA organization, *SWB*, 5 December 1989.
235. *Delo*, 23 October 1989.
236. Slavko Sorsak, *Splosna Ljudska Obramba in Zveza Komunistov Jugoslavije*, Komunist, Ljubljana, 1983, p. 186.
237. *Mladina*, 10 November 1989.
238. *Narodna Armija*, 6 July 1989.

4: Crisis and Military Legitimacy

1. Miller did so in a review of M. Milivojevic, et al., (eds): *Yugoslavia's Security Dilemmas: Armed Forces, National Defence and Foreign Policy*, Berg, Oxford, 1988 in *Soviet Studies*, Vol. XLI, No. 4, October 1989, p. 672.
2. *Mladina*, 23 December 1988.
3. *Delo*, 22 December 1988.
4. *Nova Hrvatska*, No. 1, January 1989.
5. *Narodna Armija*, 5 January 1989.
6. *Delo*, 7 January 1989
7. *Mladina*, 23 December 1988; Branko Soban, 'Zgolj Vojasko Ali Tudi Politicno Dejanje', *Delo*, 7 January 1989 (which was a useful guide in writing this section).
8. *Nova Hrvatska*, No. 2, January 1989.
9. *Delo*, 7 January 1989.
10. *Delo*, 22 December 1988.
11. Soban, loc. cit.
12. See *Mladina*, 23 December 1988.
13. Article 239.
14. Soban, loc. cit.
15. *Nova Hrvatska*, No. 2, January 1989.
16. Janez Jansa, 'Ozki pogledi, stavi vzori', *Mladina*, 13 January 1989.
17. Soban, loc. cit.
18. On the OF and its predecessor, see Metod Mikuz, *Pregled Zgodovine NOV v Sloveniji*, Vol. I, Cankarjeva Zalozba, Ljubljana, 1960. It is interesting to note that the OF's original programme of 22 June called for 'brotherhood and peace' between nations, not the Partisans more famous 'brotherhood and unity', quoted by Mikuz, p. 154.
19. Janez Jansa, 'Kaj Misli JLA o druzbi?', *Mladina*, 12 February 1988.
20. Adam Roberts, *Nations in Arms: The Theory and Practice of Territorial*

Defence, Chatto & Windus, London, 1976, p. 179.
21. Marko Milivojevic, 'The Yugoslav People's Army', *Armed Forces*, Vol. 6, No. 1, January 1987.
22. Soban, loc. cit.
23. *Nova Hrvatska*, No. 15, 24 July 1988.
24. *Mladina*, 12 February 1988.
25. *Delo*, 7 January 1989.
26. *Gorenjski Glas*, 16 December 1989.
27. The speech was published in full in a 32-page pull-out 'Aktuelni problemi obrane u odnosu na suvremena kretanja u svijetu i u nas – modernizacija koncepcije opcenarodne obrane' in *Narodna Armija*, 21 April 1988.
28. *Ibid.*, p. 22. Otherwise, Mamula had covered most of the same material previously: in a speech in Zagreb in February 1986 about his book, *Savremini Svijet i Nasa Odbrana*; *Narodna Armija*, 20 February 1986.
29. VIZ, Belgrade, 1985.
30. *Narodna Armija*, 29 October 1987.
31. Mamula, 'Aktuelni problemi', p. 23.
32. *Ibid.*
33. *Narodna Armija*, 20 February 1986.
34. *Ibid.*
35. *Ibid.*
36. *Narodna Armija*, 1 December 1988.
37. Adam Roberts, 'The Future of Militia Armies in the Face of Military Technological Developments' in Milivojevic et al., (eds), op. cit., p. 280.
38. Mamula, op. cit., p. 124.
39. *Ibid.*, p. 188.
40. *Ibid.*, p. 193.
41. *Ibid.*, p. 187.
42. Mamula, 'Aktuelni problemi', p. 24.
43. Soban, loc. cit.
44. Mamula, op. cit., p. 189.
45. Mamula, 'Aktuelni problemi', p. 24.
46. Soban, loc. cit.
47. Mamula, 'Aktuelni problemi', p. 22.
48. Soban, loc. cit.
49. *Nova Hrvatska*, No. 1, January 1989.
50. Soban, loc. cit.
51. Soban, loc. cit.
52. *Delo*, 7 January 1989.
53. Mamula, *Narodna Armija*, 14 April 1983, translated in *FBIS-EEU*, 6 May 1983.
54. Tanjug Domestic Service, 1447 GMT, 13 January 1983, translated in *FBIS-EEU*, 14 January 1983.
55. According to Jovicic the figure was 4.14 per cent and 4.6 per cent in 1985; *Narodna Armija*, 24 April 1986; a more recent figure for 1984 is lower at 3.5 per cent, *Borba*, 3 February 1987.
56. *Narodna Armija*, 22 December 1988.
57. Gavin Kennedy, 'Defence: Markets and Bureaucracy', *Economic Affairs*,

Vol. 10, No. 1, 1989, p. 7.
58. *Borba*, 3 February 1987.
59. Mamula, *Narodna Armija*, 14 April 1983, translated in *FBIS-EEU*, 6 May 1983.
60. Kadijevic gave this figure in an interview with *Narodna Armija*, 22 December 1988.
61. Kadijevic, presenting the 1988 defence budget, cited in *FBIS*, 29 November 1988.
62. Kadijevic in a speech to the SFRY Assembly, *Narodna Armija*, 1 December 1988.
63. *Mladina*, 26 August 1988
64. *Narodna Armija*, 15 December 1988.
65. Tanjug Domestic Service, 1447 GMT, 13 January 1983, translated in *FBIS-EEU*, 14 January 1983.
66. Mamula, *Narodna Armija*, 28 July 1983, translated in *FBIS-EEU*, 5 August 1983.
67. Gracanin, *Narodna Armija*, 11 July 1983, translated in *FBIS-EEU*, 11 March 1983, from Tanjug Domestic Service, 16.15 GMT, 9 March 1983.
68. Tanjug Domestic Service, 114 GMT, 26 January 1984, translated in *FBIS-EEU*, 27 January 1984.
69. *Borba*, 14 and 15 May 1983.
70. Mamula, *Politika*, 22 December 1983.
71. A further 70 firms worked in the defence industry, with yet another 1,000 making occasional contributions to the defence sector. *Nasa Obramba*, March 1989, p. 58.
72. Col.-Gen. Simeon Buncic, interviewed in *Student*, No. 27, 1984.
73. *Borba*, 23 April 1986.
74. Tanjug English Service, 2116 GMT, 18 May 1983, translated in *FBIS-EEU*, 23 May 1983.
75. *Borba*, 14 and 15 May 1983.
76. Mamula, *Politika*, 22 December 1983.
77. *Nasa Obramba*, March 1989, p. 58.
78. Mamula, Belgrade Domestic Service, 1700 GMT, 8 April 1983, translated in *FBIS-EEU*, 11 April 1983.
79. *Politika*, 22 December 1983.
80. See 'Contribution of the Yugoslav People's Army in the Development of the Country, 1980–1987' in *Yugoslav Survey*, No. 1, 1988.
81. See *Narodna Armija*, 7 September 1989, and *Front*, 20 October 1989.
82. *Narodna Armija*, 2 March 1989.
83. Mamula, *Narodna Armija*, 28 July 1983, translated in *FBIS-EEU*, 5 August 1983.
84. *Borba*, 3 February 1987.
85. *Narodna Armija*, 22 December 1988.
86. Mamula, *Narodna Armija*, 14 April 1983, translated in *FBIS-EEU*, 6 May 1983.
87. *Politika*, 22 December 1983.
88. Mamula, *Narodna Armija*, 1 May 1986.
89. See Stankovic, 'The Army to Hire Professional Soldiers', *RFE*, 22 April 1985.

NOTES 183

90. Gracanin, *Narodna Armija*, 10 March 1983, translated in *FBIS-EEU*, 5 April 1983.
91. The initial advertisements appeared in *Narodna Armija*, 29 January 1987 – although the law was changed on 13 February 1985. See the Daljevic interview in *Borba*, 27 and 28 April 1985.
92. Stankovic, 'Yugoslav Army Adopts a Wait-and-See Attitude', *RFE*, 21 January 1986.
93. Daljevic, *Borba*, 27 and 28 April 1985.
94. Stefanovski, *Narodna Armija*, 30 December 1982, translated in *FBIS-EEU*, 14 January 1983.
95. Mamula, *Politika*, 22 December 1983; Daljevic, *Borba*, 27 and 28 April 1985.
96. Mamula, *Narodna Armija*, 1 May 1986.
97. *Narodna Armija*, 12 February 1987.
98. *FBIS*, 14 March 1989.
99. Mamula, *Narodna Armija*, 28 July 1983, translated in *FBIS-EEU*, 5 August 1983.
100. *Nova Hrvatska*, No. 1, 1989.
101. Kadijevic, *Narodna Armija*, 22 December 1988.
102. Tone Gersak, 'Ali res dajemo armado namanj v Evropi in imamo najcenejsega vojska?', *Nasa Obramba*, January 1989, pp. 20–3.
103. *Narodna Armija*, 9 February 1989.
104. *Nasa Obramba*, February 1989, p. 26 ff. The army's knee-jerk response to things Slovene led to a perception of attacks even in *Nasa Obramba*. Gersak defended himself, saying he had lived in Serbia and Slovenia, favoured a modern SFRY, and, with regard to the YPA's *betes noires*: 'It is true that we live together in Ljubljana, however, I more or less do not know them, still less, they me.' He also asserted that the YPA was his army and that security was best achieved through societal and economic stability – something often said by YPA officers.
105. *Slovensko Javno Mnenje*, 1989.
106. *Mladina*, 16 March 1989.
107. *SJM*, 1989.
108. *Ibid.*
109. Vuk Obradovic, 'Nacionalizam i oruzane snage', *Vojno Delo*, No. 1, January–February 1989, pp. 503–23.
110. Dusan Zunic, 'Neki Aspekti Medjuljudskih Odnosa u Jugoslovenskoj Narodnoj Armij,' *Ibid.*, pp. 489–502.
111. *Narodna Armija*, 30 March 1988.
112. Cited in Ingrid Bakse, *Ne Cakaj Na Maj*, Republika Konferenca ZSMS, Ljubljana, 1989, p. 72.
113. Jansa outlined his idea of 'republican armies' in *Nova Revija*, No. 67, November–December 1987.
114. Obradovic, loc. cit., p. 507.
115. Quoted in *Borba*, 21 July 1988.
116. General Simion Buncic, in an interview with *Student*, No. 27, 1984.
117. Mamula, 'Aktuelni problemi', p. 29.
118. Patrick Desmond, 'A Soldier's Life', *The Independent*, (Magazine), 25 November 1989.

119. Sir John Winthrop-Hackett, *The Profession of Arms*, Macmillan, New York, 1983, p. 224.
120. Sir John Fortescue, *Historical and Military Essays*, Macmillan, London, 1928, p. 195.
121. John Keegan and Richard Holmes, *Soldiers: A Study of Men in Battle*, Hamish Hamilton, London, 1985, p. 52.
122. Anthony Verrier, *An Army for the Sixties: A Study in National Policy, Contract and Obligation*, Secker & Warburg, London, 1966, p. 57.
123. Keegan and Holmes, op. cit., pp. 52–3.
124. Russell F. Weighley, 'The Political and Strategic Dimensions of Military Effectiveness' in Allan R. Miller and Willaimson Murray, (eds): *Military Effectiveness*, Vol. III, Allen & Unwin, Boston, 1988, p. 346.
125. See F. M. Richardson, *Fighting Spirit: A Study of Psychological Factors in War*, Leo Cooper, London, 1978, pp. 14–22; see also Keegan and Holmes, op. cit., pp. 39–56.
126. Ivan Sylvain, 'Factors Affecting Morale' in Teresa Rakowska-Harmstone et al., *The Warsaw Pact; The Question of Cohesion, Phase II*, Vol. I, ORAE, Department of National Defense, Canada, 1984, p. 300.
127. Cynthia H. Enloe, *Ethnic Soldiers: State Security in a Divided System*, Penguin, Harmondsworth, 1980, p. 88 ff.
128. Rakowska-Harmstone, 'The Price of Cohesion and Performance Expectations', Rakowska-Harmstone et al., op. cit., p. 339.
129. *Borba*, 10 February 1989.
130. Cited in *Borba*, 21 July 1988.
131. Tanjug Domestic Service (Serbo-Croat) 17.33 GMT, 10 November 1988.
132. 24 December 1988.
133. See Janez Jansa, 'Kaj Misli'.
134. Gavro Perazic, *Ustavnopoliticki i Medjunarodni Status Odbrane i Oruzanih Snaga*, VIZ, Belgrade, 1976, p. 48.
135. Janez Jansa, 'Ozki Pogledi'.
136. *Slovensko Javno Mnenje*, 1988.
137. *Illustrovana Politika*, 6 April 1982.
138. Christopher D. Jones, 'Historical Precedents: Ethnic Units and the Soviet Armed Forces', Rakowska-Harmstone et al., op. cit., pp. 86–136.
139. Ellen Jones, *Red Army and Society: A Sociology of the Soviet Military*, Allen & Unwin, London, 1985, p. 185.
140. Christopher D. Jones, loc. cit., Rakowska-Harmstone et al., op. cit., p. 127.
141. Ellen Jones, op. cit., p. 187.
142. Christopher D. Jones, 'Warsaw Pact Exercises: The Genesis of a Greater Socialist Army', Rakowska-Harmstone et al., op. cit., pp. 259–60.
143. Obradovic, op. cit., p. 511.
144. *Narodna Armija*, 20 October 1988.
145. According to General Nebojsa Tica, ibid.
146. Obradovic, op. cit., p. 512.
147. Mirkovic, *Narodna Armija*, 20 October 1988.
148. Sylvain, op. cit., pp. 298–9.
149. Stephen D. Westbrook, 'Socio-political Alienation and Military

Efficiency', *Armed Forces and Society*, Vol. 6, No. 2, Winter 1980.
150. *Nasa Obramba*, No. 3, March 1989, p. 54.
151. General Sir Frank Kitson, *Directing Operations*, Faber & Faber, London, 1989, p. 72.
152. *Vjesnik*, 22 November 1987.
153. *Ibid.*
154. Quoted in *Illustrovana Politika*, 6 April 1982.
155. *Ibid.*
156. *Mladost*, 11 May 1987, translated in JPRS-EER, *Daily Report*, 17 July 1987.
157. *Vjesnik*, 22 November 1987.
158. *Slovensko Javno Mnenje*, 1988.
159. Westbrook, loc. cit., p. 185.
160. *Ibid.*
161. On 'recognition', see Tom Holm, 'Culture, Ceremonialism and Stress: American Indian Veterans and the Vietnam War', *Armed Forces and Society*, Vol. 12, No. 2, Winter 1986, pp. 237–51.
162. See *Teleks*, 22 September 1988.
163. From 646,000 in 1961, the total of Albanians (in Kosovo) became 916,000 in 1971 and 1,227,000 by 1981; Zdenko Antic, 'Exodus of Serbs from Kosovo', *RFE*, 18 May 1981.
164. John Allcock, 'Yugoslav Defence Preparedness in the Context of Yugoslav Society', in Milivojevic et al., (eds), op. cit., pp. 285–303.
165. He cites prominent work to support this: George W. Hoffman and Fred W. Neal, *Yugoslavia and the New Communism*, Twentieth Century Fund, New York, 1962; and Bogdan Denitch, *The Legitimation of a Revolution: The Yugoslav Case*, Yale U.P., New Haven, 1976.
166. Allcock, loc. cit., pp. 288–9.
167. Nikola Ljubicic, *Total National Defence – Strategy for Peace*, STP, Belgrade, 1977, p. 362; also pp. 265 and 297.
168. Reneo Lukic, 'La dissuasion populaire Yougoslave', *Cahiers d'Etudes Strategiques*, CIRPES, Paris, 1985.
169. A Yugoslav diplomat quoted by Dennison Rusinow, 'The Yugoslav Concept of All-National Defence', *AUFS Report, South-East Europe*, Vol. XIX, No. 1, November 1971, p. 6.
170. Figures given by Col.-Gen. Ivan Dolnicar in *Odbrana i Zastita*, July–August 1973.
171. See Allcock, loc. cit., p. 303.
172. Rusinow, loc. cit., p. 6.
173. Allcock, loc. cit., p. 297.
174. Allcock, loc. cit., p. 293.
175. Stevan Mirkovic, 'O mobilizaciji oruzanih snaga' *Vojno Delo*, No. 2, March–April 1989, p. 16; see also *Narodna Armija*, 15 December 1988 and Allcock, loc. cit., p. 295.
176. Robin Clarke, *London Under Attack: The Report of the Greater London Area War Risk Study Commission*, Basil Blackwell, Oxford, 1986, esp., pp. 7 and 345–59.
177. Mirkovic, loc. cit., p. 23.
178. *Slovensko Javno Mnenje*, 1988.

179. Mirkovic, loc. cit., p. 25.
180. *Mladina*, 10 March 1989.
181. Aleska Djilas, 'Tito and the Independence of Yugoslavia', *Review of the Study Centre for Yugoslav Affairs*, Vol. 2, No. 4, London, 1980, p. 397. See also Stevan K. Pavlowitch, 'The History Behind Jugoslavia's Psychological Deterrent', *Review of the Study Centre for Yugoslav Affairs*, Vol. 11, No. 2, London, 1975, p. 121. *Cf.* Jozo Tomasevich, *Peasant, Politics and Economic Change in Yugoslavia*, Stanford U.P., Stanford, 1955, p. 261.
182. On the creation of *cetnicka komanda*, see Jozo Tomasevich, *The Chetniks*, Stanford U.P., Stanford, 1975, p. 58.
183. *Ibid.*
184. The naval service has always been more predominantly Croat than has the land army been a Serb-Montenegrin preserve. *Cf.* Pavlowitch, loc. cit.
185. See Hoptner, op. cit., pp. 160–1.
186. See Jozo Tomasevich, 'Yugoslavia During the War' in Wayne S. Vucinich, (ed.): *Contemporary Yugoslavia: Twenty Years of Socialist Experiment*, Columbia U.P., London, 1969, p. 90.
187. Mamula, *Narodna Armija*, 12 March 1987.
188. *Komunist*, 20 February 1987.

5: The Disintegrative Country and Relegitimation

1. David Easton, *A Systems Analysis of Political Life*, esp., p. 171 ff where he discusses the idea of political community: his definition (political community is the 'aspect of a political system that consists of its members seen as a group of persons bound together by political division of labour . . . [it is found when a] group of members . . . participate in a common structure and set of processes.' p. 177) is borrowed here.
2. *Delo*, 2 February 1990.
3. *Delo*, 5 February 1990.
4. *Delo*, April, 21 November, 12, 13 and 18 December 1990; *Vjesnik, Vecernje List, Novi List*, 31 May 1990; *RFE*, 'Election Update', 7 December 1990; *EEN*, 30 April 1990.
5. *SWB*, 19 October 1990.
6. It was described as a 'Bolshevik oriented and coloured . . . broader version of the Constitution of Serbia', *SWB*, 23 October 1990.
7. *Delo*, 3 October 1990.
8. See *East European Newsletter*, 8 October 1990 and Milan Andrejevich, 'Crisis in Croatia and Slovenia', *RFE*, 2 November 1990; *SWB*, 13 October 1990.
9. *Borba*, 8 October 1990.
10. *Delo*, 22 September 1990.
11. Both cited by Andrejevich, loc. cit.
12. *SWB*, 12 October 1990.
13. Milica Zarkovic Bookman, 'The Economic Basis of Regional Autarchy in

Yugoslavia', *Soviet Studies*, Vol. 42, No. 1, January 1990, pp. 93–109.
14. *Ibid.*, p. 100.
15. *Mladina*, 8 December 1989.
16. *Ibid.*
17. See Ivo Goldstein, 'Serbs in Croatia, Croatia in Yugoslavia', *East European Reporter*, Vol. 4, No. 3, 1990; see also *Delo*, 3 October 1990, *The Times*, 5 September, 1 and 4 October 1990 and the *Daily Telegraph*, 1 and 4 October 1990.
18. See *EEN*, 11 July 1990.
19. *Delo*, 3 February 1990.
20. *Delo*, 30 and 31 January 1990.
21. Milan Andrejevich, 'Azem Vllasi's Acquital: A Sign of Major Changes Ahead for Kosovo', *RFE*, 11 May 1990.
22. Nezvat Haljili, leader of the Party for Democratic Prosperity, quoted by Milan Andrejevic, 'Macedonia on the Eve of the Elections', *RFE*, 30 November 1990.
23. *Delo*, 12 December 1990.
24. Milan Andrejevich, 'Serbia Accused of Interfering in Bosnian Affairs', *RFE*, 23 October 1989.
25. *EEN*, 23 July and 10 September 1990.
26. Milan Andrejevich, 'Crisis'.
27. James Madison, No. X, in James Madison, Alexander Hamilton and John Jay, *The Federalist Papers*, Penguin, Harmondsworth, 1987, pp. 122–8.
28. Of particular saliency was the Croatian interior ministry's reorganization of the police force, including the closure of local police stations in Serb-populated territories and new recruitment, creating the belief that the Serbs would be subject to more centralized Croat control; Goldstein, loc. cit., pp. 65–6.
29. The two versions of civil-society çan be explored in John Keane, *Democracy and Civil Society*, Verso, London, 1988.
30. Hugh Poulton with Minnesota Lawyers International Human Rights Committee, *Minorities in the Balkans*, Minority Rights Group, Report No. 82, London, 1989, pp. 26–7, describes the situation in Macedonia; however, the Macedonians were not unique.
31. *RFE*, 20 April 1990.
32. Milan Andrejevich, 'The Government's Economic Reform Programme', *RFE*, 9 February 1990.
33. For the following section, see EIU *Yugoslavia*, No. 3, 1990, p. 16.
34. *EEN*, 5 March 1990.
35. *Delo*, 3 February 1990; in 1988, this role was taken by the then LCY Secretary, Stipe Suvar.
36. *EEN*, 17 December 1990.
37. See the 'Survey of Yugoslav Trade and Industry' supplement in the *Financial Times*, 17 December 1990.
38. EIU, op. cit., pp. 15–17.
39. *Ibid.*, p. 18.
40. *Ibid.*, p. 12.
41. Markovic recognized this, but said that the 'process of democratization

takes time', 'Survey of Yugoslav Trade'.
42. Andrejevich, 'Macedonia' highlights the common support of the Macedonian parties for the Markovic reforms. *EEN*, 23 July 1990, gives an account of Serbia's economic sabotage of Markovic's programme.
43. Bozidar Martinovic, Managing Director of Jugometal, quoted in *Business* (Belgrade), 17–23 November 1990.
44. EIU, op. cit., p. 5.

6: The Delegitimating Army and Relegitimation

1. *Narodna Armija*, 4 October 1990.
2. *Delo*, 5 December 1990.
3. *Danas*, 16 October 1990.
4. *Neodvisni Dnevnik*, 8 December 1990.
5. According to Milan Kucan, quoted in *SWB*, 3 October 1990.
6. These events are covered in Andrejevic, 'Crisis in Croatia and Slovenia: Proposal for a Confederal Yugoslavia', *RFE*, 2 November 1990.
7. *Mladina*, 4 December 1990, gave extensive coverage concerning arms in Slovenia and in Yugoslavia.
8. *EEN*, 3 December 1990.
9. *Cf.* Samuel P. Huntington, *The Soldier and the State: The Theory and Politics of Civil–Military Relations*, Belknap Press of Harvard, Cambridge, Mass., and London, 1957.
10. *Revija Obramba*, April 1991.
11. *SWB*, 17 October 1990.
12. *Danas*, 4 December 1990.
13. *Delo*, 5 December 1990.
14. *EEN*, 3 December 1990.
15. *Delo*, 13 December 1990.
16. *Delo*, 30 September 1989; *Borba*, 30 September 1989; Milan Andrejevic, 'New Appointments in the Yugoslav People's Army', *RFE*, 23 October 1989.
17. *Narodna Armija*, 4 October 1990.
18. Nikola Cubra, 'Privredna reforma i problemi dogradnje opstenarodne odbrane', *Vojno Delo*, Nos. 3–4, 1990, pp. 67–79.

References

Periodicals

Armed Forces and Society
Army
Borba
Business (Belgrade)
The Daily Telegraph
Comparative Politics
Danas
Delo
Dnevnik (Ljubljana)
Eastern Europe Newsletter (EEN)
East European Reporter
East European Quarterly
Economist Intelligence Unit: Yugoslavia, No. 1, 1987
Financial Times
Foreign Broadcast Information Service – Eastern Europe, (FBIS-EEU)
Frankfurter Allgemeine Zeitung
Front
Gorenjski Glas
Government and Opposition
The Guardian
Illustrovana Politika
The Independent
Kommunist
Mladina
Mladost
Le Monde
Narodna Armija
Nasa Obramba
Nasi Razgledi
Neodvisni Dnevnik
New York Times
NIN
Nova Hrvatska
Nova Revija
Novi List
Odbrana i Zastita
Political Science Quarterly
Politika
Problems of Communism
Radio Free Europe Research, later RFE, *Report on Eastern Europe* (RFE)

Sluzbeni List
Soviet Studies
Student
Studies in Comparative Communism
Summary of World Broadcasts, Eastern Europe, *(SWB)*
Tanjug
Teleks
The Times
Tribuna
Vecernje List
Vjesnik
Vojnoistorijski Glasnik
Vojno Delo
The Wall Street Journal (Europe)
World Politics, Princeton University Press
Yugoslav Review
Yugoslav Survey

Books and articles

Jonathan R. Adelman, (ed.): *Communist Armies in Politics*, Westview, Boulder, 1982.

Jonathan R. Adelman, 'Comparative Communist Civil–Military Relations', paper delivered to the International Studies Association, 1980.

Michael Akehurst, *A Modern Introduction to International Law*. Allen & Unwin, London, 1970.

David E. Albright, 'A Comparative Conceptualization of Civil–Military Relations', *World Politics*, Vol. 32, No. 4, 1980.

H. R. Alker et al., *Mathematical Approaches to Politics*. Elsevier Science Publishing Co., Amsterdam, 1973.

Gabriel Almond, (ed.): *Comparative Politics Today: A World View*. Little, Brown, Boston, 1974.

Gabriel Almond and G. Bingham-Powell, Jr., *Comparative Politics: System, Process and Policy*. Little, Brown, Boston, 1978.

Francesco Altimari et al., *Albanci*. Cankarejva Zalozba, Ljubljana, 1984.

J. S. Ambler, *The French Army in Politics 1945–1962*. Ohio State U.P., Ohio, 1966.

Nikola Anic, 'Stvaranje Oruzanih Snaga 1941–1945', in *Oruzane Snage Jugoslavije 1941–1945*. VIZ, Belgrade, 1982.

Anonymous, 'The People's Liberation War and the Socialist Revolution in Yugoslavia 1941–1945', *Yugoslav Survey*, 1974.

Anonymous, 'The Contribution of the Yugoslav People's Army in the Development of the Country, 1980–1987', *Yugoslav Survey*, No. 1, 1988.

Aristotle, *Politics*, edited and translated by John Warrington. J. M. Dent, London.

H. F. Armstrong, *Tito and Goliath*. Gollancz, New York, 1951.

Raymond Aron, *Democracy and Totalitarianism*. Weidenfeld & Nicolson, London, 1968.

Patrick F. R. Artisien, *Friends or Foes? Yugoslav–Albanian Relations over the Last 40 Years,* Bradford Studies on Yugoslavia No. 2. Bradford, 1980.

P. Auty, *Tito.* Penguin, Harmondsworth, 1974.

Alan R. Ball, *Modern Politics and Government,* (2nd edn). Macmillan, London, 1977.

Ivo Banac, *The National Question in Yugoslavia: Origins, History, Politics.* Cornell U.P., London, 1984.

Ingrid Bakse, *Ne Cakaj Na Maj,* Republika Konferenca ZSMS, Ljubljana, 1989.

Anton Bebler, *Marksizem in Vojastvo.* Komunist, Ljubljana, 1975.

Anton Bebler, 'The Sociology of Militaria in Yugoslavia' in *Armed Forces and Society,* Vol. 3, No. 1, November 1976.

Samuel H. Beer and Adam B. Ulam, (eds): *Patterns of Government,* (2nd edn). Random House, New York, 1962.

V. R. Berghaan, *Militarism: The History of an International Debate, 1861–1979.* Cambridge U.P., Cambridge, 1984.

Gary K. Bertsch, *Power and Policy in Communist Systems.* John Wiley, New York, 1978.

Gary K. Bertsch, 'Yugoslavia: The Eleventh Congress, The Constitution and the Succession', *Government and Opposition,* Vol. 14, No. 1, 1979.

Dusan Biber, (ed.): *Konec Druge Svetovne Vojne v. Jugoslaviji.* Borec, Ljubljana, 1986.

Elez Biberaj, 'The Conflict in Kosovo', *Survey,* Vol. 28, No. 3, 1984.

L. S. Binder et al., *Crises and Sequences in Political Development.* Princeton U.P., Princeton, 1971.

David B. Bobrow, 'Soldiers and the Nation State', *Annals of the American Academy,* No. 358, 1965.

Milica Zarkovic Bookman, 'The Economic Basis of Regional Autarchy in Yugoslavia', *Soviet Studies,* Vol. 42, No. 1, January 1990.

K. Booth, *Strategy and Ethnocentrism.* Croom Helm, London, 1979.

A. Borowiec, *Yugoslavia after Tito.* Praeger, New York, 1977.

Baraslav Borozan, *Umetnost u NOBu.* BIGZ, Belgrade, 1977.

L. Bramson and G. W. Goethals, (eds): *War: Studies from Psychology, Sociology and Anthropology.* Basic Books Inc., New York and London, 1964.

Archie Brown, (ed.): *Political Culture and Communist Studies.* Macmillan, London, 1984.

Archie Brown and Jack Gray, (eds): *Political Culture and Political Change in Communist States.* Macmillan, London, 1977.

James M. Buchannan, *Freedom in Constitutional Contract: Perspectives of a Political Economist.* Texas, A & M, U.P., College Station and London, 1977.

James M. Buchannan, *The Calculus of Consent: Logical Foundations of Constitutional Democracy.* University of Michigan Press, Michigan, 1962.

James M. Buchannan, *The Limits of Liberty: Between Anarchy and Leviathan.* University of Chicago Press, London, 1975.

E. H. Carr, *What is History?* Penguin, Harmondsworth, 1961.

A. Carter, Democratic Reform in Yugoslavia: *The Changing Role of the Party.* Frances Pinter, London, 1982.

Vuksan Cerovic, *Kosovo – Kontrarevolcija Koja Tece.* Nova Knjiga, Belgrade, 1989.

D. Childs and J. Johnson, *West Germany: Politics and Society*. Croom Helm, London, 1981.

David Childs, *The GDR: Moscow's German Ally*. Allen & Unwin, London, 1983.

Robin Clarke, rapporteur, *London Under Attack: The Report of the Greater London Area War Risk Study Commission*. Basil Blackwell, Oxford, 1986.

Karl von Clausewitz, *On War*, edited by Anatol Rapoport. Penguin, Harmondsworth, 1968.

Stephen Clissold, (ed.): *A Short History of Yugoslavia*. Cambridge U.P., Cambridge, 1966.

Stephen Clissold, *Croat Separatism: Nationalism, Dissidence and Terrorism*. Conflict Studies, Institute for the Study of Conflict, London, 1979.

Morris R. Cohen and Ernest Nagel, *An Introduction to Logic and Scientific Method*. Routledge, London, 1934.

Timothy J. Colton, *Commissars, Commanders and Civilian Authority: The Structure of Soviet Military Politics*. Harvard U.P., Cambridge, Mass. and London, 1979.

William Connolly, (ed.): *Legitimacy and the State*. Basil Blackwell, Oxford, 1984.

Constitution of the Socialist Federative Republic of Yugoslavia. Belgrade 1974.

F. J. Cook, *The Warfare State*. Jonathan Cape, London, 1963.

Bernard Crick, *The American Science of Politics*. Routledge & Kegan Paul, London, 1959.

Nikola Cubra, 'Privredna reforma i problemi dogradnje opstenarodne odbrane', *Vojno Delo*, Nos. 3–4, 1990.

Mico Cusic, 'Vojno-politicka situacija u svetu i bezbednost SFRJ', *Narodna Armija* Supplement, 30 October 1986.

Jovan Cvijic, *La Peninsule Balkanique*. Librairie Armand Colin, Paris, 1918.

Jovan Cvijic, *Balkansko Polustrovo*. Hrvatski Stamparski Zavod, Zagreb, 1922.

Robert A. Dahl, *Modern Political Analysis*. Prentice-Hall, Englewood Cliffs, New Jersey, 1963.

Ralf Dahrendorf, *Society and Democracy in Germany*. Weidenfeld & Nicolson, London, 1967.

Karen Dawisha, *Eastern Europe, Gorbachev and Reform: The Greatest Challenge*. Cambridge U.P., Cambridge, 1988.

Robert W. Dean, 'Civil–Military Relations in Yugoslavia, 1971–75' in *Armed Forces and Society*, Vol. 3, No. 1, 1976.

Vladimir Dedijer, *Tito Speaks*. Weidenfeld & Nicolson, London, 1953.

Vladimir Dedijer, *The Battle Stalin Lost*. Grosset & Dunlap, New York, 1972.

Bogdan Denitch, (ed.): *The Legitimation of Regimes*, Sage, London, 1979.

Bogdan D. Denitch, *The Legitimation of a Revolution: The Yugoslav Case*. Yale U.P., New Haven and London, 1976.

Issac Deutscher, *Stalin: A Political Biography*, Penguin, Harmondsworth, 1966.

Aleska Djilas, 'Tito and the Independence of Yugoslavia', *Review of the Study Centre for Yugoslav Affairs*, Vol. 2, No. 4, London, 1980.

Milovan Djilas, *Conversations with Stalin*. Penguin, Harmondsworth, 1967.

Milovan Djilas, *The Unperfect Society: Beyond the New Class*. Unwin Books, London, 1972.

Milovan Djilas, *Memoir of a Revolutionary*. Harcourt, Brace and Jovanovich, New York, 1973.

Milovan Djilas, *Wartime*, Secker & Warburg, London, 1980.

Milovan Djilas, *Tito*. Weidenfeld & Nicolson, London, 1981.

D. Djordjevic, (ed.): *The Creation of Yugoslavia 1914–1918*, Clio Books, Santa Barbara, 1980.

Dusko Doder, *The Yugoslavs*. Allen & Unwin, London, 1979.

John Doe, *Report from Iron Mountain – On the Possibility and Desirability of Peace*, introduced by Leonard C. Lewin. The Dial Press, New York, 1967.

Jorge I. Dominguez, *Cuba: Order and Revolution*. Belknap Press of Harvard U.P., Cambridge, Mass., 1978.

Christopher N. Donnelly, *Heirs of Clausewitz: Change and Continuity in the Soviet War Machine*. Institute for European Defence and Strategic Studies Occasional Paper, No. 16, London, 1985.

Jacques van Doorn, *Armed Forces and Society*. Mouton, The Hague, 1968.

Alex N. Dragnich, *Serbia, Nikola Pasic and Yugoslavia*, Rutgers U.P., New Brunswick, New Jersey, 1974.

Alex N. Dragnich and Slavko Todorovich, (eds): *The Saga of Kosovo: Focus on Serbian–Albanian Relations*. East European Monographs, Boulder, 1984.

Savo Drljevic, 'The Sources of Our Concept of National Defence', *Socialism* (Belgrade), No. 4, 1969.

M. Drulovic, *Self-Management on Trial*. Spokesman Books, Nottingham, 1978.

Vernon van Dyke, *Political Science: A Philosophical Analysis*. Stanford U.P., Stanford, Cal., 1960.

David Easton, *A System Analysis of Political Life*, John Wiley, New York, 1965.

David Easton, *The Political System*. University of Chicago Press, Chicago, 1981.

Harry Eckstein and Ted Robert Gurr, *Patterns of Authority: A Structural Basis for Political Enquiry*. John Wiley, New York, 1975.

Lewis J. Edinger, *Politics in West Germany*, (2nd edn). Little, Brown, Boston, 1977.

M. Edmonds, (ed.): *Central Organisations of Defence*. Westview Press Inc. and Frances Pinter, London, 1985.

Martin Edmonds, 'The Function of the Armed Forces: A Framework for Comparative Analysis', *USSG Report*, 1971.

Martin Edmonds, *The Armed Services and Society*. Leicester U.P., Leicester, 1988.

Martin Edmonds, 'Armed Forces and Legitimacy in Britain: Emerging Stresses and Dichotomies', paper presented at the Colloque sur les systems militaires britannique et francais, Toulouse, 1976.

A. Eide and M. Thee, (eds): *Problems of Contemporary Militarism*. Croom Helm, London, 1980.

Helene Carrere d'Encausse, *Le Grand Frere*. Flammarion, Paris, 1983.

Encyclopedia of the Social Sciences, Macmillan, New York, 1933.

Cynthia H. Enloe, *Ethnic Soldiers: State Security in a Divided System*. Penguin, Harmondsworth, 1980.

John Erickson, *The Soviet High Command*. Macmillan, London, 1962.

John Erickson, *The Road to Berlin*. Weidenfeld & Nicolson, London, 1983.

John Erickson, *The Road To Stalingrad*. Weidenfeld & Nicolson, London, 1983.

John Erickson and E. J. Feuchtwanger, (eds): *Soviet Military Power and Performance*. Macmillan, London, 1979.

John Erickson and T. N. Wolfe, (eds): *The Armed Services and Society: Alienation, Management and Integration*, Edinburgh U.P., Edinburgh, 1970.

William Esslinger, *Politics and Science*. Philosophical Society, New York, 1955.

Francois Fejto, *A History of the People's Democracies*. Penguin, Harmondsworth, 1974.

Mark G. Feld, (ed.): *Social Consequences of Modernisation in Communist Systems*. Johns Hopkins U.P., London, 1976.

Maury D. Feld, *The Structure of Violence*. Sage, Beverly Hills and London, 1977.

Gugliemo Ferrero, *The Principles of Power: The Great Political Crises of History*. Puttnam, New York, 1943.

S. E. Finer, *Comparative Government*. Penguin Books, Harmondsworth, 1974.

S. E. Finer, *The Man on Horseback: The Role of the Military in Politics*. Penguin, Harmondsworth, 1978.

M. R. D. Foot, *Men in Uniform*. Weidenfeld & Nicolson, 1961.

T. M. Forster, *The East German Army: Second in the Warsaw Pact*. Allen & Unwin, London, 1980.

Sir John Fortescue, *Historical and Military Essays*. Macmillan, London, 1928.

Richard A. Gabriel, (ed.): *Fighting Armies: NATO and the Warsaw Pact – A Combat Assessment*. Greenwood Press, Westport, Conn. and London, 1983.

Stevo Gajic, 'Inzinjera', *Oruzane Snage Jugoslavije 1941–1981*. VIZ, Belgrade, 1982.

J. K. Galbraith, *How to Control the Military*. Doubleday, Garden City, N.Y., 1969.

W. B. Gallie, *Philosophers of Peace and War*. Cambridge U.P., Cambridge, 1978.

G. David Garson, *Political Science Methods*. Holbrook Press, Boston, 1976.

Tone Gersak, 'Ali res dajemo armado namanj v Evropi in imamo najcenejsega vojska?', *Nasa Obramba*, January 1989.

Anthony Giddens, *Politics and Sociology in the Thought of Max Weber*, Macmillan, London, 1982.

Anthony Giddens, *Studies in Social and Political Theory*. Hutchinson, London, 1979.

R. Giradet, (ed.): *La Crise Militaire Francaise 1945–1962: Aspects sociologiques et ideologiques*, Cahiers de la Fondaton Nationale des Sciences Politiques – Libraire Armand Colin, Paris, 1964.

Ivo Goldstein, 'Serbs in Croatia, Croatia in Yugoslavia', *East European Reporter*, Vol. 4, No. 3, Autumn–Winter 1990.

James Gow, 'The Deterioration of Civil–Military Relations in Slovenia', *Slovo*, Vol. 2, No. 1, 1989.

Slavko Graber and Toncni Kuzmanic, (eds): *Kosovo – Srbija – Jugoslavija*. Knjiznica Revolucionarne Teorije, Ljubljana, 1989.

William J. Goode and Paul K. Hatt, *Methods in Social Research*. McGraw-Hill, New York, 1952.

Mitja Grasic and Slobodan Mirkovic, 'Geodetska Sluzba i Delatnost Vojno-geografsog Instituta', *Oruzane Snage Jugoslavije 1941–81*, VIZ, Belgrade, 1982.

Great Soviet Encyclopedia, Macmillan Inc., New York (translation of *Bol'shaia Sovetskaia Entsiklopedia*, A. M. Prokhovov, Editor-in-Chief) (3rd edn) Moscow, 1974.

Jurgen Habermas, *Legitimation Crisis*, Heinemann Educational Books, London, 1970.

Sir John Winthrop-Hackett, *The Profession of Arms*. Macmillan, New York, 1983.

Peter Harris, *Foundations of Political Science*, (2nd edn). Hutchinson, London, 1986.

R. Hague and M. Herop, *Comparative Government: An Introduction*. Macmillan Educational, London, 1982.

M. Halperin, *Bureaucratic Politics and Foreign Policy*. Brookings Institution, Washington D.C., 1974.

Thomas T. Hammond, (ed.): *The Anatomy of Communist Takeovers*. Yale U.P., New Haven, 1975.

Teresa Rakowska-Harmstone, (ed.): *Perspectives for Change in Communist Societies*. Westview, Boulder, 1979.

Teresa Rakowska-Harmstone et al., *The Warsaw Pact; The Question of Cohesion*, Phase I, ORAE. Department of National Defence, Canada, 1981.

Teresa Rakowska-Harmstone et al., *The Warsaw Pact; The Question of Cohesion*, Phase II, Vols. 1 and 2, ORAE. Department of National Defence, Canada, 1984.

Teresa Rakowska-Harmstone and A. Gyorky, (eds): *Communism in Eastern Europe*. Indiana U.P., Bloomington, 1979.

Reginald J. Harrison, *Pluralism and Corporatism*. Allen & Unwin, London, 1980.

J. E. S. Hayward and R. N. Berki, (eds): *State and Society in Contemporary Europe*. Martin Robertson, Oxford, 1979.

David Held, *Modeli Demokracije*. Krt, Ljubljana, 1989.

Dale R. Herspring and Ivan Volges, (eds): *Civil–Military Relations in Communist Systems*, Westview, Boulder, 1978.

Dale R. Herspring, 'Introduction;', *Studies in Comparative Communism*. Vol. XI, No. 3, Autumn 1978.

Dale R. Herspring and Ivan Volgyes, 'The Military as an Agent of Political Socialisation in Eastern Europe', *Armed Forces and Society*, Vol. 3, No. 2, Winter 1977.

Ronald J. Hill and Peter Frank, *The Soviet Communist Party*. Allen & Unwin, London, 1981.

George W. Hoffman and Fred W. Neal, *Yugoslavia and the New Communism*. Twentieth Century Fund, New York, 1962.

Tom Holm, 'Culture, Ceremonialism and Stress: American Indian Veterans and the Vietnam War', *Armed Forces and Society*, Vol. 12, No. 2, Winter 1986.

David Holloway and Jane M. Sharp, (eds): *The Warsaw Pact: Alliance in Transition?* Macmillan, London, 1984.

J. R. Hoptner, *Yugoslavia in Crisis 1938–41*. Columbia U.P., New York, 1963.

D. Horowitz, (ed.): *Corporations and the Cold War*. Monthly Review Press, New York, 1969.

Branko Horvat, *Kosovsko Pitanje*. Globus, Zagreb, 1988.

Jerry F. Hough, *The Soviet Prefects: The Local Party Organs in Industrial Decision-making*. Harvard U.P., Cambridge, Mass., 1969.

Jerry F. Hough and Merle Fainsod, *How the Soviet Union is Governed*. Harvard U.P., Cambridge, Mass., 1979.

Michael Howard, *Soldiers and Government*. Eyre & Spottiswoode, London, 1957.

R. M. Carew-Hunt, *The Theory and Practice of Communism*. Penguin, Harmondsworth, 1966.

Samuel P. Huntington, (ed.): *Changing Patterns of Military Politics*. Free Press of Glencoe Inc., New York, 1962.

Samuel P. Huntington, *The Soldier and the State: The Theory and Politics of Civil--Military Relations*. Belknap Press of Harvard U.P., Cambridge, Mass. and London, 1957.

Samuel P. Huntington, *Political Order in Changing Societies*. Yale U.P., New Haven and London, 1968.

Samuel P. Huntington, 'Political Development and Political Decay', *World Politics*, Vol. 17, 1964-5.

Samuel P. Huntington, 'The Change to Change', *Comparative Politics*, Vol. 3, 1970-1.

Mensur Ibrahimpsic, 'Vojna subordinacija kao determinanta strukture: Princip Organizacije Armije', *Zbornik Radova 1*. Belgrade, 1969.

Mensur Ibrahimpsic, *Armija Kao Drustvena Institutacija*, Magister Thesis, Political Science Faculty, Belgrade University, 1973.

International Encyclopedia of the Social Sciences. Macmillan, New York, 1968.

Ghita Ionescu, *The Parties of the European Communist States*. Weidenfeld & Nicolson, London, 1967.

A. C. Isaak, *The Scope and Methods of Political Science*. Dorsey Press, Homewood, Illinois, 1981.

Morris Janowitz, *The Military in the Political Development of New Nations*. University of Chicago Press, Chicago, 1964.

Morris Janowitz, *Military Institutions and Coercion in the Developing World*. University of Chicago Press, Chicago, 1977.

Morris Janowitz and Stephen D. Westbrook, (eds): *The Political Education of Soldiers*. Sage, Beverly Hills, 1983.

Morris Janowitz, (ed.): *Civil-Military Relations: Regional Perspectives*. Sage, Beverly Hills and London, 1981.

Janez Jansa, *Na Svoji Stran*. Casopis za Kriticno Znanosti, Ljubljana, 1988.

Jacob K. Javits et al., *The Defense Sector and the American Economy*. New York U.P., New York, 1968.

G. Harries-Jenkins and J. van Doorn, (eds): *The Military and the Problem of Legitimacy*. Sage, London, 1976.

A. Ross Johnson, 'The Role of the Military in Communist Yugoslavia: An Historical Sketch', *RAND*, P. 6070. Santa Monica, 1978.

A. Ross Johnson, *Yugoslavia in the Twilight of Tito*, Washington Paper, No. 16. Sage, Beverly Hills and London, 1974.

A. Ross Johnson, *The Transformation of Communist Ideology*. MIT Press, Cambridge, Mass., 1972.

A. Ross Johnson, 'Total National Defence in Yugoslavia', *RAND*, P. 4746, Santa Monica, 1971.

A. Ross Johnson, 'Impressions of Post-Tito Yugoslavia: A Trip Report',

RAND, P. 5383-1, Santa Monica, 1977.

A. Ross Johnson, 'The Warsaw Pact: Soviet Military Policy in Eastern Europe', *RAND*, P. 6583, Santa Monica, 1981.

A. Ross Johnson, 'Soviet-East European Military Relations: An Overview', *RAND*, P. 383-1, Santa Monica, 1977.

A. Ross Johnson, 'Yugoslavia: The Non-Leninist Succession', *RAND*, P. 6442, Santa Monica, 1980.

Chalmers Johnson, *Revolutionary Change*. University of London Press, London, 1968.

Christopher D. Jones, *Soviet Influence in Eastern Europe: Political Autonomy and the Warsaw Pact*. Praeger, New York, 1981.

Ellen Jones, *Red Army and Society: A Sociology of the Soviet Military*. Allen & Unwin, London, 1985.

Blazo S. Jovanovic, *Cetvrta Proletarska Crnogorska Brigada*. VIZ, Belgrade, 1975.

John Keane, *Democracy and Civil Society*. Verso, London, 1988.

John Keane, (ed.): *Civil Society and the State: New European Perspectives*. Verso, London, 1988.

Russell Keat and John Urry, *Social Theory as Science*. Routledge & Kegan Paul, London, 1975.

C. M. Kelleher, *Political Military Systems: A Comparative Perspective*. Sage, London, 1974.

Gavin Kennedy, 'Defence: Markets and Bureaucracy', *Economic Affairs*, Vol. 10, No. 1, 1989.

John Keegan and Richard Holmes, *Soldiers: A Study of Men in Battle*. Hamish Hamilton, London, 1985.

Sir Frank Kitson, *Directing Operations*. Faber & Faber, London, 1989.

Zdravko Klanjscek, *Oris Narodnoosvobodilne Vojne na Slovenskem 1941–1945*. Partizanska Knjiga, Ljubljana, 1982.

Zdravko Klanjscek, 'Narodnoosvobodilacki Rat u Sloveniji u 1942 Godini', *Vojnoistorijski Glasnik*, Vol. XXXIV, No. 3, 1983, pp. 69–81.

Boguoljub Kocovic, *Zrtve Drugog Svetskog Rata u Jugoslaviji*. Nase Delo, London, 1985.

R. Kolkowicz and A. Korbonski, (eds): *Soldiers, Peasants and Bureaucrats: Civil–Military Relations in Communist and Modernizing Societies*, Allen & Unwin, London, 1982.

Lawrence J. Korb, *The Fall and Rise of the Pentagon: American Defence Policies in the 1970s*. Greenwood Press, London, 1979.

Bojan Koriska, (ed.): *Srbija i Albanci: Pregled Politike Srbije Prema Albancima od. 1878 du 1914 Godine*, Book 1. Casopis za Kriticno Znanosti, Ljubljana, 1989.

Bojan Koriska, (ed.): *Srbija i Albanci: Pregled Politike Srbije Prema Albancima od. 1913 do 1945 Godine*, Book 2. Casopis za Kriticno Znanosti, Ljubljana, 1989.

Bojan Koriska, (ed.): *Srbija i Albanci: Pregled Politike Srbije Prema Albancima od. 1944 do 1989 Godine*, Book 3. Casopis za Kriticno Znanosti, Ljubljana, 1989.

Sveto Kovacevic, 'Koncipiranje Uloge Komunista u Posleratnom Razvitku Jugoslovenske Narodne Armije', *Zbornik Radova 1*, Politicka Skola JNA, Belgrade, 1968.

J. Krejci, *Social Structure in Divided Germany*. Croom Helm, London, 1976.

Hajro Kulenovic, 'Sanitetska Sluzba', *Oruzane Snage Jugoslavije 1941-1981*. VIZ, Belgrade, 1982.

Vladimir V. Kusin, (ed.): *The Czechoslovak Reform Movement 1968*. International Research Documents, London, 1973.

David Lane, *Politics and Society in the USSR*, (2nd edn). Martin Robertson, London, 1978.

Harold D. Lasswell, 'The Garrison State', *The American Journal of Sociology*, Vol. XLVI, 1941.

Harold D. Lasswell, *Politics: Who Gets What, When, How*. Whittlesey House, New York, 1936.

Branko Latas, 'Cetnici Draza Mihailovica u Sloveniji – Plava Garda 1941-1943 Godine', *Vojnoistorijski Glasnik*, Vol. XXXIV, No. 3, 1983, pp. 163-90.

Ivo J. Lederer, *Yugoslavia at the Paris Peace Conference*. Yale U.P., New Haven, 1963.

Roman Leljak, *Sam Proti Njim*. Casopis za Kriticno Znanosti, Ljubljana, 1989.

Paul Lendvai, *Eagles in Cobwebs: Nationalism and Communism in the Balkans*. Macdonald, London, 1970.

V. I. Lenin, *The State and Revolution*. Foreign Languages Press, Peking, 1976.

Paul G. Lewis, (ed.): *Eastern Europe: Political Crisis and Legitimation*. Croom Helm, London, 1984.

Seymour Martin Lipsett, *Political Man*. Heinemann, London, 1969.

Nikola Ljubicic, *Total National Defence – Strategy for Peace*. STP, Belgrade, 1977.

A. R. Luckham, 'A Comparative Typology of Civil–Military Relations', *Government and Opposition*, Vol. 6, No. 2, Spring 1971.

Peter C. Ludz, *The Changing Party Elite in East Germany*. MIT Press, Cambridge, Mass., 1972.

Reneo Lukic, 'La Dissuasion Populaire Yougoslave', *Cahiers d'Etudes Strategiques*, No. 5, CIRPES, Paris, 1985.

Martin McCauley, (ed.): *Communist Power in Europe 1944-49*. Macmillan, London, 1977.

Martin McCauley and Stephen Carter, (eds): *Leadership and Succession in the Soviet Union, Eastern Europe and China*. Macmillan, London, 1986.

R. M. MacIver, *The Modern State*. Oxford U.P., London, 1926 and 1964.

W. J. M. MacKenzie, *Politics and Social Science*. Penguin, Harmondsworth, 1967 and The Open University Press, Milton Keynes, 1982.

Fitzroy MacLean, *Eastern Approaches*. Jonathan Cape, London, 1950.

William H. McNeill, *The Pursuit of Power: Technology, Armed Forces and Society*. Basil Blackwell, Oxford, 1983.

Machiavelli, *The Prince*, Chapter XIII in *The Portable Machiavelli*, P. Bondanella and M. Mufa, (eds). Penguin, Harmondsworth, 1979.

James Madison, Alexander Hamilton and John Jay, *The Federalist Papers*. Penguin, Harmondsworth, 1987.

Branko Mamula, 'Aktuelni problemi obrane u odnosu na suvremena kretanja u svijetu i u nas – modernizacija koncepcije opcenarodne obrane', *Narodna Armija*, 21 April 1988.

Branko Mamula, *Savremini Svijet i Nasa Odbrana*. VIZ, Belgrade, 1985.

Branko Mamula, *Odbrana Malih Zemalja*. Vojnoizdavacki Centar, Belgrade, 1988.

Roderick Martin, *The Sociology of Power*. Routledge & Kegan Paul, London, 1977.

Karl Marx and Friedrich Engels, *Collected Works*. Lawrence & Wishart, London, 1980.

Seymour Melman, *Pentagon Capitalism: The Political Economy of War*. McGraw-Hill, New York, 1970.

J. G. Merquior, *Rousseau and Weber*. Routledge & Kegan Paul, London, 1980.

Alfred G. Meyer, *The Soviet Political System: An Interpretation*. Random House, New York, 1965.

Metod Mikuz, *Pregled Zgodovine NOV v Sloveniji*, Vols. 1–5. Cankarjeva Zalozba, Ljubljana, 1960–73.

Metod Mikuz, *Slovensko Partizansko Gospodarstvo*. Zavod Borec, Ljubljana, 1969.

Allan R. Miller and Willaimson Murray, (eds): *Military Effectiveness*, Vols. I–III. Allen & Unwin, Boston, 1988.

M. Milivojevic et al., (eds): *Yugoslavia's Security Dilemmas: Armed Forces, National Defence and Foreign Policy*. Berg, Oxford, 1988.

Marko Milivojevic, 'The Yugoslav People's Army', *Armed Forces*, Vol. 6, No. 1, January 1987.

C. Wright Mills, *The Power Elite*. Oxford U.P., New York, 1959.

Slobodan Milosevic, *Godine Raspleta*. BIGZ, Belgrade, 1989.

A. S. Milovidov and G. Kozlov, *The Philosophical Heritage of V. I. Lenin and Problems of Contemporary War*. Moscow, 1972, USAF translation, U.S. Government Printing Office.

Stevan Mirkovic, 'O mobilizaciji oruzanih snaga', *Vojno Delo*, No. 2, March–April 1989.

R. Moore, *Self-Management in Yugoslavia*. Fabian Research Series, No. 281, London, 1970.

K. Krishna Moorthy, *After Tito, What?* Humanities Press, Atlantic Highlands N.J., 1980.

Ernest Nagel, *Logic: Without Metaphysics*. Free Press of Glencoe, Glencoe, Illinois, 1956.

M. Needler, *The Anatomy of a Coup d'Etat: Ecuador, 1963*. Institute for the Study of Comparative Political Systems, Washington, 1964.

Daniel N. Nelson, (ed.): *Soviet Allies: The Warsaw Pact and the Issue of Reliability*. Westview, Boulder and London, 1984.

Drago Nikolic, *Razvoj Politickih Organa u Jugoslavenskoj Narodnoj Armiji*. VIZ, Belgrade, 1985.

Milan Nikolic, 'Yugoslavia's Failed Perestroika', *Telos*, No. 79, Spring 1989.

Blazo Nikolovski, 'Drustveni Razvoj i Izgradnja Nasih Oruzanih Snaga' in *Oruzane Snage Jugoslavije 1941–45*. VIZ, Belgrade, 1982.

1941–1942 U Sve Docenjima Ucesnika NOB, Vols. 1–25. VIZ, Belgrade, 1975.

Alec Nove, *Stalinism and After*. Allen & Unwin, London, 1981.

Vuk Obradovic, 'Nacionalizam i oruzane snage', *Vojno Delo*, No. 1, January–February 1989.

William E. Odom, 'The Party Connection' in *Problems of Communism*, Vol. XXII, September–October 1973.

Milojica Pantelic, 'The Role of the Armed Forces in the System of National

Defence', *Yugoslav Survey*, No. 4, 1969.

Pascal, *Pensees*, Michel Autrand (ed), Bordas, Paris, 1976.

David W. Paul, *The Cultural Limits of Revolutionary Politics: Change and Continuity in Socialist Czechoslovakia*. East European Quarterly, Boulder and Columbia U.P., New York, 1979.

Stevan K. Pavlowitch, *Yugoslavia*. Ernest Benn, London, 1971.

Stevan K. Pavlowitch, 'The History Behind Jugoslavia's Psychological Deterrent', *Review of the Centre for Yugoslav Affairs*, Vol. 11, No. 2, 1975.

Stevan K. Pavlowitch, 'The Grey Area on NATO's Balkan flank', *Survey*, Vol. 25, No. 3, 1978.

Stevan K. Pavlowitch, *The Improbable Survivor: Yugoslavia and its Problems 1918–1988*. C. Hurst, London, 1988.

Dusan Pejanovic, *The Yugoslav People's Army in the Reconstruction and Development of the Country*. VIZ, Belgrade, 1968.

Dusan Pekic, 'Neki Aspekti Daljeg Razvoja Oruzanih Snaga', *Oruzane Snage Jugoslavije 1941–1981*. VIZ, Belgrade, 1982.

Gavro Perazic, *Ustavnopoliticki i Medjunarodni Status Odbrane i Oruzanih Snaga*. VIZ, Belgrade, 1976.

Amos Perlmutter, *The Military and Politics in Modern Times*. Yale U.P., 1977.

Amos Perlmutter and William Leo Grande, 'The Party in Uniform: Toward a Theory of Civil–Military Relations in Communist Political Systems', *American Political Science Review*, Vol. 76, 1982.

Milan Perunovic, 'Intendantska Sluzba', *Oruzane Snage Jugoslavije, 1941–1981*. VIZ, Belgrade, 1982.

Stanko Petelin, *Enaintridesta Divizija*. Zalozba Borec, Ljubljana, 1985.

Ranko Petkovic, (ed.): *Kosovo: Proslost i Sadasnjost*. Medunarodna Politika, Belgrade, 1989.

PIC/276, *National Liberation Movement of Yugoslavia*. Public Records Office, Political Intelligence Command Middle East, June 1944.

Arshi Pipa and Sami Rapishti, (eds): *Studies on Kosova*. East European Monographs, Boulder, 1984.

I. de Sola Pool, (ed.): *Contemporary Political Science: Toward Empirical Theory*. McGraw-Hill, New York, 1967.

Karl R. Popper, *The Open Society and Its Enemies*. Princeton U.P., Princeton, 1950.

Karl R. Popper, *The Poverty of Historicism*, Routledge & Kegan Paul, London, 1957.

D. Potter et al., (eds): *Society and the Social Sciences*. Routledge & Kegan Paul, London, 1981.

Hugh Poulton with Minnesota Lawyers International Human Rights Committee, *Minorities in the Balkans*. Minority Rights Group, Report No. 82, London, 1989.

Milos Prelevic, 'Neki podaci o oruzanim godina formacija NOR-a', *Zbornik Radova*, No. 3, Politicna Skola JNA, Belgrade, 1970.

Milos Prelevic, *Drustvena Sustina Vojne Sile*. VIZ, Belgrade, 1972.

C. W. Pursell, (ed.): *The Military Industrial Complex*. Harper & Row, 1972.

Pedro Ramet, *Nationalism and Federalism in Yugoslavia 1963–1983*. Indiana U.P., Bloomington, 1984.

Pedro Ramet, (ed.): *Yugoslavia in the 1980s*. Westview, Boulder, 1985.

Robin Alison Remington, *The Warsaw Pact*. MIT Press, Cambridge, Mass., 1971.

Robin Alison Remington, 'Civil–Military Relations in Yugoslavia: The Partisan Vanguard', *Studies in Comparative Communism*, Vol. XI, No. 3, Autumn 1978.

Ciril Ribicic and Zdravko Tomac, *Federalizam po Mjeri Buducnosti*. Globus, Zagreb, 1989.

F. M. Richardson, *Fighting Spirit: A Study of Psychological Factors in War*. Leo Cooper, London, 1978.

Lewis F. Richardson, *Arms and Insecurity: A Mathematical Study of the Causes and Origins of War*. Stevens, London, 1960.

T. H. Rigby and Ferenc Feher, (eds): *Political Legitimation in Communist States*. Macmillan, London, 1982.

Dragisha N. Ristic, *Yugoslavia's Revolution of 1941*. Hoover Institution Publications, London, 1966.

Adam Roberts, *Nations in Arms: The Theory and Practice of Territorial Defence*. Chatto & Windus, London, 1976.

Richard Robinson, *Definition*. Clarendon Press, Oxford, 1950.

Rade Roksandic, 'Organizacijsko-Formacijsko Razvoj Oruzanih Snaga', *Oruzane Snage Jugoslavije 1941–45*. VIZ, Belgrade, 1982.

Richard Rose, *The Problem of Party Government*. Penguin, Harmondsworth, 1976.

Richard Rose, 'Dynamic Tendencies in Authority of Regimes', *World Politics*, Vol. 21, No. 4, 1969.

S. Rosen, (ed.): *Testing the Theory of the Military Industrial Complex*. Lexington Books, Lexington, Mass., 1973.

Joseph Rothschild, *Eastern Europe Between the World Wars*. University of Washington Press, Seattle, 1974.

Dennison I. Rusinow, 'The Yugoslav Concept of "All-National Defence"', *American Universities Fieldstaffs Reports, South Eastern Europe Series*, Vol. XIX, No. 1, 1971.

Dennison I. Rusinow, 'The Crisis in Croatia', *American Universities Fieldstaffs Reports, South Eastern Europe Series*, Vol. XIX, Nos. 4–7, 1971.

Dennison I. Rusinow, *The Yugoslav Experiment, 1948–74*. Hurst, London, 1977.

E. Schneider, *The GDR: The History, Politics, Economy and Society of East Germany*. Hurst, London, 1978.

Louis Schneider and Charles Bonjean, (eds): *The Idea of Culture in the Social Sciences*. Cambridge U.P., Cambridge, 1973.

George Schopflin, 'Communism and Nationalism in Eastern Europe: The Uses and Abuses of Two Ideologies', *Europaische Rundschau*, November 1980.

Aleksandar Sekulic, 'Veza', *Oruzane Snage Jugoslavije 1941–1981*. VIZ, Belgrade, 1982.

Radoslav Selucky, *Economic Reforms in Eastern Europe: Political Background and Economic Significance*. Praeger, New York, 1972.

Jim Seroka and Radoslav Smilijovic, *Political Organs in Socialist Yugoslavia*. Duke U.P., Durham, 1986.

Jane P. Shapiro and Peter J. Posichnyj, (eds): *Change and Adaptation in Soviet and East European Politics.* Praeger, New York, 1976.

Paul Shoup, 'Crisis and Reform in Yugoslavia', *Telos*, No. 79, Spring 1989.

Ota Sik, *The Communist Power System.* Praeger, New York, 1981.

William B. Simons (ed.): *The Constitutions of the Communist World.* Sijthoff and Noordhoff, Alphen van den Rijn, 1980.

Fred Singleton, *Twentieth Century Yugoslavia.* Macmillan, London, 1976.

Fred Singleton, *A Short History of the Yugoslav People.* Cambridge U.P., Cambridge, 1985.

S. Sinnanian et al., (eds): *Eastern Europe in the 1970s.* Praeger, New York, 1972.

Ljubo Sirc, *Between Hitler and Stalin.* Andre Deutsch, London, 1989.

H. Gordon Skilling, *The Governments of Communist East Europe.* Thomas Y. Crowell, New York, 1966.

Slovensko Javno Mnenje, 1987, 1988, 1989.

Gordon Smith, *Politics in Western Europe: A Comparative Analysis*, (3rd edn). Heinemann Educational Books, London, 1980.

Social Science Research Council, Committee on Historiography, *Bulletin 54: Theory and Practice in Historical Study*, SSRC, New York, 1946.

Slavko Sorsak, *Splosna Ljudska Obramba in Zveza Komunistov Jugoslavije.* Komunist, Ljubljana, 1983.

Sovetskaya Istoricheskaya Entsiklopedia, E. M. Zhukov, editor-in-chief. Moscow, 1966.

Sovetskaya Voennaya Entsiklopedia, Voennoe Izdatepstvo Ministerstvo Oborana SSSR. Moscow, 1978.

Drago Chas Sporer, 'Politics and Nationalism within the Yugoslav People's Army', *Journal of Croatian Studies*, Vol. XX, 1979.

Djordje Stanic, 'Military Schools of the Yugoslav People's Army', *Yugoslav Survey*, No. 2, 1975.

Slobodan Stankovic, *The End of the Tito Era: Yugoslavia's Dilemmas.* Hoover Institute Press, Stanford, Cal., 1981.

Milija Stansic, *KPJ u Izgradnji Oruzanih Snage Revolucije 1941–1945.* VIZ, Belgrade, 1973.

Geoffrey Stern, 'Political Relations in Eastern Europe', paper delivered to the 11th UK Conference on International Studies, 1968.

Dolf Sternberger, 'Legitimacy', *International Encyclopedia of the Social Sciences.* Macmillan, New York, 1968.

Arthur L. Stinchcombe, *Constructing Social Theories.* Harcourt, Brace and World Inc., New York, 1968.

Rade Susa, 'Naoruzani narod – Crvena Nit u Posleratnoj Izgradnji Nasih Oruzanih Snage', *Vojno Delo*, No. 6, 1983.

Svetozar Vukmanovic-Tempo, *Revolucija Koja Tece: Memoari*, Vols. I and II. Komunist, Belgrade, 1971.

Josip Broz Tito, *Military Thought and Works.* VIZ, Belgrade, 1982.

Bosko Todorovic, 'Neke Bitne Karakteristike Razvoja Oruzanih Snaga u Posleratnom Periodu' in *Oruzane Snage Jugoslavije 1941–45.* VIZ, Belgrade, 1982.

Jozo Tomasevich, *Peasant, Politics and Economic Change in Yugoslavia.* Stanford U.P., Stanford, 1955.

Jozo Tomasevich, *The Chetniks*. Stanford U.P., Stanford, 1975.

Bernhard Tonnes, *Sonderfall Albanien*. Oldenbourg, Munich, 1980.

Robert C. Tucker, 'Culture, Political Culture and Communist Society', *Political Science Quarterly*, LXXXVIII, 1975.

Adam B. Ulam, *Titoism and the Cominform*. Cambridge, Mass., 1952.

Svjatopolk Urbancic, 'Gradjevinska Sluzba', *Oruzane Snage Jugoslavije 1941–1981*. VIZ, Belgrade, 1982.

A. Vagts, *A History of Militarism: Romance and Realities of a Profession*. W. W. Norton, New York, 1937.

Anthony Verrier, *An Army for the Sixties: A Study in National Policy, Contract and Obligation*. Secker & Warburg, London, 1966.

Michael Voslensky, *Nomenklatura*. Bodley Head, London, 1984.

Wayne S. Vucinich, (ed.): *Contemporary Yugoslavia: Twenty Years of Socialist Experiment*. California U.P., London, 1969.

Stephen L. Wasby, *Political Science – The Discipline and Its Dimensions: An Introduction*. Charles Scribner, New York, 1970.

H. W. Seton-Watson, *The East European Revolution*. Methuen, London, 1950.

H. W. Seton-Watson, *The East European Revolution*. Westview, Boulder and London, 1985.

Max Weber, *From Max Weber: Essays in Sociology*, H. H. Gerth and C. Wright Mills, (eds). Routledge & Kegan Paul, London, 1948.

Max Weber, *Economy and Society*, Gunther Roth and Claus Wittich, (eds). University of California Press, Berkeley, 1978.

Murray L. Weidenbaum, *The Economics of Peacetime Defence*. Praeger, New York, 1974.

C. E. Welche Jr., (ed.): *Civilian Control of the Military: Theory and Cases from Developing Countries*. State University of New York Press, Albany, N.Y., 1976.

C. E. Welche and A. R. Smith, *Military Role and Rule*. Duxbury Press, North Scituate, 1974.

Stephen D. Westbrook, 'The Alienated Soldier: Legacy of Our Society', *Army*, London, 1979.

Stephen D. Westbrook, 'Socio-political Alienation and Military Efficiency', *Armed Forces and Society*, Vol. 6, No. 2, Winter 1980.

Mark C. Wheeler, *Britain and the War for Yugoslavia 1940–1943*. East European Monographs, Boulder, 1980.

B. Whitaker, *The Police*. Penguin, Harmondsworth, 1964.

L. D. White, (ed.): *The State of the Social Sciences*. University of Chicago Press, Chicago, 1956.

Stephen White, *Political Culture and Soviet Politics*. Macmillan, London, 1979.

Stephen White, John Gardener and George Schopflin, *Communist Political Systems: An Introduction*. Macmillan, London, 1982.

Sir Duncan Wilson, *Tito's Yugoslavia*, Cambridge U.P., Cambridge, 1979.

Francis Graham Wilson, *The Elements of Modern Politics: An Introduction to Political Science*. McGraw-Hill, New York, 1936.

T. W. Wolfe, *The SALT Experience*. Ballinger Publishing Co., Cambridge, Mass., 1979.

Quincy Wright, *A Study of War*, Vol. II. University of Chicago Press, Chicago, 1942.

Vincent Wright, *The Government and Politics of France*, (2nd edn). Hutchinson, London, 1983.

Igor T. Zagar and Peter Tancig, *Kontekst Ljuljanaskega procesa, Kolokvij pravnikov o procesu zoper cetverico, Racunalniska analiza 'napadov na JLA'*. Casopis za Kriticno Znanosti, Ljubljana, 1989.

Zbornik Dokumentata i Podatka o Narodnooslobodilackom Ratu Naroda Jugoslavije, Vols. I–XIV. VIZ, Belgrade, 1949–85.

G. Zinoviev, *Army and People: The Soviet Government and the Corps of Officers.* Communist International, Petrograd, 1920; Carl Slienger, London, 1977.

Dusan Zunic, 'Neki Aspekti Medjuljudskih Odnosa u Jugoslovenskoj Narodnoj Armij, *Vojno Delo*, No. 1, January 1990.

Peter Zwick, *National Communism*. Westview, Boulder, 1983.

Index